NATURE WITHOUT BORDERS

NATURE without BORDERS

Edited by

Mahesh Rangarajan
M. D. Madhusudan
Ghazala Shahabuddin

Orient BlackSwan

NATURE WITHOUT BORDERS

ORIENT BLACKSWAN PRIVATE LIMITED

Registered Office
3-6-752 Himayatnagar, Hyderabad 500 029 (Telangana), India
e-mail: centraloffice@orientblackswan.com

Other Offices
Bengaluru, Bhopal, Chennai, Guwahati, Hyderabad, Jaipur, Kolkata
Lucknow, Mumbai, New Delhi, Noida, Patna, Vijayawada

First published 2014
This Paperback Edition 2017

ISBN 978-81-250-6420-6

024688

08082016

Typeset in
Bembo Std 11/13
by Le Studio Graphique, Gurgaon

Printed in India at
Rakmo Press Pvt. Ltd.
Greater Noida

Published by
Orient Blackswan Private Limited
3-6-752 Himayatnagar, Hyderabad 500 029, Telangana, INDIA
e-mail: info@orientblackswan.com

Dedicated to the memory of
Our friend, colleague and companion,

Dr Ravi Sankaran
(4th October, 1963 – 17th January, 2009)

'As a conservation biologist, as a *practitioner* of conservation, you would actually have to build upon science, management, policy, advocacy, *implementation*—very important—and of course education for the larger grouping of people... it is not a narrow field, you actually have to be multi-multi-disciplinary for working with conservation.'

Dr Ravi Sankaran,
Address to an ornithologists' conference in Haridwar,
December 2008.
(Emphasis in original)

CONTENTS

PREFACE AND ACKNOWLEDGMENTS

The editors acknowledge a deep debt to the entire team at the journal *Seminar*, as many ideas here were first tested out in issue number 638 of September 2010. The work still bears, we hope, the distinctive impress of the editorial team of Tejbir Singh and Harsh Sethi, who have consistently upheld the principle that complex, nuanced and sophisticated ideas, arguments and concepts are best conveyed in simple language. We also thank the publisher, Malvika Singh for urging us to think out of the box. We cannot claim to have succeeded but we do hope that the several teas and lunches the editors provided in generous measure to aspiring or unwary contributors, real and potential, have not been wholly in vain.

Each of us owes a deep debt to the institutions and organisations where we work and find shelter in a world of deep uncertainty. It is vital to note that the milieu and spirit of open enquiry fostered by the leaders and colleagues of our workplaces deserves much credit.

Mahesh would especially like to thank the faculty and students of the Department of History, University of Delhi as well as the Chairman and committee members, the staff and by no means the least, the Fellows of the Nehru Memorial Museum and Library. The members of the Elephant Task Force 2010, the entire editorial team of *Conservation and Society*, 2003–08, and members of the Forest Advisory Committee 2008–12 deserve special mention. Even our disagreements (which were legion) were never disagreeable. The Ecology and Society network especially Asmita Kabra, Rohan D'Souza, and last but not least by any means, Gunnel Cederlöf, deserve special appreciation. Special thanks also to family members:

Shantha, Geetha and Uttara for their patience and support even when energies flagged. Many thanks as well to Wing Commander and Mrs Venkataraman and the MSc guest house (and gang).

Madhusudan owes a special word of gratitude to the entire team at the Nature Conservation Foundation in Mysore, Bengaluru and all field sites for their continued engagement, excitement and camaraderie. Thanks are also due to Ipsita Herlekar for her help with the bibliography. Special and warm mention of Pavithra, and his parents and his in-laws for their forbearance is a must.

Ghazala places on record her deep appreciation of the support of the Vice Chancellor, the faculty and students of the Ambedkar University, Delhi. The School of Human Ecology, her intellectual and professional home for the past few years, is an active, dynamic and invigorating place with a range of disciplines and never a dull moment. She also thanks Jawed for his steady and unwavering confidence in her and this project.

A number of colleagues, friends and teachers across a range of disciplines have played a key role in provoking, stimulating and exciting our imagination. We especially thank those who work in the field on issues of ecology and society in their widest sense, for it is their concerns we have tried to address in a small way. We would be failing in our duties not to name a few: Shafqat Hussain, Archana Godbole, Ramana Athreya, Vidya Athreya, Roma, Ashok Chowdhury, Sanjay Gubbi, Emmanuel Theophilus, Janaki Lenin, Kashmira Kakati, Shankar Gopalakrishnan, Usha Ramanathan, Anand Vaidya, Shibani Bose, Nisarg Prakash, Nishant Srinivasaiah, Meghna Krishnadas, Nandini Velho, Umesh Srinivasan, Jayant Sarnaik, Sameer Punde and G.V. Reddy.

It was with sadness that we heard of our friend Dr Ravi Sankaran's untimely and sudden passing in 2009. In dedicating the volume to him, we wish to acknowledge his everlasting inspiration. He was older than us, enough to have been known to those growing up in the 80s and 90s as an intrepid ornithologist who ventured to study the rare florican. This doctoral research made him one of the pioneers of wildlife biology, then an emerging discipline in India. But he was much more than that. By the time of his death, he was widely recognised as a scholar and practitioner who could and did think out of the box.

The stories are legion but a few instances will suffice. Poachers looking for nests of the Andaman edible-nest swiftlet, highly sought after as the ingredient of the famed bird's nest soup, found a scientist willing to try and engage with and restrain them. Recognising the limits to a policing approach in a remote setting, he was keen on cross-fostering the beleaguered swiftlet in the nests of the more common house swift. To do this, he took on and tried to change wildlife laws to suit new conservation practice. The recent debate on the future of Narcondam Island, home to a unique hornbill species, owes much to his research and advocacy.

His voice and his work live on also in the continuing work of his students, bereft of his presence, and his colleagues at the Salim Ali School of Ornithology, Coimbatore. His brief tenure as director gave everyone a glimpse of his leadership qualities and team building skills. His death was a blow, a star falling out of the night sky just as it reached its zenith. A year later, the cruel hand of fate snatched away his wife R. Rajyashri and little daughter Yamini, a whole family obliterated in a matter of months.

Of course, Ravi's life was never about endings, but new beginnings. Always searching for new challenges, he put in many months on the ground in Nagaland, working with a cross section of Naga society. As he surveyed and stayed in one village after another, his presence helped catalyse a significant set of efforts to protect rare bird species in their habitats. Initiatives for community forests in the heavily altered landscape had a history before him, but it was his drive, energy and passion as much as his patience and hard work that helped sensitise many to the issues of pheasant protection in new ways. As always, he was drawn to the less well known, the fascinating but not always the most spectacular or charismatic of species of avifauna, and to settings far removed from the centre of government, the media or mainline preservation concerns. His no-nonsense manner, his utter fearlessness, his generosity to younger scholars, staff and field assistants are all as vivid as his plucky and original trademark humour. His laugh still echoes in memory. But with other such original creative people, Ravi had the gift of immersing himself in the milieu and reaching for the elements within it that could effect a qualitative change. For us, Ravi's passing, sad as it is, leaves a larger legacy of knowledge harnessed to practice, a deep curiosity that is willing to learn and unlearn and ask questions afresh, and a willingness to try and secure nature by transcending the borders of the mind. In going down untrodden paths, he gave those who try to forge a peace with nature a beacon of hope for a new tomorrow.

In a country such as India, the barriers to conservation often look insurmountable and the institutional frame can at times drive the best of minds to despair. It is an open society, a leading columnist recently wrote, but one with a closed mind. We respectfully beg to differ with the second part of the proposition. For, India's potential for those with the patience as much as the dedication, and attachment to the land, its people, is, put in one word, incalculable. We work in the conviction that such potential is being—and can be—unlocked, but only if we back belief with initiative, thoughts with deeds, and analysis with action. Our contributors work in a range of landscapes, each cutting the cloth to fit their respective milieux. As Ravi's work showed, it is only from such diverse efforts that coherent alternatives will emerge. We humbly dedicate this book to his memory with the confidence that the dream still lives. As for hope, like his memory, it never dies.

Mahesh
Madhusudan
Ghazala
Delhi and Mysore, August 2013

NATURE WITHOUT BORDERS
An Introduction

Mahesh Rangarajan, M. D. Madhusudan and Ghazala Shahabuddin

Drawing Lines, Securing Nature

Nature seldom respects the borders that people draw. Much of our common past and much of our present is about defining where borders do or do not lie, or what they should mean. The attempt to etch lines on land, river front or sea is not new but the motivations in the recent past have changed. They have begun to include a vision of securing nature by secluding it from the twin impacts of human demographic expansion and runaway economic growth. This will explain why the creation of Protected Areas, whether national parks or game reserves, sites of special scientific interest or plain wildlife sanctuary, have gathered so much traction via legislative enactment and executive action in different nation states of the world.[1] Securing nature required the control of untrammelled human activity and its supervision by those with the expertise, wisdom and foresight to preserve what might be imperilled.

This issue can be seen in a narrow biological sense, as it must. But beyond that, it also raises dilemmas that are more far reaching in their implications. Can an unyielding line be drawn to shut out changes, and if so, how can it endure? Before posing this question, it is best to set up the context of place and time.

Nature in an Emerging Economy

Making space for nature is especially difficult in emerging economies. Here, the onrush of economic growth creates opportunities for self-enhancement but also imposes a heavy burden on ecological systems. India is a case in point, but many of the features of the country's ecological and economic profile are similar to those of other large nation-states like China and Indonesia, Brazil and South Africa.[2] Nature's array of life forms and diverse ecosystems is under intense pressure due to a mix of demographic expansion and economic growth. India has four times as many people as it did just four decades ago. The human population per square kilometre, which was thirty-five in 1600, crossed 350 by 2011, though the rate of population growth has begun to taper off since the high point of the 1970s.[3] The economy has grown at six per cent or more a year since 1980. In the first decade of the new century there was further acceleration to over 7.5 per cent a year, well above the average of the two previous decades. Seven of ten Indians are less than thirty years of age. There has been universal franchise since 1952 and over six of ten voters make sure to vote. India's is a vibrant polity, and for the most part, one of the world's fastest growing major economies. Rapid economic expansion and changing aspirations are secular facts of our age, but what makes India's a significant case is the democratic frame in which these changes are taking place. Such far reaching economic, political and cultural transformations make any attempt at creating secluded spaces for nature a complex challenge.

One specific feature of India as against many other emerging economies is that it is still largely rural, although it is seeing extensive urbanisation. Today, about thirty per cent of Indians—roughly twice as many in percentage terms as in 1947—live in urban settlements. Further, although agriculture now accounts for less than one-sixth of national wealth, it employs just about half the country's labour force. The figures are open to controversy, but what is also crucial is that four of five agricultural holdings are less than 1.2 hectares in size. The country has seen huge gains in economic terms, even for the poor, but India still has one in three people on the planet who earn less than 1.25 dollars a day. It is also a deeply unequal society where the wealth bestowed by nature and the bounty generated by humans is shared unequally.[4] India thus has a more agrarian, more rural profile than any of the major emerging economies and also a larger underclass, both rural and urban, than any other nation state.[5]

Problems arise due to the very premises on which an approach of secluding nature is based. Borders are not only created by people but also contested, redefined or even undermined by them. Through history, state-making has also involved claiming natural features as marking boundaries, as with rivers or mountain ranges. Similarly, the very idea of a fixed line to control human ingress has a converse, namely, to contain and preserve nature on the other side of the line. Yet, as we seek to show, many elements of nature, not least living organisms themselves, do not respect the sanctity of the lines humans draw.

People do not make borders acting always in concert. The reverse is often the case: borders are disputed. Some people try to lay down lines and others often contest these. Borders are not set in stone, and borderlands may be zones of transition where different cultures merge, diverge or synthesise. They could also be the zone where contrasting ecological systems meet, merge or mingle.[6] State-making is a complex process but the setting aside of land for nature has entailed drawing borders, thereby breaking up a continuum. This may go some way in explaining why frictions have been the hallmark of parks from the time of their inception, and why these are not likely to die in a hurry. Writing of the USA, Spence argues how the Blackfeet Indian people, even to this day, stage protests against the takeover of their common lands for the Glacier National Park.[7] Breaking the continuum of poor white settlers and rural underclass Americans with nature was equally contentious. After all, until the 1920s, the USA was a largely rural society and governmental controls on forests or game use brought state and federal officials into conflict with local users including poor whites, African Americans and American Indian peoples.[8] Similar frictions have now been documented widely from independent India. For instance, the violent eviction of unarmed villagers at Morichjhappi in the Sundarbans Tiger Reserve in the Bengal delta in 1978, which resulted in many deaths, is the subject of both scholarly study[9] and a fictional telling.[10] The redrawing of the bounds of the vast mangrove forest had far reaching implications, as the cosmopolitan remaking of nature also means that the human inhabitants are disempowered. In a geographical sense, there are also new curbs on how far and when the woodcutters, fishers and cultivators may access the waters and lands.[11]

Even in the case of the ambitious Project Tiger programme, the federal or union government in India was cautious enough to initially propose minimum core areas of 300 square kilometres or less in each of the nine tiger reserves established in the 1970s. State governments were unwilling to forgo timber and related forest revenues on more forest acreage. Further, there were few precedents then for displacing rural settlements to make way for wildlife preservation projects. It is also possible that the larger backdrop of agrarian discontent at that time put a brake on more ambitious schemes of intervention. Likewise, in East Africa, Maasai protests at a new nature reserve taking over their grazing lands have taken various forms, from litigation in British times to peaceful protest at the time of writing.[12] When nature reserves are established, nature is not just protected for the future, but is also protected from the present: securing it has often entailed restrictions on passage, residence or use. The motives have altered: in the past, it was for game or leisure hunts, and through the twentieth century, for conservation goals.

Borders Past, Borders Present

The borders of a nature reserve may also mark a zone of transition between the forest and the sown space. Such shifts are not unique to our own time: the contrast of *grama* (village) and *aranya* (forest) was commonplace in Sanskrit literature in the first millennium of the Common Era.[13] Similarly, the idea of *shikargahs* where there were restrictions on certain kinds of hunts and key large animals like the lion set aside for the *padsha* (emperor) and his *omrah* (nobles), was commonplace in the sixteenth century under the Mughals.[14] People living adjacent to such reserves could trap small game and birds, but not larger animals. But conservation as a means to preserve vanishing species and rare habitats is a more modern development in India, with origins under the British imperium and the princely states.

No wonder then that complaints about crop-raiding deer, of tigers that lifted cattle, and sounders of wild boar menacing cultivators and crops alike were common in the early twentieth century. Remaking landscapes for tiger hunting was important for rulers such as those of Dungarpur and Banswara, with zones being earmarked in the forest where grazing was allowed and others where princely hunts had exclusive access.[15] Bhavnagar's princes reforested the Mytiala hills, curbed grazing, dug water holes and tried to make transient lions from the nearby Gir forest, resident.[16] Similarly, re-naturing the forest with selective felling, watering points, and roads for access for *shikar* (hunting), all using forced labour, was commonplace in Alwar's Sariska reserve.[17] Access to nature for some (for elite hunts) meant pain and anguish for the many. Huge sounders of boar came out to feast on crops while cultivators were not allowed to act in self-defence against these royal game animals. It was not just nature that was remade but human hierarchies were reinforced in the way nature was re-apportioned.[18]

Human frictions are only one part of the tale. Equally, if not more central to the story, is the part that emphasises that nature may itself need some sanctuary. In a context where relatively intact forests and waterscapes are despoiled by pollution, forest clearance, mining, dams or roadways, fossil fuel extraction or new townships, there may be a need to set aside some spaces where such activities are either not allowed, or permitted only under the most extreme circumstances. Thus, the creation of parks or sanctuaries was seen as a barrier to large-scale modern trespass upon nature. It built upon earlier aesthetic notions not only of the British Raj but also of the princes whose records show an elite aesthetic project of remaking nature.[19] This may have been undermined, for instance, by the construction of the Ramganga dam in India's Corbett Reserve. But the principle still holds. Even as spaces have been mined or rivers dammed, many parks and sanctuaries have stood as legal barriers (sometimes permeable but barriers nonetheless) to such far reaching changes to land and waterscapes.

Sanctuaries and parks in India today often, though not always, are lineal descendants of yesteryears' Reserved Forests (for timber and revenue), or erstwhile princely hunting parks, or of small tracts where trees, plants or animals were safe for cultural or symbolic reasons. Protected Areas worldwide had their genesis in state policies. Early parks were founded for their scenic beauty (Yellowstone or Yosemite) and some for rare fauna (Virungas for the gorilla).[20] Yet some were key elite hunting grounds (Gir Forest or Bandipur) and others were forest reserves where the officers of the Raj could also shoot game or secure trophies, and later secure endangered megafauna as in Kaziranga.[21] Some areas were re-natured to enable hunting of prize game, as with waterfowl in the Keoladeo Ghana National Park, Bharatpur. In each and all of these cases, the lands or waters set aside have remained intact, but in an age of epochal ecological and economic transformations, even their champions are having to ask: are they really secure?

Making Spaces for Nature

The land area set aside under parks in India—an area shy of 2,00,000 square kilometres—is small compared to many African or South American nations. A decade ago, the Selous Game Reserve in Tanzania alone could encompass all of India's tiger reserves.[22] India also has a far smaller fraction of its land set aside for conservation than even neighbours such as Bhutan, Nepal and Sri Lanka.

Yet, one has to look beyond percentages and acreages. Large vertebrate assemblages of the lowland savannah, once widespread across the Brahmaputra-Ganga-Indus basin, still remain in sites like Manas and Kaziranga due to decades of protection. The birth of a rhino calf in Manas, where they were re-introduced after extermination, was a matter of celebration for the local autonomous Bodo Scheduled Tribal Council and the state of Assam.[23] The Rajasthan government recently placed a half page advertisement on the protection of the Great Indian Bustard.[24] Regional nationalism has similarly helped protect the Asian or Asiatic lion in Gujarat.

The large vertebrates matter and serve to open wider horizons for decision makers. Often, discussions about the conservation of nature in India—and wildlife conservation, in particular—have gravitated towards nature reserves. This has been the case most so since the early 1970s when the Expert Committee of the Indian

Board for Wildlife widened the definition to include the life forms, both plant and animal, of the uncultivated landscapes of the country.[25] The Wildlife (Protection) Act of 1972 widened the ambit to include marine species. Project Tiger in 1973 bridged the transition from a species-centred approach to one where a prominent and charismatic vertebrate could enable *in situ* preservation of the wider ecosystem. To let nature be in a few select tracts was the idea and ideology that animated not only tiger conservation but also wildlife protection in general. There was an expansion of tiger reserves from nine in 1973 to forty-two by 2013, and a growth in the areas under parks and sanctuaries from one to over five per cent of the total land mass. Unlike much of South East Asia and China, but in common with the former USSR, India set aside landscapes and water bodies for preservation.[26] The strategy was simple. Spaces on land and water of intrinsic ecological worth were delineated. Protection was made the explicit management priority. Preservation was privileged as the way to safeguard ecological integrity. Competing social, economic or cultural claims were shut out by law and executive fiat. Much of wildlife conservation since then has been about the vigorous defence of these reserves and their protection from any activity that might compromise wildlife and nature.[27]

At first sight, the results would appear quite encouraging. The largest fractions of many endangered species populations today occur within Protected Areas, while they have all but disappeared from many areas outside. Wildlife laws, under which these tracts have been established, still afford them strong legal protection in the face of growing demands to divert these lands and waters in the service of economic growth or human development. Parks and conservation zones are still vital. There is little doubt that controls on land use such as expansion of the cultivated arable, or mining ores, or working of forests for industry could—and did—brake rapid changes that might otherwise have caused irreversible ecological changes. Reserves served as safe havens for animals of the mature tree forest like the gaur, whose numbers had been depleted in the late 1960s by the now extinct rinderpest virus, and it helped them rebound over the next two decades.[28] After the shift to preservation as the centrepiece of wildlife protection at the end of the 1960s, there were marked advantages for the survival of key biomes distinct from mature forest so beloved of imperial foresters and their successors. It is also notable that ecotypes once regarded as fit to be destroyed also got a measure of protection, including the desert, thor-forest and mangroves. Nature was to take its own course in preservation zones such as core areas of tiger reserves. It is possible to appreciate the value of such protection without subscribing to deeply ahistorical and scientifically invalid views of pristine nature. Amendments to the Wildlife Protection Act in 1991, and more so, in 2006, allow for a measure of public consultation and integration of protected zones into larger landscapes. They also help explain why so few species—two birds (the pink headed duck and the mountain quail) and a few large mammals (the banteng, the Sikkim stag, the Sumatran and Javan rhinoceros, and the Asiatic cheetah)—have become extinct in India. These are the only large vertebrate extinctions since 1600, a marked contrast to China, West and South East Asia, not to mention Europe and North America. Plans are on anvil to re-introduce the locally-extinct lion to central India and to bring back the cheetah,[29] though the sociopolitical motives and ecological feasibility of such a move have come under question.

Parks No Panacea

The idea of a well-defined park yields a simple ecological paradox. Advocates of strict nature reserves, such as those who specialise in large carnivores, form an articulate and important constituency. They range from eminent scientists and foresters to nature photographers, journalists and campaigners.[30] Such advocates of strict preservation favour minimal biomass removal and human intrusions into nature reserves. They still see secure parks as vital, but equally stress the need to secure corridors between inviolate habitats. But the case for a more holistic view becomes stronger if one even slightly changes the parameters, or the species in question. Many strictly protected areas have been only patchily successful in preserving the gamut of wildlife and ecological functions that they were meant to, despite considerable financial, intellectual and protective inputs on the part of governments. A recent global review of sixty tropical Protected Areas found that about half of them had suffered declines in abundance of both large animal groups such as apex predators and primates as well as smaller ones such as stream dwelling amphibians and freshwater fish during the last twenty to thirty years.[31] Such losses can be attributed to adverse changes in habitat. For instance, in Wolong Nature Reserve in China, pre- and post-establishment comparisons of forest cover show that giant panda habitat continued to decline since the reserve was set up in 1975. Both the average habitat patch size as well as the total area of habitat in Wolong declined, and the rate of decline has in fact accelerated since 1975.[32]

In India too, the pattern seems to hold. Among the best known examples of ecological decline within India's Protected Areas was the local extinction of the tiger from Sariska and a handful of other tiger reserves.[33] Though re-introduced, it is yet unclear whether this will be a long-term sustainable breeding population. Besides species declines, habitat degradation within the boundaries of PAs too is widespread. There is almost a complete lack of regeneration of native tree species inside Sariska Tiger Reserve,[34] while the invasion of the exotic *Lantana camara* seriously affects the B. R. Hills Temple Sanctuary.[35] Reported cases of local extinctions from established Protected Areas are becoming more frequent—during the last decade, the four-horned antelope was confirmed to have gone extinct from Sariska Tiger Reserve[36] and the Great Indian Bustard from Karera Wildlife Sanctuary.[37] Conservation solely via strict protection is clearly not enough. These are, fortunately, still local extinctions and source populations do exist elsewhere within the country.

Some reasons that can undermine the integrity of protected areas system are self-evident. Such reserves do not exist in ecological or economic isolation from a wider matrix. Animals and birds, water and wind do not obey the boundaries people draw. Cycles of abundance and scarcity, of dry and wet seasons, of pinch and plenitude are a marked feature of monsoon lands in Asia and Africa. These stretch and strain the web of life, imposing burdens on plant and animal alike. Prolonged years of drought lead lions in the Gir hills to traverse and move great distances, often deepening conflicts with cattle herders.[38] The annual flooding of the great Brahmaputra River forces mega-herbivores like the wild buffalo and the rhino to move from its north bank to the southern hills. Private land purchases and permanent resorts can block such routes of movement.[39] Bamboo flowering and seeding in multi-year cycles in the Lushai Hills in the North East India leads to plagues of rodents that lead to human deprivation as they raid stores of grain.[40] Animals here, whether herbivore, rodent or carnivore, are metaphors for nature that is not easily contained any more than Canute could command the waves of the ocean.

There is another key issue to consider. The complex workings of nature *within* reserves may be vitally linked to life forms that are hundreds of kilometres away. Individuals of many tropical tree species are rare and widely scattered. They need specific mobile pollinators from kilometres away to enable their reproduction. Hawk-moths fly from dry forests on eastern Costa Rica to rainforests on its western hill slopes. Such migration depends on the seasonal cycles of leafing of host plants. Any disruption of links in this complex mosaic spanning seasons, altitudinal ranges and vegetation zones could bring the entire population to nought.[41]

Large taxa cannot easily be contained within frontiers of park and sanctuaries. Recent scholarship has shown Asian elephants, a key species around which many Protected Areas have been carved, dispersing hundreds of kilometres between protected areas, much of it through farms and other human-dominated lands.[42] There are resident elephant populations in areas with little legal forest cover cohabiting with high densities of cattle and humans. For instance, small herds of elephants in southern West Bengal have over the last two decades re-colonised areas where they have been unseen for a century. Similarly, over the last three decades, in Hassan district of Karnataka, a few elephants have colonised a densely settled landscape with virtually no forests. These are range expansions and not movements of 'stray animals' as often misleadingly referred to in press reports or briefings by officials. This led the report of the National Elephant Task Force in 2010 to suggest ways of protecting both people and elephants in larger landscapes through careful interventions beyond the Protected Areas. This may entail detailed long-term monitoring, crop protection as well as maintaining paths for movements of the mega-herbivores. What is crucial in the latter case is that it was recognised that the larger landscape called for easing the terms of cohabitation. Some 25,000 to 30,000 elephants do matter but so do the half million cultivators who suffer loss of crops.[43] This gets more starkly clear when regional and national media report herds near cities such as Bengaluru.[44] Large zones exist where humans and animals overlap, and these need special attention distinct from that given to Protected Areas, where preservation takes priority. In fact, the viability of the latter may hinge on our ability to adopt new approaches in the former.

This is true even for large vertebrate carnivores and large wild ungulates (hoofed mammals). Leopards live, hunt, breed and raise cubs in patchwork landscapes of sugarcane fields, pasture and small forest patches and tree corridors in western India. Leopard densities in parts of western Maharashtra are higher than in many tiger reserves. This smaller predator takes advantage of the human-crafted landscape of sugarcane fields and hedgerow trees to breed and raise cubs.[45] The picture is equally complex and fascinating as one moves from fields and patchworks to Reserved Forest habitats. New research indicates the subcontinent's largest carnivore, the tiger, also maintains genetic continuity, with populations in the North East and those in the Peninsula being linked.[46] Such linkages of carnivore populations spell fresh hope and call also for going beyond a narrow reserve-centred view. Incredibly diverse carnivore assemblages, including tigers, clouded leopards and Malayan sun bears, are still extant in the remnants of lowland rainforests of Upper Assam, historically ravaged and fragmented by timber and oil extraction and tea plantations.[47] The Terai Arc study by Johnsingh and others had also reported the highest wild ungulate densities in Reserved Forests with a high presence of cattle.[48] Further research is essential to understand conditions that permit high densities of wild ungulates to coexist with livestock.

The scientific underpinnings of the role of such *buffers* or *sink populations*[49] in maintaining populations of large carnivores and other species inside reserve boundaries have long been recognised.

Human-dominated landscapes adjacent to strict nature reserves, although potentially suboptimal for breeding, can help dramatically increase genetic continuity. They may serve as corridors for movement of large mammals from one reserve to another. Sunquist suggests how suboptimal habitats may harbour young dispersing male tigers.[50] A wildlife sanctuary, National Park or Reserved Forest is often only one part of a larger range, as is now well established in the case of the lions of Gujarat, whose total range now is over ten times that of the Gir Protected Area. Home ranges of individual male lions in the Greater Gir area, can encompass 1,200 or even 1,900 square kilometres, well beyond the famous lion reserve.[51] Animals have feet and will move: this poses a challenge.[52] The label of 'stray animals' outside parks is inappropriate and misleading. These animals are peripatetic and their home ranges are in areas outside reserves. Conservation policy has to tackle the all-important question of how to address issues beyond reserves' borders so that they can be more effective.

Research also shows that not only species, but also ecological processes can be seldom contained within protected area boundaries. Globally, studies show that while Protected Areas may indeed reduce deforestation rates within their boundaries, most are gradually becoming more and more isolated from other nearby habitats.[54] The process of habitat fragmentation works in insidious ways, its many effects remaining unseen until some species or the other vanishes. For instance, species of antbirds in Amazon rainforest fragments went extinct soon after the loss of their primary symbiont, the army ants, which require continuous forests for survival due to their method of foraging collectively over large areas.[55] Isolated reserves simply cannot maintain the web of ecological processes and functions that form the core of any living functioning ecosystem, given the scales at which they operate. Lack of genetic continuity, stalled dispersal movements, reduced habitat size and simply loss of habitat variety can doom many area-sensitive[56] species such as rhinos or specialised creatures such as fruit-dependent butterflies that need rare resources.[57] These ideas of borders between nature and people become further untenable when species losses and impairment of ecological functions within protected landscapes can directly affect a range of goods and services that underpin human production systems outside.

A recent debate has explicitly explored the tradeoffs between food production and biodiversity conservation. It asks if and when *land sparing*, an approach where some land is set aside strictly for biodiversity and there is intensification of production on agricultural lands, ensures better outcomes for agriculture and biodiversity, compared with *land sharing*, where no explicit boundaries are drawn between the two, but a balance is sought between the goals of (agricultural) production and (biodiversity) protection.[58] Although both are conceptually elegant, recent reviews have suggested that production and conservation lands are closely linked by processes that do not obey borders drawn under land-sparing approaches.[59]

The limitations of land sparing are all too apparent in an age of industrialisation and market-driven agrarian change. Rishad Naoroji, in his research on raptor nests in India's first park, Corbett, showed declining hatchling success due to pesticides. Eggs were laid in the eyries but did not hatch. The mating rituals were not followed by hatching and rearing of young eaglets.[60] In the late 1990s, the work of Vibhu Prakash in the famous Keoladeo Ghana park pointed to sharp and even precipitous fall in vulture breeding.[61] Since the 2000s, the decline of three major vulture species has largely been driven by the impact of veterinary diclofenac. Clearly, administrative fiat cannot halt movements of chemical compounds in the food chain across ecosystem boundaries. In the evocative words of Rachel Carson, over five decades ago, the voices of birds are stilled not just by pesticides but a reductionist view of nature, one that fails to see the threads that bind life together.[62] India's vast livestock population—one in five domestic ungulates on earth—sustains India's vulture species. But the low cost of the diclofenac medicine makes it easier for owners of stock to treat their valued animals, thereby unwittingly, but all too surely, setting off a spiral that results in the dying out of vultures. Once net replacement falls below a certain level, we are left with skies bereft of vultures. Thus, by using diclofenac, livestock owners solve a veterinary problem for cattle but create a serious conservation issue as the same compound leads to vulture dying out.[63] In both cases, whether the fish that sustain eagles or the livestock that support vultures, a larger and more environmentally alert approach and readiness to work beyond park boundaries is key to saving species. To move beyond diclofenac needs more than a ban: it needs low cost remedies that are biodegradable, an approach tried by Vanishing Herds Foundation with some success in Gujarat. The vulture die-out, like that of the fishing eagles, is a warning signal that borders cannot confine toxic compounds just to production zones.

Further, against the looming threat of global climate change, few reserves can offer all the insurance that species need. There are virtually no ways of fencing out threats like climate change that are occurring at planetary scales. The only reasonable way forward is to provide natural systems and the species that inhabit them, the resilience needed to make adjustments to the vast but relatively slow change in climate. For one thing, if one did not work to rethink the hard border of the reserve and enable species to reside in—or at least move through—the matrix that surrounds the reserve, climate change is certain to preside over the loss of biodiversity even as we fly flags of conservation in our reserves. As Leakey warned:

> Conservationists have made strenuous arguments for *in situ* conservation, but from what we now know this approach may require revisiting. National parks and other protected areas were designated without thought to climate change. Historically, when the climate has changed significantly, species have moved if they could. Sometimes—if the climate change was too extensive or if migration was obstructed by geographical barriers such as mountains or rivers—movement has been impossible and extinction has been the result.[64]

This reasoning only reinforces our argument in favour of fluid borders and mosaics of landscapes. What makes the case here stronger is that the argument is not only about biological systems or only about human livelihood systems but the interface of the two in times of rapid environmental shifts. There have been dry and wet, warm and cold cycles in the past driven by natural elements and forces. The fluidity of human settlements and occupations was a major means of survival: this is clear even seasonally as with the great river systems that see an increase in water flow of thirty- to fifty-fold in the rainy season. Not only do banks break, but the river front changes shape and size. For instance the famous *chars* of the Ganga in eastern India are neither simply dry land nor waterscape: they form a hybrid of both.[65] Similarly the forest-savannah frontiers have shifted over time due to changes in precipitation. Today's forest can be the next decade's savannah. It is worth asking if production systems such as pastoralism or shifting cultivation (never done in isolation but in conjunction with activities like trading and fishing, hunting or farming) were shifting mosaics. There is extensive research on the ways in which executive practice, legislative enactment and wider changes brought immense pressure to bear on such systems.[66] Extensive and in-depth historical research on swidden or pastoral systems often has a contemporary flavour and topical relevance.[67]

Ecologically fluid and mobile systems such as those of the herders studied here by Ghotge and Ramdas may have deep implications for conservation and for human endurance in general. Similarly, wetlands shrink and grow in size, undergoing temporal and spatial shifts, and as Sundar shows, local adaptive systems are crucial. Fluidity and shifting mosaics may make both eminent ecological sense and enable a critical drawing on user knowledge.

All human impacts on nature need not be as slow, insidious and invisible as climate change. In the rich faunal assemblage of the Ganga in Bhagalpur, Kelkar and Krishnaswamy sketch a picture of a shifting tapestry of bank and river inhabited not only by Gangetic dolphins and turtles, but also serving as the resource catchment for fishers. What a sanctuary means in a fluid, shifting ecosocial milieu is often unclear. This can be a difficult sociopolitical task given resource and status-related conflicts. The net of such conflicts is as complex as the nets that unintentionally but all too often kill the dolphins. Any way out again has to stitch together partnerships based on cooperation. The river as site seems to illustrate well the limits to a hardnosed 'fences-are-best' view to secure nature.

It is still not the case that strict reserves are unnecessary *per se*. It was possible to argue at the turn of the century that policing had done its share to help protect nature and better politics was a must to secure a larger constituency in a diverse, unequal society.

Yet, as two of us have earlier argued,[68] conservation sans parks is unthinkable. It must remain so if only to have living laboratories for study and research in a country that remains rich in diverse ecosystems and species (Mundanthurai, Dachigam, Mudumalai-Bandipur or Kanha). Further, action cannot just be about parks and sanctuaries. In fact, as the climate change and pollution cases illustrate, even large vertebrate protection cannot take a blinkered fortress-centred approach. It is simply unthinkable that a few oases of green survive and remain vibrant as we go about creating a larger moonscape of unclean rivers, contaminated soils and polluted air. Issues of biological diversity are, after all, intertwined with those of soil, water and air quality and with public health, both human and animal. The web of life is intricate and it would be folly just to secure a few patches on it unless it is part of a larger view.

Opportunities Beyond the Border

It is also crucial to note that the array of forest based life forms that exists is not all confined to the small area under protection, or even to the half million square kilometres of government forest. This pattern is even more telling in other ecologies such as wetlands, rivers and seas. Recent field-based research shows that nature continues to make significant space for itself *outside* reserve boundaries. Human-modified landscapes, or rather landscapes with a very high level of landscape change due to human actions, may be critical for smaller taxa. The forest edge and beyond are not all that meet the eye. There may be wide variation along a spectrum depending on the kinds of shifts in the composition of tree cover and a host of similar factors. Smaller birds, insects, reptiles, amphibians, fish, worms and small mammals can and do inhabit such areas. This is due to both their ability to survive in smaller habitat patches as well as their adaptability to human presence. Several rainforest bird species of Mizoram continue to exist in secondary forest regenerating from swidden cultivation. Of course, these are only a fraction of the number that can live in a primary rainforest.[69] As many as eight of the region's twelve woodpecker species persist in historically worked *sal* forest around the Corbett Tiger Reserve. Even the teak plantations in the area harbour up to six species of these birds, well known to be species-poor in comparison to natural forests.[70] Taking forest birds as an indicator group, the data shows that the proportion of native species that can live in human-modified landscapes tends to be correlated with the degree of naturalness and complexity of the habitat, such as tree density, height of the trees, degree of canopy closure, presence of leaf litter, density of snags for nesting and other such habitat features.[71]

Moving beyond mature tree forest to other landscapes, other kinds of opportunities and avenues for conservation arise. As Sundar argues in this volume, the cultivated arable also has diverse bird species—as many as 300—in parts of north India. Bhatnagar and Mishra paint a similar picture from the mountains, of interwoven lives of predators and prey, animals wild and tame, and of herding and trading. The mountains in the north and to the west provide paths for the common tread of domestic goats and sheep, and of an array of wild sheep, antelope, gazelle and wild goats. The most camera shy big cat on earth, the snow leopard, first filmed in the wild as recently as the early 1970s, is a phantom presence but one that is often still reliant on stock reared and raised by human hands.

A similar picture emerges in the Deccan, examined by Ghotge and Ramdas in this volume. The open grasslands and tree-dotted savannah offer browse and graze for goats and sheep as well as habitat for an array of life forms such as wolf and bustard. The cultivated arable and pastures, both upland and lowland, are critical to any larger appreciation of the challenges of conservation. Here, there are borders, but they shift and move in time and space. Fields after harvest provide stubble for transient herds and are also staging grounds for antelope. Pastures are not only grazing grounds but perform a host of other ecological functions and may be integral to dryland peasant production. To view them as 'dead zones' or 'black spots' and only focus on mature forest may be deeply misleading.

Farmlands, pastures and mountains are only a selection of the kind of terrain where nature and culture are not easily separable. The overwhelming fact of ecological India is that it often shows up a subtle blurring of lines between the domains of people and wildlife. There are indeed some instances of stark and sharp divides of the wild and the sown. These mutually contradictory features may not be unique to India or South Asia but are certainly a key archetypal dimension of it.[72] To conceive of nature as wilderness, a space untouched by humans is an idea with a specific history and context. Writing of North America, environmental historians have called the return to pristine wilderness getting back to 'the wrong kind of nature'.[73] In the Indian case, it is more accurate to argue that 'wrong' kind of nature had virtually no past and has no present. Meticulous archaeological researches show how humans have reshaped lands in the 70,000 plus years that humans have been in South Asia. Humans have long driven some, not all, key biological changes, but our age is unique in the scale of these impacts though not in the impact itself. The past was one of both forest loss and recovery. This fluidity as historic feature makes for a messy story and not a linear tale of decay of nature wrought by human onslaught.[74] Fluidity was a historic feature of the landscape through prehistoric and early historic times and continues to be so into the modern period. Simple ideas of harmony crumble when faced with evidence.[75]

This is not to argue that secure zones for ecosystems should not be established today, given the hectic and unplanned nature of human-induced change. But it is to argue that these are exceptional and rare cases, and that there can be no reclaiming nature from history. Such a project, beguiling though it is, is deeply misleading. Its historic role in the 1960s to 1980s was in energising the creation of a conservation apparatus. But to persist wholly or solely with it to the near total exclusion of newer thought and action is to ignore what stares us in the face. Nature and culture, human and animal, the wild and the sown were and indeed are enmeshed, even if not in harmony—and sometimes in sharp conflict. It is by asking how they are interwoven that we can move on ahead.

Refuges, howsoever large, cannot persist in an inhospitable matrix either. The matrix that exists requires active intervention, care and thought. Its fabric is both more vulnerable (in terms of external threats to parks) and more resilient (in terms of key habitats, breeding, wintering and living spaces beyond them) than we once imagined. It is vital to distinguish such an approach as ours from those who see coexistence or devolution of powers as the *sine qua non* of conservation success. There are ample spaces and times for cohabitation and there is a strong case for devolving power outward from federal or state governments to local level institutions and also downward in society. In both cases, however, there has to be the ability to delineate some spaces for nature. What is critical to us is that the realities are far too complex to allow for preservation as any more than as a highly specific strategy for a fraction of land and waterscapes.

Cohabitation—if not harmonious coexistence—seems to be more the norm across larger swathes of land and water than preservation advocates are willing to acknowledge. In the once dominant paradigm of wildlife apart, 'wilderness in pristine form', or 'wildlife first', or 'preserve nature by letting it be', there was little or no perspective beyond the fortress sites. There has been a loosening up with the acknowledgement that larger matrices are as critical as corridor or core habitats. Yet, it does not go far enough. It does not even begin to acknowledge or comprehend how critical taxa or ecosystems that cohabit with humans can be conserved. In fact, far too rigid an insistence on preservation as a strategy has solidified it into a magic spell. It is no surprise that this often, though not always, fails to work. To understand why, it is essential to move from ecology to economics.

The Other Oikos

If nature's processes defy borders, so too do the webs of human economy and actions. The creation of wealth and waste, the movement of goods and people, all combine to limit, if not totally undermine, the value of enclave-centred conservation. The complex of parks, sanctuaries and Reserved Forests in the Nilgiri Biosphere Reserve is a case in point. A hundred-and-fifty-thousand people have relied on Bandipur alone for firewood. This 900 square kilometre park has no residents inside its bounds. Villages within its boundaries were displaced soon after it became a tiger reserve less than four decades ago. Currently, tens of thousands of cattle graze in it every day. For those eking out modest livelihoods, energy and cash are vital for sustenance, and the forest is a source of both. If the parks do sustain the people, the harvest of fuel wood and fodder also undermines its fragile ecology. Livestock vie with wild ruminants for fodder in the reserve's forests and dung. Dung is a vital product for those who gather, but it represents a perturbation of the nutrient cycle.[76] Increasingly able to assert their rights, and as active voters and citizens, local residents cannot legitimately be stopped from regular ingress into the park. Watchers and guards, themselves often recruited from local settlements, are highly unlikely to disallow grazing, vital as it is as a living for the many. On the park's rim, raids by elephant and wild boars on crops are a major risk to agricultural livelihoods and much hard labour is invested in protecting crops of millets, *ragi* or *jowar*, in the growing season. Neither of these—the flow of forest produce to larger livelihood and exchange economies, or the clash with wild vertebrates—is unique to this park. As one of us has demonstrated elsewhere, the park and its forests are part of a wider web of exchange, of flows of credit and cash, dung and crop residue, plant protein and mobile animals.[77] Fences and trenches at the park perimeter to keep elephants in, or people and their cattle out, have barely worked. One has to address why livestock enter the park (to produce dung that is sold to service high interest agricultural credit of thirty-five per cent per annum or more), or why elephants move out (to forage in poorly protected fields). Either way, fluidity across boundaries is driven by deeper human forces that need to be tackled. If drawing lines on land is itself so difficult, in the marine and riverine realms, it remains quite impossible to contain the rise and ebb of ecological and economic flows.[78]

The perimeter of the park is not simply a border in the sense that it marks a break. It is also a place where there is a continuum with the wider world. Wishing this away will not solve the issues. In his insightful study of the Mekong river delta in Vietnam, David Biggs goes even further. A border is also a place where the consequences of unfolding of new events begin to become evident. How to deal with fluidity in land and waterscape is an even greater challenge for states that seek to draw sharp lines around processes more elastic than they bargained for.[79] To press on with the Bandipur case, the usual response of more guards or fences has limited value. To deal with the consequences of fluxes across borders, one needs to rethink not only nature's place in the web of human commodity exchanges.

It is vital to remember how strands of nature are ever present in the wider social, cultural and economic web. The recent Forest Rights Act of 2006 (or FRA), which came about from the sustained rights campaigns of the country's forest-reliant groups, including the Scheduled Tribes, is a case in point. These political campaigns successfully contested the long-held control of provincial or state forest departments over forest lands, which had defined forest boundaries in a way that privileged the government and marginalised the adivasi and other forest-dependent peoples. The Act was a first in allowing for a process of recognition of rights in Reserved Forests and also in Protected Areas. As a result of this law that empowers the *grama sabha*, many a boundary is being redrawn. For the Soliga tribe in BRT Wildlife Sanctuary in Karnataka, the Act helped firmly anchor adivasi claims over the reserve. Many a conservationist saw the new Act as a new threat to nature that would trigger fresh encroachments of the human world into the natural.[80] This missed out on how community consent and rights could serve as shield for forests and wildlife as much as for people. In the Niyamgiri Hills of Odisha, people from the Dongaria Kondh and Kutia Kondh Scheduled Tribes leveraged these rights to prevent their forest land from becoming a large bauxite mine. In reality, legal and policy instruments like the FRA and Ecologically Sensitive Areas (ESAs) under the Environment Protection Act of 1986 are now redefining the nature-human frontier in unprecedented ways. These instruments represent new opportunities to reconcile and regulate relations of people and nature in a manner far less conflict prone than the creation of new Protected Areas. There are indeed risks. Yet, to see only the risk and uncertainty, and not to seize the opportunities, would be to misread the situation.[81]

Most of all, laws and policies such as the FRA might well offer new and better ways of reconciling a degree of human use and presence over large areas with the maintenance of certain levels of ecological structure and function. To be sure, inviolate areas, where ecology takes precedence over humans, will still be needed, particularly for fragile species and sensitive habitats that do not flourish alongside humans. But ensuring that such inviolate areas are created through an inclusive process under the rule of law, as the 2006 law itself provides for, can go a long way in lowering social conflicts that have otherwise accompanied the creation of inviolate areas.

If this has rarely happened so far, there is a reason. It is because the FRA has been seen mostly in terms of individual tenurial rights. The strengthening of individual rights on cultivable land in much of India after Independence has been positive, putting some brakes on arbitrary powers of the government. Nevertheless, the recognition of community rights, which the recent Act also provides for, has still been under-utilised, with initiatives such as the one in Mendha (Lekha) in Gadchiroli, Maharashtra, vis-à-vis bamboo remaining an exception.[82] There are encouraging signs that this may be changing, but it is a long way yet to reform tenures in the forest. The potential of the community rights proviso in the FRA is mainly in terms of widening protection but via a new instrument. These forests could act as corridors, check soil erosion and help maintain hydrological regimes if their use is regulated in a manner that does not impede regeneration and recruitment of trees, herbs and grasses. Its efficacy in conserving biological diversity is as yet unclear and will likely vary from one site to another.[83] Yet, it is worth asking and exploring new mechanisms such as these, both to empower citizens and also to expand and retain earth's green mantle without having to resort to government land acquisition. Such approaches also reinforce our central argument about fluid borders. Conservation can work in shared spaces via key alliances on the forest floor. In Niyamgiri, Odisha, the recognition of local collective rights to forest is also helping to keep intact an elephant corridor. This is a qualitatively new development, for such local knowledge and culture was earlier rarely integrated into the government's decision-making in such an open and transparent manner.[84]

The FRA and attendant rights-based laws are part of a large, complex and ongoing process, and the three of us as editors (and our more numerous authors) do not agree on each dimension.

But there is little doubt about its significance. Along with other such citizen-friendly laws, it widens the ambit of democracy to the forest space, which is heavily bureaucratised and carries a deep imperial hangover in dealings with citizens.[85] Even in Protected Areas, the enactment on forest rights ought to provide security against arbitrary and illegal dislocation and displacement. There are disturbing signs of the enactment not being followed to the letter in many tiger reserves. This issue has been raised not only by rights activists but also by a leading ecologist and in official fora.[86]

In the context of nature beyond borders, debates on the virtues of devolution and empowerment (and equally so of government control or corporate models) should not detract from the need for *some* strict reserves. These will inevitably form only a small fraction of the larger landscape but are vital as living libraries and laboratories of ecological systems. But where the new instrument may be of considerable ecological significance is in widening not only the social base of conservation thinking, but also in extending its reach to wider landscapes (and waterscapes, were there to be similar provisions for fishers), where some if not all ecosystem features are protected.[87] Social change governed by law in various arenas and diverse settings across this vast country thus offers opportunity to advance both human and ecological baselines.[88]

Restoration of Urban Forests and City Lakes

The actual dynamics of nature and society have constantly challenged any boundaries drawn in *space*. In much the same way, nature and society have also continually remade, if not challenged, the boundaries drawn in the dimension of *time*. This is a thorny and complex issue and short term generalisations can be a hazard. It is worth considering that denudation or degradation of forest cover was not the overarching historical trend in India across millenia. There is a significant history in centuries past of the recovery of uncultivated vegetation, and the term *jungle* used in the late eighteenth century for abandoned fields was itself an acknowledgement of the regrowth of secondary vegetation.[89] There is similarly now ample documented work on the recovery and regrowth in the fallows in cycles of swidden plots. But distinct from these unaided ecological recoveries and transitions, there are also cases of planned forest or ecological restoration that hold out hope in the longer term.

The Ridge forest in Delhi, the subject of an essay here by Ravi Agrawal, is a major battleground between those who wish to retain it for its intrinsic worth as a natural area and others who see it as land to be taken over for construction. Given that it is located in a greater metropolis of 25 million people, the battle at first sight looks like one that will be lost. Here, and in contrast to other essays in the volume, the issue is really of holding the line at the border, of literally preventing asphalt, concrete and cement from replacing shrubs and herbs, trees and bushes, peacocks and flycatchers, mongooses and jackals. Yet, the forest itself has a long and complex history, serving as hunting ground in medieval times, a war zone in 1857–58 and eventually being landscaped with intensive tree planting and afforestation in the second decade of the twentieth century. James Beatto's old photographs, taken in the aftermath of 1857, show a moonscape of rocks and stones, a far cry from the tree-covered landscape we see today.[90] It was active afforestation by foresters that laid the base, literally by bringing in soil, manure and saplings for the mosaic of forest types that make up the Ridge today. It is necessary to acknowledge the role and limits of such a forest: most of the large vertebrates are long gone, and an exotic, the mesquite tree, makes up much of the canopy. But as Agrawal shows, along with the riverfront of the Yamuna, it has a critical role to play in the urban environment. Ironic as it may be, even as the legacy of imperial foresters are such a sociopolitically confrontational one, here it is the green fingers of that very legacy that have helped recreate the green mantle. The ambitious work of University of Delhi's Centre for Degraded Ecosystems on restoration of the ecosystems of parts of the Aravali Ridge opens up exciting possibilities for the future.

Nagendra and her colleagues, Sivaraman and Subramanya, go a step further: from understanding to imagining restoration. Bengaluru or Bangalore has been the subject of fascinating histories that show the lakes and water bodies as integral to its evolution from fort city to cantonment to modern globalised metropolis.[91] What is critical is that the restoration of the ecological function and role of the lakes has been subject of active citizen debate. Where Delhi has the Ridge Management Board on which voluntary groups have nominees, Bengaluru has brought expertise as well as local elected representatives on board. This story is still unfolding for ecological restoration but it points to ways in which collective constructive action can work. There are major issues, the most difficult of which is the mutually conflicting ways in which urban elites (with property rights, secure housing and water supply, and high purchasing power) and the poor (who lack many of these basic amenities) view these water bodies. What is notable is the attempt to conduct open dialogue and discussion involving not only legislators but also local corporators and public bodies such as schools in the process. The actual issue of what to restore and how to do it poses dilemmas for science as much as for society.

In their larger work, Nagendra et al. urge that we look at when and how collective action has helped the processes of forest recovery. The latter is not a linear process and can happen variously via the routes of state fiat (as in old imperial hunting parks) or bureaucratic control (the Tiger Reserves) but there are other, alternative paths as well. The regenerating sal forests of western West Bengal had significant vegetation growth, according to Nagendra et al., but with continuing gaps in terms of biodiversity.[92] On the other hand, Nepal offers examples where such processes have shown far better results in bringing back not only forests, but also their denizens.[93] A more rigorous investigation is needed, not just into the ecological opportunities, but also into the ecological limits of such recovery.[94] Likewise, careful work is also needed into the tenurial arrangements, revenue sharing and local role in decision-making that can create or limit such opportunities.[95] But, all told, recovery and restoration are as much on the agenda as the protection of natural remnants.

The city has been the site, arena and subject of narratives of environmental change but these have mostly been about housing and sanitation, design and layout, the many ways of remaking urban spaces in a country where the percentage living in towns and cities has almost doubled since the mid twentieth century. But the city is also home to nonhuman life. It is sobering to recall that both Delhi, nestled between the Aravalis and the Yamuna River, and Bengaluru are in semi-arid zones. They have far more large trees per hectare today than they would if thorn forest and scrub dominated the vegetation complex. Nature thus spans rather than spills over borders, and people remake the land, not as and when they please, but as the contingent result of a series of contests and choices by myriad actors. Trees like the *neem* and *shisham* have been naturalised in the Ridge, just as ponds and lakes in and around Bengaluru have been deepened or de-silted by human choice and action.[96] Where and how cities relate to nature is an issue that will require more thought and action. Mumbai's Sanjay Gandhi National Park, Borivili has been a site of human-animal conflict as well as of contest between urban sprawl and conservation.[97]

To know how all these specifics relate to the wider picture, we need to return to the issue of how far projects of conservation can be enriched by perspectives that draw on the historical record and changing societal dynamics.

Towards Nature Without Borders

This brings us to a simple but prosaic truth. Seldom have 'hard' borders been an unqualified success, in a historical sense, in separating the entities they have sought to keep apart. People, and with them, ideas and artefacts, have invariably scaled these barriers over time. China's Great Wall in the fourteenth century CE aimed to shut off the sedentary societies to the south from the mobile pastoralists of the north. In 1912, the planner of New Delhi hoped to seal off the new city with gardens and open spaces from the more densely settled older city. Historians have shown how and why these attempts did not and could not work.[98] The flows of commodities and services, the movement of pathogens and people, of labour and capital meant that no barrier entirely severed contact. If people and their interactions have defied borders, nature has obeyed them even less. The idea of a border itself has limits. It has been virtually impossible to enclose nature within their borders. Engagements across lines are not only possible but also more necessary than ever before. The borders within which we have tried to sequester nature against the siege of human demographic and economic growth are important symbols, for they remind us of what we would like to secure, and against what. But as we have argued earlier, to proceed on the premise that these borders can or do stand up to the challenges posed by human aspirations or nature's functions is simply untenable.

There is a spectrum of responses to this proposition. At one end is a response which despairs that efforts to sequester nature within protected spaces may not be succeeding. As society's incursions on nature continue and the fortresses that secure nature crumble, and as nature insinuates itself back into human societies in newer ways, it apprehends that the high ideal—of nature's 'naturalness', its 'pristine' qualities—may be lost forever. An enclave-sensitive but pragmatic approach would be to rethink the meaning and context of the fortresses for nature. But it is much easier to bemoan their crumbling, and call for ever stronger enforcement.[99] Such approaches have self-evident limitations. It might be better still to reach out to form broader alliances. This approach tries to leverage a range of tactics from a direct appeal to power, through ecological reasoning, economic incentives, legal instruments and working closely with governments as 'fingers in the dyke' to keep Protected Areas secure.[100] A recent proposal to locate a major scientific facility underground in revenue lands and Reserved Forests at the edge of the adjacent Mudumalai Tiger Reserve was halted after protest.[101] Had it gone ahead, it might well have seriously affected habitat contiguity for large herbivores and predators in a key conservation region. Such victories are still rare. In the instance of the POSCO steel plant, the Odisha government gave primacy to economic growth over local rights under the FRA. This case in coastal Odisha is still significant for there were protests not only from local claimants to rights but also from turtle biologists and conservationists. The latter worried about nesting beaches that would be lost to make way for a port.[102] Such unusual alliances are not new but they do need to go well beyond tactical moves to espouse a more holistic set of alternatives. The two recent Western Ghats reports were efforts, albeit with differing approaches, that aimed to build in better safeguards in the pursuit of development and growth in an ecologically fragile region.[103] Although caught up in controversy, they merit closer look and further debate.

The question of nature goes well beyond a few refugia or even spaces where underprivileged groups have space as per the law. Nature 'spills out' of its assigned bounds, as when leopards or elephants lead a life amongst people in anthropogenic settings. Underclass and middle class interests may similarly clash when a city tries to revive a forest or renew the life cycles of a lake in its midst.

At the other end of the spectrum and going beyond refugia or rights-centred approach is the admission that borders have their limits. We argue that the boundaries we draw between nature and society are useful symbols—but merely symbols nonetheless—around which we must constantly reorder thoughts and actions about both nature and people. India—and for that matter the entire planet—has long been a mosaic of shifting landscapes and waterscapes, which have at once connected and at another level, separated the human world and the natural. Material flows of energy, water and biotic matter crisscross bounds as do human-made dynamic forces like commodities. The separation is attempted via law, judicial fiat and administrative intervention. We have consistently held here that the latter separation works on paper but is rarely in evidence in real life and even then only in highly specific contexts.

So, how can one advance nature-friendly agendas on a wider social and ecological canvas on which borders are continually being drawn, erased and redrawn? It is important to set out where we broadly stand vis-à-vis the present debates. This will help set the in-depth studies of this collection in perspective. That nature is in peril and needs a shield is a deep-seated view within the conservation community. Yet advocates of nature are divided on who will hold this shield and how best to design it.

Three paths suggest themselves at the present juncture. Secure nature preserves have, since the mid twentieth century and more so in India since the end of the 1960s, found defence from those who see statist control as a guarantor of harmony at the lines that ring the reserves, be they National Parks or tiger reserves. This seems to work, but only up to a point, in contests for space with resource-reliant livelihood seekers and also with strong economic interests on the horizon.

Second, and most so since the early 1990s, are various versions of community cooperation and participation. Although very persuasive in the abstract, they begin to run aground in face of more prosaic realities. Bureaucratic regimes, both forest and civil, undermine attempts to empower local bodies such as gram sabhas. Democratising society and enabling nature to endure can go together: but both encounter foot-dragging and resistance, though ground level mobilisation can help turn the corner as in the Western Himalayas, both with respect to forest protection and nature conservation.[104] Conversely, even in the process of conserving biodiversity, hierarchies of caste, gender and occupation may reinforce themselves even as they have done while retrieving soil fertility, grassland production and water recharge as in parts of western India.[105] Even the much celebrated sacred groves are often deeply interwoven with caste and gender exclusion.[106] Devolution, desirable as outcome, has to still engage with both equity and ecology. Further, community level initiatives require further and continuing study to ask when, why and how they work best, but to not try them out would be folly.[107] As a result, even their advocates are now critically re-assessing their limits and constraints.[108]

Third, and this is critical, is the new attraction of a corporate drive for nature, most evident in the bid to prevent even minimal regulation of tiger tourism in the half dozen sites where the large cat is easily seen. While issues of benefit-sharing with resident adjacent communities remain vital, what is most amusing is the way in which tourists are touted as the best 'protectors' of wildlife. This remains the case, even though the key burden of protection has largely been borne by forest staff and state governments, and the indirect costs of tourism, such as loss of water and amenities, has often been additionally borne by the underprivileged such as poor villagers or itinerant peoples to whom tourism offers very little in the first place.[109] Our criticism therefore is not of nature tourism per se but of the skewed corporate model under which it currently operates.

Each approach shows promise and yet, all have severe, even crippling limitations. Clearly, statist control for strict preservation or for conservation ('wise use') has diminishing returns, in the main because strong, elite economic interests, urban or rural, local or national or global, can capture and subvert protection. Even where protection endures, its inclusive capability and use of just means for desired outcomes is being and should be under question. Community-level approaches are certainly positive but have limits in their reach. Small in scale, they can renew hierarchies. Corporate conservation, now in its infancy, has yet to demonstrate its potential or redress justice issues. The scope of capture by specific interests is great. Our own instincts are pragmatic enough to admit that markets and global links cannot be wished away. Markets today penetrate mountain, forest and ocean alike, and carry the ability to shake their ecological foundations.[110] Coastal overfishing by trawlers is akin to clearcutting a forest of mature trees but is deeply linked to the market not only for palatable fish but for 'trash fish' that are eaten by poultry. Those who are sharply critical of market and capital driven growth models[111] do have a point but a reversal of markets and global links is not on the cards. Given the world we inhabit today, it may indeed be possible—and at times, even necessary—to imagine and engage markets as a force to be harnessed to ecological recovery.[112] Studies in this volume show how a spectrum of players from Himalayan shepherds to plantation companies can creatively engage with existing institutions of government, market and local self government to widen spaces for nature. There are few stark 'either/or' choices.

Our approach here—one broadly shared by contributors—is to be open to diverse approaches, but deeply conscious of how people and practices, ecologies and economies are shifting mosaics. Further, a careful mix and match of different instruments can only work if citizens on ground have greater opportunity for self-improvement, and we are convinced that there are enough instances where this can be combined with ecologically sane ways to conserve nature. Such instances are neither universal nor widespread enough.

To paraphrase the late Chinese leader Deng Xiao Ping, we can 'cross the river while feeling the stones'. Finding these fords is where the creative challenge lies. As the contributors to this book exemplify, in this process, there is as much of a role for corporate businesses, for instance, with ecological restoration on commercial plantations. There is also a key role for government, say, in enabling livestock insurance programmes that not only protect livestock but also reduce retaliatory killing of carnivores, or for local communities to determine how to make space for birds on farmlands while seeking better agricultural returns. There is role for the local—in the city and cultivated arable, mountain, pasture and forest. There will be times of protest and struggle. Yet, as history has shown, alongside such mobilisation and action, positive and constructive brick-by-brick initiatives can also flourish. These transitions will only be made easier with further strengthening of democratic norms. At the same time, a careful partnership with markets coupled with state assistance to the needy—for instance, with crop and cattle insurance, access to credit and timely expertise, support for cooperative endeavours and strengthening of property rights regimes—can help us find the many fords across the river. If nothing else, these approaches can take us beyond a fences-and-guards approach with its single-minded, even obsessive, focus on fortresses whose walls, in reality, have long been breached by market and demographic forces.

This requires engagement not only with protection but also production; not only with 'inviolate spaces' but also with human settlements, towards a vision of 'reconciliation ecology'.[113] Often, conservationists try to go beyond small nuclei of the middle class, bureaucracy and science but now they need to reach out to even larger social and political constituencies. This requires a revolution not only of action but also in thought. Conservation in practice has to tie in with wider secular trends that combine ecological sanity with justice, a space for nature with one for livelihoods. We have to conserve nature but not by being conservative in social or, for that matter, intellectual terms. We have tried to bring together a selection of working approaches with different and often more effective ways of drawing on knowledge and institutions, processes and practices to create more, not less, space for nature. But for that we need to think afresh and create anew. Nature without borders is not just about more of the same. It is about some of the new.

Notes

1. See S. Chape, J. Harrison, M. Spalding and I. Lysenko, 'Measuring the extent and effectiveness of protected areas as an indicator for meeting global biodiversity targets', *Philosophical Transactions of the Royal Society Series B* 360 (2005): 443–55; and D. Brockington, R. Duffy and J. Igoe, *Nature Unbound: Conservation, capitalism and the future of protected areas* (London: Earthscan, 2008).

2. On China, see J. Watts, *When a Billion Chinese Jump: Voices from the frontline of climate change* (New York: Scribner, 2010). On Brazil, see S. B. Hecht and A. Cockburn, *The Fate of the Forest: Developers, destroyers, and defenders of the Amazon* (Chicago: University of Chicago Press, 1990). On South Africa, see J. Carruthers, *The Kruger National Park: A social and political history* (Durban: University of Kwazulu-Natal Press, 1995).

3. See S. Guha, *Health and Population in South Asia: From earliest times to the present* (New Delhi: Permanent Black, 2001), pp. 31–34.

4. A. Bhaduri, *The Face You Were Afraid to See: Essays on the Indian economy* (New Delhi: Penguin Books India, 2009); and A. Roy, *Listening to Grasshoppers: Field notes on democracy* (London: Penguin UK, 2009).

5. J. Dreze and A. Sen, *An Uncertain Glory: India and its contradictions* (New Delhi: Penguin India, 2013).

6. P. C. Perdue, *China Marches West: The Qing conquest of Central Eurasia* (Cambridge, MA: Harvard University Press, 2009), pp. 41–44.

7. M. D. Spence, *Dispossessing the Wilderness: Indian removal and the making of the national parks* (New York: Oxford University Press, 1999).

8. K. Jacoby, *Crimes Against Nature: Squatters, poachers, thieves, and the hidden history of American conservation* (Berkeley: University of California Press, 2003).

9. A. Jalais, *Forest of Tigers: People, politics and environment in the Sundarbans* (London: Routledge, 2011).

10. A. Ghosh, *The Hungry Tide* (London: Harper Collins, 2006), pp. 2–6.

11. A. Jalais, 'Unmasking the cosmopolitan tiger', *Nature and Culture* 3 (2008): 25–40.

12. See, L. Hughes, *Moving the Maasai: A colonial misadventure* (Basingstoke: Palgrave Macmillan, 2006); L. Hughes, 'Rough time in paradise: Claims, blames and memory making around some protected areas in Kenya', *Conservation and Society* 5 (2007): 307–30; and J. Patinkin, 'Tanzania's Maasai battle game hunters for grazing land', *BBC News*, 18 April 2013. Available at http://www.bbc.co.uk/news/world-africa-22155538 (accessed 13 May 2014).

13. F. Zimmermann, *The Jungle and the Aroma of Meats: An ecological theme in Hindu medicine* (Berkeley: University of California Press, 1989), pp. 170–73; and M. Rangarajan, *India's Wildlife History: An introduction* (New Delhi: Permanent Black, 2001), pp. 2–3.

14. T. T. Allsen, *The Royal Hunt in Eurasian History* (Philadelphia: University of Pennsylvania Press, 2011), pp. 18, 19, 31–33.

15. M. K. Ranjitsinh, *Beyond the Tiger: Portraits of Asian Wildlife* (New Delhi: Brijbasi Publishers, 1995), pp. 22–23; M. Rangarajan, 'Forest as faunal enclave' in S. Hecht, K. D. Morrison and C. Padoch (eds), *The Social Life of Forests: The Past, Present and Future of Woodland Resurgence* (Chicago: University of Chicago Press, 2014).

16. M. Rangarajan, 'From princely symbol to conservation icon: The political history of the lion in India' in M. Hasan and N. Nazakato (eds), *Unfinished Agendas: Nationalism in South Asia* (New Delhi: Manohar Publishers, 2001), pp. 371–99.

17. R. Johari, 'Paper tigers and invisible people: The cultural politics of nature' in G. Shahabuddin and M. Rangarajan (eds), *Making Conservation Work: Securing biodiversity in this new century* (New Delhi: Permanent Black, 2007), pp. 48–80.

18. A. G. Gold and B. R. Gujjar, *In the Time of Trees and Sorrows: Nature, power, and memory in Rajasthan* (Durham: Duke University Press, 2002).

19. J. E. Hughes, *Animal Kingdoms: Hunting, the environment, and power in the Indian princely states* (Cambridge: Harvard University Press, 2013), 26.

20. A. Runte, *National Parks: The American experience* (Boulder: Taylor Trade Publications, 2010); A. C. Isenberg, *The Destruction of the Bison: An environmental history, 1750–1920* (Cambridge: Cambridge University Press, 2001); and B. Weber and A. Vedder, *In the Kingdom of Gorillas: The quest to save Rwanda's mountain gorillas* (New York: Simon and Schuster, 2012).

21. A. Saikia, 'Kaziranga National Park: Dynamics of social and political history', *Conservation and Society* 7 (2009): 113–29.

22. W. A. Rodgers, D. Hartley and S. Bashir, 'Community approaches to conservation: Some comparisons between India and Africa' in V. Saberwal and M. Rangarajan (eds), *Battles Over Nature: Science and the politics of conservation* (New Delhi: Permanent Black, 2003), pp. 324–82, 344.

23. *Assam Tribune*, 'Translocated rhinos rehab prog receives big boost', 8 July 2013.

24. *Hindu*, 'Right to fly (advertisement by the Government of Rajasthan)', 5 June 2013.

25. Government of India, *Indian Board for Wildlife (IBWL) Report of the Expert Committee* (Ministry of Agriculture, New Delhi, 1970).

26. J. Vaillant, *The Tiger: A true story of vengeance and survival* (New York: Knopf, 2010).

27. M. Rangarajan, 'Contesting Conservation: Nature, politics and history in contemporary India' in T. S. Patel and T. Uys (eds), *Contemporary India and South Africa: Legacies, identities and dilemmas* (New Delhi: Routledge, 2012), pp. 241–58.

28. M. Krishnan, *India's Wildlife in 1959–70: An ecological survey of the larger mammals of Peninsular India* (Bombay: Bombay Natural History Society, 1975), pp. 113, 136.

29. M. K. Ranjitsinh and Y. V. Jhala, 'Assessing the potential for reintroducing the cheetah in India' (Noida and Dehradun: Wildlife Trust of India and Wildlife Institute of India, 2010).

30. K. U. Karanth, *View From the Machan: How science can save the fragile predator.* (Ranikhet: Permanent Black, 2005); V. Thapar, *The Last Tiger: Struggling for survival* (New Delhi: Oxford University Press, 2012); V. Thapar, *Battling for Survival: India's wilderness over two centuries* (New Delhi: Oxford University Press, 2003); and B. Sahgal, *The Kaziranga Inheritance* (Mumbai: Sanctuary Books, 2005).

31. W. F. Laurance, D. Carolina Useche, J. Rendeiro, M. Kalka, C. J. A. Bradshaw, et al., 'Averting biodiversity collapse in tropical forest protected areas', *Nature* 489 (2012): 290–94.

32. J. Liu, M. Linderman, Z. Ouyang, L. An, J. Yang and H. Zhang, 'Ecological degradation in protected areas: The case of Wolong Nature Reserve for giant pandas', *Science* 292, no. 5514, (2001).

33. Government of India, 'Joining the Dots: Report of the Tiger Task Force' (New Delhi: Ministry of Environment and Forests, 2005).

34. G. Shahabuddin, *Conservation at the Crossroads: Science, society, and the future of India's wildlife* (New Delhi: Permanent Black, 2010).

35. B. Sundaram, and A. J. Hiremath, '*Lantana camara* invasion in a heterogeneous landscape: Patterns of spread and correlation with changes in native vegetation', *Biological Invasions* 14 (2012): 1127–41.

36. Personal communication with A. J. T. Johnsingh.

37. A. R. Rahmani, 'Conservation outside protected areas: Case studies of bustard protection' in Saberwal and Rangarajan (eds), Battles Over Nature, pp. 117–38.

38. V. K. Saberwal, J. P. Gibbs, R. Chellam and A. J. T. Johnsingh, 'Lion-human conflict in the Gir forest, India', *Conservation Biology* 8 (1994): 501–07.

39. Saikia, 'Kaziranga National Park: Dynamics of social and political history'; and A. Saikia, 'Kaziranga National Park: History, landscape and conservation practices', *Economic and Political Weekly* 46 (2011): 12–13.

40. S. Nag, *Pied pipers in North-East India: Bamboo-flower, rat-famine and the politics of philanthrophy (1881–2007)* (New Delhi: Manohar Publishers, 2008).

41. D. Janzen, 'The eternal external threat' in M. E. Soule (ed.), *Conservation Biology: The science of scarcity and diversity* (Sunderland: Sinauer Associates, 1986), pp. 286–303.

42. A. Shah, *In the Shadows of the State: Indigenous politics, environmentalism and insurgency in Jharkhand, India* (Durham: Duke University Press, 2010).

43. M. Rangarajan, A. Desai, R. Sukumar, P. S. Easa, V. Menon, D. S. Vincent, S. Ganguly, B. K. Talukdar, B. Singh, D. Mudappa, S. Chowdhury and A. N. Prasad, 'Gajah: securing the future for elephants in India' (New Delhi: Ministry of Environment and Forests, Government of India, New Delhi, 2010); and Karnataka Elephant Task Force (KETF), 'Report of the Karnataka Elephant Task Force appointed by the Karnataka High Court' (Bangalore: Government of Karnataka, 2012).

44. *Times of India*, 'Tusker trail', 25 June 2013, Bengaluru edition.

45. V. Athreya, 'Is relocation a viable management option for unwanted animals?: The case of the leopard in India', *Conservation and Society* 4 (2006): 419–23;

V. Athreya, M. Odden, J. D. C. Linnell and K. U. Karanth, 'Translocation as a tool for mitigating conflict with leopards in human-dominated landscapes of India', *Conservation Biology* 25 (2011): 133–41; V. Athreya, M. Odden, J. D. C. Linnell, J. Krishnaswamy and U. Karanth, 'Big cats in our backyards: Persistence of large carnivores in a human dominated landscape in India', *PLoS ONE* 8 (2013): e57872; and V. R. Athreya, S. S. Thakur, S. Chaudhuri and A. V. Belsare, 'Leopards in human-dominated areas: A spillover from sustained translocations into nearby forests?' *Journal of the Bombay Natural History Society* 104 (2007): 45–50.

46. S. K. Mondal, M. W. Bruford and U. Ramakrishnan, 'Demographic loss, genetic structure and the conservation implications for Indian tigers', *Proceedings of the Royal Society B* 280, no. 1762, (2013).

47. Personal communication with K. Kakati.

48. A. J. T. Johnsingh, K. Ramesh, Q. Qureshi, A. David, S. P. Goyal, et al., 'Conservation status of tiger and associated species in the Terai Arc Landscape, India' RR-04/001, (Dehradun: Wildlife Institute of India, 2004).

49. A population where there is no net growth due to sub-optimal conditions, and often populated by spillover of individuals from thriving 'source' populations such as can exist in large suitable habitats and where population growth is in the positive.

50. M. E. Sunquist, 'The social organization of tigers (*Panthera tigris*) in Royal Chitawan National Park, Nepal', *Smithsonian Contributions to Zoology* 98 (1981).

51. Y. V. Jhala, R. Chellam, B. Pathak, V. Meena and P. Basu, *Ecology of the lion in Greater Gir Landscape* (Dehradun: Wildlife Institute of India, 2011); M. Rangarajan, 'Animals with rich histories: The case of the lions of Gir Forest, Gujarat, India', *History and Theory* 52 (2013), 109–27.

52. Athreya, et al., 'Big Cats in our Backyards'.

53. A. Sharma, 'Off to pastures new', *Hindu*, 9 June 2013.

54. L. Naughton-Treves, M. B. Holland and K. Brandon, 'The role of protected areas in conserving biodiversity and sustaining local livelihoods', *Annual Review Environment and Resources* 30 (2005): 219–52.

55. A. C. Lees and C. A. Peres, 'Habitat and life history determinants of antbird occurrence in variable-sized Amazonian forest fragments', Biotropica 42 (2010): 614–21.

56. Species requiring large areas for meeting their foraging and breeding needs on account of large size, and those that are generally the first to disappear once a continuous forest area is fragmented.

57. G. Shahabuddin and J. W. Terborgh, 'Frugivorous butterflies in Venezuelan forest fragments: Abundance, diversity and the effects of isolation', *Journal of Tropical Ecology* 15 (1999): 703–22.

58. J. Fischer, B. Brosi, G. C. Daily, P. R. Ehrlich, R. Goldman, et al., 'Should agricultural policies encourage land sparing or wildlife-friendly farming?', *Frontiers in Ecology and the Environment* 6 (2008): 380–85; B. Phalan, M. Onial, A. Balmford and R. E. Green, 'Reconciling food production and biodiversity conservation: Land sharing and land sparing compared', *Science* 333, no. 6047 (2011): 1289–91.

59. T. Tscharntke, Y. Clough, T. C. Wanger, L. Jackson, I. Motzke, et al., 'Global food security, biodiversity conservation and the future of agricultural intensification', *Biological Conservation* 151 (2012): 53–59.

60. R. Naoroji, 'Contamination in egg shells of Himalayan grey headed eagle in the Corbett National Park, Uttar Pradesh', *Journal of the Bombay Natural History Society* 94 (1997): 398–400.

61. V. Prakash, 'Status of vultures in Keoladeo National Park, Bharatpur, Rajasthan, with special reference to population crash in *Gyps* species', *Journal of the Bombay Natural History Society* 96 (1999): 365–78.

62. R. Carson, *Silent Spring* (London: Hamish Hamilton, 1962); L. Lear, *Rachel Carson: Witness for nature* (London: Macmillan, 1998).

63. R. E. Green, M. A. Taggart, D. Das, D. J. Pain, C. S. Kumar, et al., 'Collapse of Asian vulture populations: Risk of mortality from residues of the veterinary drug diclofenac in carcasses of treated cattle', *Journal of Applied Ecology* 43 (2006): 949–56; R. Naoroji, *Birds of prey of the Indian subcontinent* (New Delhi: Om Books International, 2007).

64. R. Leakey, 'Not-so-cold mountain', *Economist* 18 November 2005. Available at http://www.economist.com/node/5134723 (accessed 8 April 2014).

65. K. Lahiri-Dutt and G. Samanta, *Dancing with the River: People and lives on the chars of South Asia* (Yale: Yale University Press, 2012).

66. M. Rangarajan, *Fencing the Forest: Conservation and ecological change in India's Central Provinces, 1860–1914* (New Delhi: Oxford University Press, 1996); V. K. Saberwal, *Pastoral Politics: Shepherds, bureaucrats and conservation in the Western Himalaya* (New Delhi: Oxford University Press, 1999); A. Pratap, *The Hoe and The Axe: An ethnohistory of shifting cultivation in Eastern India* (New Delhi: Oxford University Press, 1999).

67. A. Prasad, 'The political ecology of swidden cultivation: The survival strategies of the Baigas in the Central Provinces 1860–1960' in M. Rangarajan, and K. Sivaramakrishnan (eds), *India's Environmental History, Volume 2* (Ranikhet: Permanent Black, 2012), pp. 246–80; S. Dasgupta, 'Accessing nature: Forest laws and their impact on an *Adivasi* economy in Central India', *Conservation and Society* 7 (2009): 227–38.

68. G. Shahabuddin and M. Rangarajan, *Making Conservation Work: Securing biodiversity in this new century* (New Delhi: Permanent Black, 2007), pp. 1–20.

69. T. R. S. Raman, 'Effect of slash-and-burn shifting cultivation on rainforest birds in Mizoram, Northeast India', *Conservation Biology* 15 (2001): 685–98.

70. R. Kumar, G. Shahabuddin and A. Kumar, 'How good are managed forests at conserving native woodpecker communities?: A study in sub-Himalayan dipterocarp forests of northwest India', *Biological Conservation* 144 (2011): 1876–84.

71. See Raman, 'Effect of slash-and-burn shifting cultivation'; Kumar, Shahabuddin and Kumar, 'How good are managed forests', and Sundar; this volume.

72. L. Hazzah and S. Dolrenry, 'Coexisting with predators', *Seminar* 577 (2007): 21–27; L. Hazzah, S. Dolrenry, D. Kaplan and L. Frank, 'The influence of park

access during drought on attitudes toward wildlife and lion killing behaviour in Maasailand, Kenya', *Environmental Conservation* (forthcoming); D. Western, *In the Dust of Kilimanjaro* (Washington DC: Island Press, 2001); T. Catton, *Inhabited Wilderness: Indians, Eskimos, and National Parks in Alaska* (Albuquerque: University of New Mexico Press, 1997); G. P. Nabhan, *Gathering the Desert* (Tucson: University of Arizona Press, 1987).

73. W. Cronon, 'The trouble with wilderness: Or, getting back to the wrong nature' in W. Cronon (ed.), *Uncommon Ground: Rethinking the human place in nature* (New York: W. W. Norton & Company, 1995), pp. 69–90.

74. Catton, *Inhabited Wilderness.*

75. G. Cederlöf, 'Fixed boundaries, fluid landscapes: British expansion into northern East Bengal in the 1820s', *Indian Economic and Social History Review* 4 (2009): 513–40; K. Morrison, 'Opening up the pre-colonial: Primeval forests, baseline thinking and other archives in environmental history' in M. Rangarajan and K. Sivaramakrishnan (eds), *Shifting Ground: People, mobility and animals in India's environmental pasts* (New Delhi: Oxford University Press, forthcoming).

76. M. D. Madhusudan, 'Recovery of wild large herbivores following livestock decline in a tropical Indian wildlife reserve', *Journal of Applied Ecology* 41 (2004): 858–69; M. D. Madhusudan, 'The global village: Linkages between subsistence use and global markets in a forest-based rural economy in southern India', *Conservation Biology* 19 (2005): 411–20.

77. P. Sankaran and M. D. Madhusudan, 'Desperate neighbours: Endangered wildlife and the rural poor', The Hindu, *Survey of the Environment 2010* (2010):113–18.

78. See Lobo and Arthur, and Kelkar and Krishnaswamy's essays in this volume.

79. D. Biggs, Quagmire: *Nation-building and Nature in the Mekong Delta* (Seattle: University of Washington Press, 2012), pp. 43–44.

80. K. U. Karanth and P. Bhargav, 'De-fragmenting nature', *Seminar* 552 (2005): 59–61.

81. M. Kapoor, K. Kohli and M. Menon, *India's Notified Ecologically Sensitive Areas (ESAs)* (Pune: Kalpavriksh, 2009).

82. R. Mahapatra and K. S. Shrivastava, 'Bamboo rising', *Down To Earth*, 2013. Available at http://www.downtoearth.org.in/content/bamboo-rising (accessed 9 April 2014).

83. G. Shahabuddin, *Conservation at the Crossroads*; G. Shahabuddin and M. Rao, 'Do community-conserved areas effectively conserve biodiversity: global insights and the Indian context', *Biological Conservation* 143 (2010): 2926–29.

84. Savyasaachi, 'The tiger and the honeybee', *Seminar* 423 (1995): 30–35.

85. S. Gopalakrishnan, 'Conservation and democracy', *Seminar* 638 (2010): 66–71; Roma, 'Forest justice movements', *Seminar* 638 (2010): 75–77.

86. C. R. Bijoy, 'The great Indian tiger show', *Economic and Political Weekly* 46 (2011): 36–41; A. Datta, 'Science, policy, politics and human rights: Myriad dimensions of conservation in the real world', Public lecture at the Society for Conservation Biology (Asia) Meeting, Bangalore, 10 August, 2012. Unpublished.

87. G. Shahabuddin, *Conservation at the Crossroads.*

88. A. Subramanian, *Shore Lines, Space and Rights in South India* (New Delhi: Yoda Press, 2013); M. Gadgil, 'Ecology, science and democracy in India', 2013. Available at http://www.nehrumemorial.org/audio/(594)Lecture-by-Sh.Madhav-Gadgil-17-7-13.MP3 (accessed 5 February 2014).

89. M. Rangarajan and K. Sivaramakrishnan (eds), *India's Environmental History: From ancient times to the colonial period, Volume 1* (New Delhi: Permanent Black, 2012), pp. 1–36.

90. J. Masselos and N. Gupta, *Beato's Delhi: 1857 and beyond* (New Delhi: Ravi Dayal and Penguin Viking, 2011).

91. J. Nair, *The Promise of the Metropolis: Bangalore's twentieth century* (New Delhi: Oxford University Press, 2005).

92. H. Nagendra, S. Paul, S. Pareeth and S. Dutt, 'Landscapes of protection: Forest change and fragmentation in northern West Bengal', *Environmental Management* 44 (2009): 853–64.

93. E. Dinerstein, A. Rijal, M. Bookbinder, B. Kattel and A. Rajuria, 'Tigers as neighbours: Efforts to promote local guardianship of endangered species in lowland Nepal' in J. Seidensticker, S. Christie and P. Jackson (eds), *Riding the Tiger: Tiger conservation in human-dominated landscapes* (Cambridge: Cambridge University Press, 1999), pp. 316–33; E. Dinerstein, C. Loucks, E. Wikramanayake, J. Ginsberg, E. Sanderson, et al., 'The fate of wild tigers', *BioScience* 57 (2007): 508–14.

94. N. H. Carter, B. K. Shrestha, J. B. Karki, N. M. B. Pradhan and J. Liu, 'Coexistence between wildlife and humans at fine spatial scales', *Proceedings of the National Academy of Sciences (USA)* 109 (2012): 15360–65; V. R. Goswami, D. Vasudev, D. Karnad, Y. C. Krishna, M. Krishnadas, et al., 'Conflict of human–wildlife coexistence', *Proceedings of the National Academy of Sciences (USA)* 110 (2013): E108; A. Harihar, P. Chanchani, R. K. Sharma, J. Vattakaven, S. Gubbi, et al., 'Conflating "co-occurrence" with "coexistence"', *Proceedings of the National Academy of Sciences (USA)* 110 (2013): E109; K. U. Karanth, A. M. Gopalaswamy K. K. Karanth, J. Goodrich, J. Seidensticker and J. G. Robinson, 'Sinks as saviors: Why flawed inference cannot assist tiger recovery', *Proceedings of the National Academy of Sciences (USA)* 110 (2013): E110; N. H. Carter, B. K. Shrestha, J. B. Karki, N. M. B. Pradhan and J. Liu, 'Reply to Goswami et al., Harihar et al., and Karanth et al.: Fine-scale interactions between tigers and people', *Proceedings of the National Academy of Sciences (USA)* 110 (2013): E111–E112.

95. A. Agrawal and E. Ostrom, 'Collective action, property rights, and decentralization in resource use in India and Nepal', *Politics and Society* 29 (2001): 485–514; E. Ostrom and H. Nagendra, 'Insights on linking forests, trees, and people from the air, on the ground, and in the laboratory', *Proceedings of the National Academy of Sciences (USA)* 103 (2006): 19224–31.

96. P. Krishen, *Trees of Delhi: A field guide* (New Delhi: Penguin Books, 2006); S. Srinivas, *Landscapes of Urban Memory: The sacred and the civic in India's high-tech city* (Hyderabad: Orient Longman, 2004).

97. Athreya et al., 'Translocation as a tool for mitigating conflict'; D. Parthasarathy, 'Hunters, Gatherers and Foragers in a Metropolis: Commonising the Private and Public in Mumbai', *Economic and Political Weekly* 46 (2011): 54–63.

98. Perdue, *China Marches West*; S. Legg, *Spaces of Colonialism: Delhi's urban governmentalities* (London: Wiley-Blackwell, 2011).

99. Thapar, *The Last Tiger*; V. Thapar, *Ranthambhore: 10 days in the tiger fortress* (New Delhi: Oxford University Press, 2011); R. E. Leakey and R. Lewin, *The Sixth Extinction: Biodiversity and its survival* (New York: Anchor Books, 1996); R. E. Leakey and V. Morell, *Wildlife Wars: My battle to save Kenya's elephants* (London: Pan Macmillan, 2001).

100. T. R. S. Raman and D. Mudappa, 'Island in peril: Conservation caveats', *Hindu*, 25 February 2012; *Our Bureau*, 'Javadekar clears Karwar Nath Base Project', *Economic Times*, 10 June 2014. This is in reference to Narcondum Island as a site for a radar station.

101. R. Ramachandran, 'Ministry's "no" to neutrino observatory project in Nilgiris', *Hindu*, 21 November 2009.

102. M. Rajshekar, 'Posco's Orissa project: Many hurdles lie ahead despite environment ministry's approval', *Economic Times*, 8 May 2011.

103. Government of India, 'Report of the Western Ghats Ecology Expert Panel: Part 1 & 2' (New Delhi: Ministry of Environment and Forests, 2011); Government of India, 'Report of the High Level Working Group on Western Ghats: Volumes I and II' (New Delhi: Ministry of Environment and Forests, 2013).

104. A. Agrawal, *Environmentality: Technologies of government and the making of subjects* (Durham: Duke University Press, 2005); A. Chhatre and V. K. Saberwal, *Democratizing Nature: Politics, conservation, and development in India* (New Delhi: Oxford University Press, 2006).

105. M. Sharma, *Green and Saffron: Hindu nationalism and Indian environmental politics* (Ranikhet: Permanent Black, 2012).

106. R. Freeman, 'Folk models of the forest environment' in M. Rangarajan and K. Sivaramakrishnan (eds), *India's Environmental History, Volume 2* (Ranikhet: Permanent Black, 2012), pp. 169–96.

107. A. Kothari, N. Pathak, R. V. Anuradha and B. Taneja (eds), *Communities and Conservation: Natural resource management in South and Central Asia* (New Delhi: Sage, 1998).

108. A. Kothari, 'The many colours of environmentalism', *Economic and Political Weekly* 47 (2012).

109. K. K. Karanth and R. DeFries, 'Nature-based tourism in Indian protected areas: New challenges for park management', *Conservation Letters* 4 (2011): 137–49. K. U. Karanth and K. K. Karanth, 'A tiger in the drawing room', *Economic and Political Weekly* 47 (2012): 38–43.

110. Madhusudan, 'The global village'; J. Berger, B. Buuveibataar and C. Mishra, 'Globalization of the cashmere market and the decline of large mammals in Central Asia', *Conservation Biology* 27 (2013): 679–89; also, see Lobo and Arthur, this volume.

111. A. Shrivastava and A. Kothari, *Churning the Earth: The making of global India* (New Delhi: Penguin, 2012).

112. See Mudappa, Kumar and Raman, this volume.

113. M. L. Rosenzweig, *Win-Win Ecology: How the earth's species can survive in the midst of human enterprise* (New York: Oxford University Press, 2003).

One
TRAWLING THE SHORELINES
Fished Out and Squandered

Aaron Savio Lobo and Rohan Arthur

We love fish. Fish is good for us. High in Omega-3 fatty acids, fish plays a vital role in brain development and in maintaining a healthy heart. The Indian coastal cuisine is replete with an extraordinary diversity of seafood recipes. Incomes from fishing support entire coastal communities. Fish is big business, and ensuring that our love for it is satisfied requires an increasingly efficient harvesting of the ocean to maximise production.

We love fish. Yet somehow, we love fish in a slightly different way than we love other species of wildlife. While the country's human-dominated landscape is largely either owned or managed by people in some way, and its species bounded within protective pickets of restrictions, fines and jail sentences, all but the most charismatic of marine species are fair additions to the already bountiful seafood platter. We may loathe the slaughter of wildlife for bushmeat, but we will still want to ensure that seafood is harvested at rates that allow our calamari rings not to cost the earth.

Hunting and fishing are, of course, of the same lot.[1] In fact, marine hunters employ the most advanced technology available to chase down their prey. Today, fishing vessels the size of small cruise liners, often working in pairs, using nets several kilometers long, drag their gear along the ocean floor and scrape up everything in their path. Many of these fishing trawlers come equipped with freezing and processing facilities to process their catch at sea according to customer specifications which also allows them to stay out at sea for extended periods and helps reduce costs. This is hunting alright, but at scales unimagined by the artisanal fisher stalking his evening meal with a bamboo trap or wooden harpoon. And no terrestrial hunting has ever matched the sheer industrial quantities of daily offtake gathered from the sea. Increasingly, in India, this has little to do with satisfying our hankering after fish curry and rice. It is an industry adapting to its own economic impulses, keeping itself afloat—quite literally—by responding to changes in supply and demand, seeking new markets, repackaging its products and byproducts to woo these new markets, reinventing itself constantly in order to survive. The upshot of this industrial inventiveness is that a system of production that should have been rightfully unsustainable years ago continues to persist at increasing ecological and socioeconomic costs. And since all of this happens beneath the waves, it largely escapes the noisy debates over the vanishing wilds.

Here we present a potted recent history of trawl fishing along the Indian coastline, and trace its ecological and economic fallout to coastal communities. We discuss the factors currently driving the economics of trawling within the Indian scenario, and explore potential directions towards a more meaningful management of this harvest. Our discussion focuses on the fishery of the Coromandel Coast, but it is indicative of much of the rest of the Indian coastline.

Indian Fisheries: A Brief History

The growth of the fisheries sector in India began as part of the five year plan post-Independence with the key goal of achieving self-sufficiency in terms of food production in the shortest possible time through agricultural and fisheries development. These modest ambitions were rapidly replaced by much more industrial ones like maximising foreign exchange earnings from the fisheries sector in particular.

The introduction and initial trial experiments to test the effectiveness of trawl fishing was facilitated with aid provided by the Indo-Norwegian project and the Food and Agricultural Organization.[2] Along the Coromandel Coast, trawlers were first introduced in Chennai. Before the introduction of trawlers, the sea off the Coromandel was largely fished by sail-propelled crafts called *kattumarams*, which translates to 'tied wood' in Tamil, and from which the word catamaran is derived. Often these were little more than a couple of logs bound together to make a seaworthy craft. Limited by this lack of sophistication, artisanal fishers primarily employed passive (stationary) gear and predominantly targeted fish.[3] They had no holding space or preserving facilities. Trips were short, within striking distance of beaches where they would land their craft, and the catch was either supplied to local markets or intended for self-consumption.

Scraping the Bottom

When trawling began in earnest in the 1960s it was not fish but shrimp that was the main revenue provider. Such was its value that the noble aim of developing Indian fisheries to achieve self-sufficiency and to make available a cheap source of protein to the country's poor was all but forgotten as trawlers tapped export markets for the most part.[4] In fact, the growth of the trawling sector in India coincided with the development and growth of the export markets for shrimp. The shrimp caught was exported mainly to the US, Europe, Australia and Japan.

Shrimp are among several species of crustacean that predominantly live on the sea floor where they generally feed on small plankton and invertebrates or scavenge on dead creatures. In a marine system they belong to the lowest rung of the trophic pyramid. The targeted shrimp can range in size. However, the most commonly caught species are generally a few centimetres long and a couple of millimetres in width. The trawler net is designed to make close contact with the sea floor. It is conical in shape and the mesh becomes increasingly fine from the mouth to the cod-end (the tapered end of the net where the catch is concentrated) to ensure that not even the smallest shrimp escapes. Large otter boards help weigh the net down while aiding its contact with the sea floor. A system of floats and weights at the margin of the roof and the floor respectively, together with the otter boards keep the mouth of the net open. While this entire rig is a very efficient system of harvesting shrimp, it results in the indiscriminate capture of large quantities of non-target (bycatch) species often in far higher quantities than the target catch.

When this form of fishing began, trawlers dragged their nets freely through fresh territory and relatively unexploited benthic resources, given that artisanal fishers primarily fished in sail-propelled crafts and employed gear that was stationary rather than dragging it over the sea floor like trawlers did. Moreover, the artisanal fishers mainly targeted pelagic fish (fish that swim near the surface) rather than shrimp.[5] The first few years of trawling saw glut catches. The catches of shrimp in particular were high and fetched good prices, particularly in the export market. Moreover, since the main export demand was for shrimp, cephalopods and a few fish species (a demand largely driven by western consumption), trawl fishers primarily reserved their storage space for this target catch. The remaining bycatch, always in far higher proportions than the target catch, was generally dumped overboard, by this stage usually dead. For every kilo of shrimp, a trawler captures approximately 10 kilos of bycatch.[6] The global estimate of fisheries discards is currently around seven million tonnes per year.[7] The tropical trawl bycatch includes a large diversity of species. Along the Coromandel Coast, each trawl rakes up a sad taxonomic cornucopia that includes everything from sponges, starfish, sea cucumbers, corals, a large diversity of fish species, marine reptiles (sea snakes and sea turtles) and the occasional dolphin. Since trawlers fish the near-shore shallow grounds, which are the preferred spawning grounds of many coastal species, they end up capturing large quantities of juveniles (including target species), larvae and eggs. A considerable portion of bycatch is suitable for human consumption and is sold to local markets and can be regarded as commercial bycatch. The rest of the bycatch is generally made up of small, undersized marine species which, for various reasons such as their small size, noxious nature and low commercial value, are collectively termed 'trash fish'.[8] When trawling began, trash fish as well as significant quantities of commercial bycatch were discarded since trawling was primarily an export driven venture.

The initial trawling experiments carried out in various coastal states through aid provided by the Food and Agriculture Organization and the Indo-Norwegian Project clearly demonstrated that trawlers were undoubtedly the finest seafood harvesting machines.[9] The most productive grounds for shrimp also happened to be the near-shore shallow areas of the continental shelf, the domain of the by then vulnerable artisanal fishers.[10] By dragging their nets in these shallow regions where the target catch was abundant, trawlers damaged the passive gear (lines, gill nets, beach seines and traps) employed by artisans and brought about significant reductions in their catches. Trawlers posed a major threat to the livelihoods and food security of coastal communities as they wastefully exhausted the most accessible source of protein—fish. The introduction of trawlers to this coastline was soon followed by heated coastal conflicts between the artisanal and the mechanised sectors, an uneasy relationship that continues to this day.[11]

Fishing Down the Marine Food Web

The sustained dragging of mobile gear (the nets with all their paraphernalia of weights, otterboards and chains) across the sea floor has been likened to the clear felling of tropical rainforests. These nets can disturb the seabed and alter its complexity, reduce benthic production and lead to substantial changes in benthic community structure and habitat.[12] Moreover, these disturbed soft-bottom habitats may never return to their earlier or 'pristine' state and are often taken over by weedy species, similar to those that take over the clear felled patches in tropical rainforests.

In India, the damage trawling has inflicted on the sea bottom and its potential ecological impacts on marine species are largely unknown. There are few studies in the region that quantify the direct impacts of trawl fishing on species and habitats. Interestingly, while the target groups such as shrimp and cephalopods possess life history traits that allow their populations to recover quickly after they are fished, this contrasts starkly with several other species caught as bycatch in the trawl. Many bycatch species are long-lived, grow slowly, are late to mature sexually and produce few offspring.

These traits make their populations much more susceptible to fishing pressure, and they could even be driven to local extinctions. Moreover, because bycatch is rarely monitored, these declines (and possibly extinctions) can often go unnoticed.[13] In India there has been a loss of species at the apex of the food web (sharks, groupers, snappers, etc.), followed by a sequential replacement by lower trophic groups; fish catches today are largely devoid of large predatory fish, a phenomenon referred to as 'fishing down marine food webs'.[14] This is a signature of overexploited fisheries worldwide, and leaves marine ecosystems and their associated species communities vulnerable to small disturbances that could trigger catastrophic shifts in ecological state. This can go easily unnoticed because, on the face of it, catches of some target species (especially lower trophic species like shrimp) are relatively more resilient to fishing compared with species higher up in the food chain, and it may take a while before their populations begin to show signs of decline.

There is abysmally little research documenting local extinctions of marine species in India, although sufficient evidence for it can be found by talking to local communities who depend on the trade. Fishers along most of the country's coastline are able to name several species they no longer see in their catch, which they believe have been locally extirpated. Evidence of some of these rarities now only exist in the form of trophies (the jaws of large sharks, the impressive saw-like jaws of sawfish and turtle shells) adorning the walls of some fishers' houses.

Fishers are an adaptable bunch. When catches decline, they employ several other strategies to make ends meet. The geographical area covered by fishing fleets in India grew fourfold between 1970 and 2000. Besides trawling near-shore grounds in violation of the Marine Fisheries Regulation Act, 1983, small fleets of trawlers, mainly in Nagapattinam and a few other fish landing sites along the coast, have, over the last decade, begun towing their nets approximately 600 metres below the sea level. Here they target deep sea shrimp resulting in the capture of considerable quantities of other deep sea species of bycatch for which very little information is available. In the Palk Bay and the Gulf of Mannar, after largely overfishing their near-shore resources, trawlers now drag their nets on the apparently more productive grounds of neighboring Sri Lanka. This has often triggered fishing conflicts between the two countries resulting in the persecution of trespassing fishermen.[15]

In the meanwhile, the artisanal fisher has not been sitting idly as trawlers have taken over, watching his craft and trade become increasingly insignificant. This stereotype of the marginalised artisan masks a more complex tale of constant adaptation, as traditional fishers have modernised and upgraded their boats with motorisation and more efficient fishing gear.[16] Along the Coromandel Coast, this process gained a huge impetus soon after the tsunami in the form of aid (both national and international) and the consequent large-scale replacement of traditional technology with more modern crafts and gear.[17] The new fibre-reinforced plastic boats now employed by the artisanal fishers are equipped with storage space and efficient engines, are able to venture and spend longer durations at sea, and are also regarded as stiff competition for trawler fishers.

Chickenfeed: Fishing Down the Price List

Gone are the days of plenty. With consistently rising fuel prices and steadily declining target catches, discarding of bycatch of even the lowest quality (i.e. trash fish) has been greatly reduced. The once-discarded trash fish has now spawned an industry of its own, including transporters, sorters and processors. In Chennai, the artisanal fishers whose near-shore fishing grounds had been swept clean by trawling now act as courier agents of trash fish for the Chennai trawlers. These trawlers now make longer fishing voyages (generally up to seven days) to the apparently more productive waters of Andhra Pradesh. By heading out to these trawlers, loading up the trash fish and bringing it back to shore on their behalf, these agents ensure that trash fish does not occupy the trawlers' fish holds nor do trawl fishers risk it spoiling rapidly if left exposed on the deck. Once landed, trawler owners sell trash fish to trash fish dealers for an average price of Rs. 3.50 per kilo. This price is subject to variation depending on its composition. Trash fish predominantly composed of actual fish is more valuable than that with high proportions of crustaceans and shell. Trash fish dealers employ transporters, who make use of bicycles with attached carts to transport trash. Manual labour is also utilised to tend to the trash fish. This involves firstly spreading out the wet catch on drying fields, specially reserved for this purpose. In Tamil Nadu, as in many other parts of the Indian coastline, it is not uncommon these days to see acres of land adjoining fish landing sites being used to dry low value trash bycatch. Once dried, the trash is heaped in piles before sieving off the visible impurities and then packing into jute bags. From fish landing sites such as Nagapattinam, trucks laden with these packed jute bags leave every day, making a beeline inland to Namakkal district, located approximately 200 km away. Nammakal along with Chitoor (located in the neighbouring state of Andhra Pradesh) are major poultry centers in southern India. Protein forms a small but important part of a chicken's diet, and fishmeal offers this protein at a reasonable cost. India's economic boom and the resultant increase in affluence is also fuelling a change from vegetarianism to carnivory.[18] Unlike beef or pork, fish and chicken are among the most kosher of all meats in India, and the country is witnessing a massive growth in their consumption.[19] This, in turn, increases demand for trash fish, and the fishing industry, already in the doldrums because of declining profits, is happy to repackage its discards to supply chicken factories.

There is no doubting the fact that the prior practice of discarding bycatch was bad, so on the face of it, it appears encouraging that trawlers are discarding far less than they used to. The improved utilisation of bycatch would also appear to improve livelihoods of trawl fishers and generate employment for people who work in the trash fish industry. However our work along the Coromandel Coast shows that the pleasantly portrayed picture of judiciously utilising marine resources actually masks the collapse of target species, and can thus push a fishery beyond the commercial extinction of its target stocks.[20] Our work shows that the trawl fishery today is sustained not so much by the increasingly scarce lotteries that a bumper crop of shrimp or cephalopods may provide, but rather by the remarkably predictable harvest of cheap trash fish. The trawlers are fishing for chickenfeed in more ways than one.

The harvest of bycatch beyond the economic viability of target stocks can facilitate the biological extinction of highly depleted target species. This is because the relatively abundant bycatch resource allows for a continued opportunistic harvest of the valuable target species, a windfall gain whenever encountered. This phenomenon, termed 'opportunistic exploitation', is characteristic of mixed species harvest systems, including fisheries, bushmeat hunting and timber harvest and can potentially result in the local extinction of species.[21]

Invisible Catches: Trashy Data and Data on Trash

Fisheries in India, as in so many other parts of the world, are managed to sustain yields and profits rather than meet conservation goals. To this end, research institutions like the Central Marine Fisheries Research Institute (CMFRI), Department of Animal Husbandry and Dairying (DAHD) and the Marine Products Exports Development Authority (MPEDA) have been monitoring fish catches over the last sixty years. This is presumably with an eye to establishing quotas and sustainably managing the stock. Not surprisingly, the species that are part of this monitoring protocol are primarily target groups—species that were deemed to be economically important when the monitoring programmes were first implemented. From the point of view of managing single stocks it made good sense since it was easy to implement, and uncomplicated to measure, model and understand. However, as discussed earlier, species that were once 'trash fish' or 'bycatch', and were considered unimportant to monitor, are perhaps the main economic drivers maintaining the fishery today, yet they pass completely beneath the radar Trawl fisheries along the Coromandel capture a large number of species and a monitoring protocol that either ignores these species or lumps them into broad categories is ecologically nonsensical and yields very little useful information.

The trouble with monitoring trends in fish stocks highlights the blurred boundaries within which fisheries management operates. Being an enthusiastically unplanned sector, the industry reinvents itself constantly, dynamically responding to every opportunity that will allow it to continue harvesting for short-term economic gain. While effective monitoring is the lynchpin of any effective harvest management, designing a monitoring programme that is as dynamic and adaptive as the changing industry is scarcely easy. It requires a built in horizon-scanning protocol that identifies potential new markets for fishery products and tracks the growth and development of these markets, ideally even before the fishery discovers them. This proactive and predictive monitoring has never really been attempted, but it is the best way forward for any rational, real world attempts at marine conservation in the developing tropics.

Species Conservation and Stock Protection: Management for Gain or Restraint

Philosophically, there is much that conservation can learn from the simple functional pragmatism of fisheries management. Where they have been most successful, no-take areas have been sold largely as one tool among many in the fisheries' management toolbox.[22] Rather than being couched in the quasi-religious litanies of species endangerment and conservation necessity, these no-take areas have been proposed as simple stock enhancement techniques, maintained with the primary purpose of protecting, supporting and enhancing fish catches and profits.[23]

The concept of population spillovers appears to be well understood by fishing communities.[24] If taken into confidence during the planning process, fishers find it relatively easy to buy into an idea of spatial and/or temporal restraint for overall gain rather than for the far less palpable goals of species or ecosystem conservation directives.

Although Marine Protected Areas (MPAs) in highly populated coastal regions such as India are likely to have high socioeconomic costs, it has been well documented that MPAs designed with the local fisheries in mind have a negligible socioeconomic impact (and even significant benefits) compared to those that don't.[25] Although MPAs could be a potentially good fisheries management tool, their management should be case-specific and adaptive, especially in the developing world context.

Efforts have also focused on modifying the indiscriminate design of industrial fishing gear with Bycatch Reduction Devices (BRD) and other technological solutions. While these have been demonstrated to have considerable success in reducing bycatch in several parts of the world, they have been met with strong opposition in India. This is not hard to fathom, considering that there is now a strong economic incentive to harvest bycatch.

A prominent example of the opposition to technological solutions was that of the Turtle Excluder Devices (TED) in Odisha. The coast of Odisha hosts the largest nesting population of sea turtles in the world. Turtles are known to congregate off nesting beaches before they come ashore to nest. Although the seas off one of the major mass nesting sites have been declared a Marine Protected Area, fishing, mainly by mechanised vessels (trawlers and gillnetters), is largely unregulated and continues unabated. Approximately 1,00,000 turtles were killed as fisheries bycatch between 1994 and 2004.[26] Trawlers are known to be the main contributors of bycatch-related mortality of sea turtles, and besides being banned from fishing in the marine sanctuary they were also required to be fitted with a Turtle Excluder Device, which allows for turtles and other large bycatch to escape without bringing about drastic reductions in the commercially targeted species. This became a trigger for a very vocal conflict between fishers and conservation organisations, with fishers concerned that they stood to lose a significant part of their depleting income by reducing bycatch.[27] There has been little uptake of this initiative by trawlers, and turtles continue to be killed as bycatch along this coast.

Management solutions like MPAs have also found very little traction from local communities in India. Artisanal fishers, in particular, have objected to the creation of MPAs in their backyard. The common perception is that local fishers are being robbed of their rights and livelihood, becoming easy scapegoats of larger development projects including ports and thermal and nuclear power plants that probably pose a much larger threat to marine biodiversity.

These bleak successes suggest that there is no single fix all solution and the above recommendations are likely to fail if attempted in isolation. To be effective, we need to strive towards a compromise or middle ground, ensuring that fisheries are carried out sustainably while meeting conservation goals as well.[28] This requires an institutional shift in attitudes and approaches, where the conflicting mandates of government fisheries departments (maximising production) and wildlife departments (restricting access and offtake) find a resonant common message, which can strike a reasonable balance between these extremes. There is also a need for change in current governance systems, from the current top down approaches to ones more inclusive of local communities. When effectively communicated and inclusively managed, such community-based co-management initiatives have been shown to be largely successful in meeting socioeconomic and ecological goals, especially in the artisanal sector.[29]

We have few such examples from Indian waters, and our current legislative frameworks are not designed to marry conservation and production within the same land or seascape. Where it has happened, it has been largely a result of unplanned happenstance. A clear example is the Lakshadweep Archipelago. Here, prior to the 1970s, local artisanal communities lived off the surrounding atoll reefs, extracting most of their protein resources (largely reef fish and octopus) from these waters. A fisheries department initiative to promote a pole-and-line pelagic skipjack tuna fishery became rapidly successful, supported by a suite of subsidies, training programmes and distribution networks. This relatively sustainable pelagic fishery soon nearly replaced reef fishing in the Lakshadweep waters. Today, despite supporting the densest fishing populations in rural India, the Lakshadweep reefs are among the most pristine in the Indian Ocean, and have shown an extraordinary resilience to climate-related benthic mortality events in the last decades—much of it due to having a healthy fish community.[30] This epiphenomenal conservation example has much to teach about how a middle ground between conservation and extraction can be achieved, and practices like this need much more recognition as sustainable exemplars.

Finally, considering the highly dynamic nature of marine systems, there is an urgent need for regional cooperation when it comes to the conservation of marine species both within national and international waters. This is especially true in the case of highly migratory species such as sea turtles, pelagic sharks and tuna, which can migrate great distances and where any conservation action is unlikely to be effective if efforts remain confined to political boundaries.

A Call for a Sea Ethic

The situation is complex and demands ever more complicated solutions especially since it involves making redundant many whose jobs are already in the doldrums. We are not the first—several countries have been swept by the overfishing crisis long before India.

The fisheries crisis and the prediction of the impending collapse of global fish stocks has been a long-standing rallying call.[31] One study rather boldly predicted the collapse of all major fisheries by the year 2048 and also heralded the impairment of ecosystem services provided by the oceans.[32] Although this has been considered a trifle alarmist,[33] the current trajectory of global marine fisheries is definitely not sustainable. Although known marine extinctions are far fewer than terrestrial ones, commercial fishing has led to the collapse of about a thousand populations that once supplied the world's seafood. Studies reckon that about twenty-eight to thirty-three per cent of the current global stocks have been overexploited and seven to thirteen per cent have collapsed.[34]

Although India has created hardly a ripple on the marine conservation front and has an overexploitation ranking which is far worse than the global average,[35] there are important lessons we can learn from successfully managed fisheries. Precisely because of the easy double standard with which we view the ocean and its species, we are perhaps able to avoid the unhelpful conservation discourses that pit humans against the wilderness as violator and victim. Freed from this, it is possible to explore strategies for effective management that are economically functional and ecologically acceptable as well. On the face of it, terrestrial and marine strategies for conservation do not appear very different, since among the most effective management tools is the Marine Protected Area, a designated area from which no offtake is allowed. Yet, unlike our terrestrial Protected Areas, MPAs are often designed as a way to maximise fish and seafood production, protecting seed stock and spawning areas from exploitation, and creating a zone of spillover that can be harvested. There is conservation happening here, but as a happy collateral (a bycatch, as it were) of a fisheries management action, delivering conservation benefits while augmenting fishers' catches and incomes.

We do not as yet have working models within the country of a fisheries reserve that works to this design. At least part of the reason for this lies in the bipolar bureaucracy within which marine resources are managed—between a fisheries department that focuses on maximising production and a forest department that is still largely influenced by terrestrial paradigms of conservation. Yet, between these two approaches lies our best way forward for ocean management, if we are to continue enjoying our fish curry and rice in the decades to come.

Notes

1. C. Clover, *The End of the Line: How overfishing is changing the world and what we eat* (London: Random House, 2004).
2. M. Bavinck, *Marine Resource Management: Conflict and regulation in the fisheries of the Coromandel Coast* (New Delhi: Sage, 2001).
3. Bavinck, *Marine Resource Management.*
4. J. Kurien, 'Entry of big business into fishing: Its impact on fish economy', *Economic and Political Weekly* 13 (1978): 1557–65.
5. Bavinck, *Marine Resource Management.*
6. M. A. Hall, D. L. Alverson and K. I. Metuzals, 'By-Catch: Problems and solutions', *Marine Pollution Bulletin* 41 (2000): 204–19.
7. K. Kelleher, 'Discards in the world's marine fisheries: An update' in *Rep. 470* (Rome: Food and Agriculture Organization of the United Nations, 2005).
8. S. Funge-Smith, E. Lindebo and D. Staples, *Asian Fisheries Today: The production and use of low value/trash fish from marine fisheries in the Asia-Pacific region* (Bangkok: Food and Agricultural Organization of the United Nations, 2005).
9. J. Kurien, 'Technical assistance projects and socioeconomic change: Norwegian intervention in Kerala's fisheries development', *Economic and Political Weekly* 20 (1985): A70–A88.

10. P. Gillet, *Small is Difficult: The pangs and success of small boat technology transfer in South India* (Rugby, UK: Intermediate Technology Development Group [ITDG], 1985).

11. M. Bavinck, 'Understanding fisheries conflicts in the south: A legal pluralist perspective', *Society and Natural Resources* 18 (2005): 805–20.

12. L. Watling and E. A. Norse, 'Disturbance of the seabed by mobile fishing gear: A comparison to forest clearcutting', *Conservation Biology* 12 (1998): 1180–97.

13. J. Briggs, 'Marine extinctions and conservation', *Marine Biology* 158 (2011): 485–88.

14. D. Pauly, V. Christensen, J. Dalsgaard, R. Froese and F. Torres Jr., 'Fishing down marine food webs', *Science* 279 (1998): 860–63; B. Bhathal and D. Pauly, 'Fishing down marine food webs and spatial expansion of coastal fisheries in India, 1950–2000', *Fisheries Research* 91 (2008): 26–34.

15. J. Scholtens, M. Bavinck and A. S. Soosai, 'Fishing in dire straits: Trans-boundary incursions in the Palk Bay', *Economic and Political Weekly* 57 (2012): 85–95; J. Stephen, A. Menon, J. Scholtens and M. Bavinck, ' Transboundary dialogues and the "politics of scale" in Palk Bay fisheries: Brothers at sea?', *South Asia Research* 33, no. 2 (2013): 141–61; V. Vivekanandan, 'Trawl brawl', *Samudra Report* 57 (2010): 24–27.

16. M. Bavinck, 'Changing balance of power at sea: Motorization of artisanal fishing craft', *Economic and Political Weekly* 32 (1997): 198–200.

17. R. S. Pomeroy, B. D. Ratner, S. J. Hall, J. Pimoljinda and V. Vivekanandan, 'Coping with disaster: Rehabilitating coastal livelihoods and communities', *Marine Policy* 30 (2006): 786–93.

18. N. Myers and J. Kent, 'New consumers: The influence of affluence on the environment', *Proceedings of the National Academy of Sciences (USA)* 100 (2003): 4963–68; S. Bonhommeau, L. Dubroca, O. Le Pape, J. Barde, D. M. Kaplan, E. Chassot and A. E. Nieblas, 'Eating up the world's food web and the human trophic level', *Proceedings of the National Academy of Sciences (USA)* 110, no. 51 (2013): 20617–20.

19. C. L. Delgado, 'Rising consumption of meat and milk in developing countries has created a new food revolution', *The Journal of Nutrition* 133 (2003): 3907–10.

20. Bonnhommeau, et al., 'Eating up the world's food web'.

21. T. A. Branch, A. S. Lobo and S. W. Purcell, 'Opportunistic exploitation: An overlooked pathway to extinction', *Trends in ecology and evolution* 28, no. 7 (2013): 409–13.

22. R. S. Pomeroy, J. E. Parks and L. M. Watson, *How is your MPA doing?* (Gland, Switzerland, and Cambridge, UK: International Union for Conservation of Nature [IUCN], 2007).

23. T. R. McClanahan, 'Effects of fisheries closures and gear restrictions on fishing income in a Kenyan coral reef', *Conservation Biology* 24, no. 6 (2010):

1519–28; G. R. Russ and A. C. Alcala, 'Enhanced biodiversity beyond marine reserve boundaries: The cup spilleth over', *Ecological Applications* 21 (2011): 241–50.

24. C. Pita, G. J. Pierce, I. Theodossiou and K. Macpherson, 'An overview of commercial fishers' attitudes towards marine protected areas', *Hydrobiologia* 670 (2011): 289–306.

25. C. J. Klein, A. Chan, L. Kircher, A. J. Cundiff, N. Gardner, Y. Hrovat, A. Scholz, B. E. Kendall and S. Airame, 'Striking a balance between biodiversity conservation and socioeconomic viability in the design of marine protected areas', *Conservation Biology* 22 (2008): 691–700.

26. K. Shanker, B. Pandav and B. C. Choudhury, 'An assessment of the olive ridley turtle (*Lepidochelys olivacea*) nesting population in Orissa, India', *Biological Conservation* 115 (2004): 149–60.

27. G. S. Rao, 'Turtle Excluder Device (TED) in trawl nets: Applicability in Indian trawl fishery', *Indian Journal of Fisheries* 58 (2011): 115–24.

28. N. L. Gutiérrez, R. Hilborn and O. Defeo, 'Leadership, social capital and incentives promote successful fisheries', *Nature* 470 (2011): 386–89.

29. J. E. Cinner, T. R. McClanahan, M. A. MacNeil, N. A. J. Graham, T. M. Daw, A. Mukminin, D. A. Feary, A. L. Rabearisoa, A. Wamukota, N. Jidawi, S. J. Campbell, A. H. Baird, F. A. Januchowski-Hartley, R. Lahari, T. Morove and J. Kuange, 'Comanagement of coral reef social-ecological systems', *Proceedings of National Academy of Sciences (USA)* 109 (2012): 5219–22.

30. R. Arthur, 'Patterns and processes of reef recovery and human resource use in the Lakshadweep Islands, Indian Ocean', PhD thesis, James Cook University, Australia, 2005.

31. D. Pauly, V. Christensen, S. Guenette, T. J. Pitcher, U. Rashid Sumaila, C. J. Walters, R. Watson and D. Zeller, 'Towards sustainability in world fisheries', *Nature* 418 (2002): 689–95; D. Pauly and J. Maclean, *In a Perfect Ocean: Fisheries and ecosystem in the North Atlantic* (Washington DC: Island Press, 2003); J. B. C. Jackson, 'Ecological extinction and evolution in the brave new ocean', *Proceedings of the National Academy of Sciences (USA)* 105 (2008): 11458–65.

32. B. Worm, E. B. Barbier, N. Beaumont, J. E. Duffy, C. Folke, B. S. Halpern, J. B. C. Jackson, H. K. Lotze, F. Micheli, S. R. Palumbi, E. Sala, K. A. Selkoe, J. J. Stachowicz and R. Watson, 'Impacts of biodiversity loss on ocean ecosystem services', *Science* 314 (2006): 787–90.

33. B. Worm, R. Hilborn, J. K. Baum, T. A. Branch, J. S. Collie, C. Costello, M. J. Fogarty, E. A. Fulton, J. A. Hutchings, S. Jennings, O. P. Jensen, H. K. Lotze, P. M. Mace, T. R. McClanahan, C. Minto, S. R. Palumbi, A. M. Parma, D. Richard, A. A. Rosenberg, R. Watson and D. Zeller, 'Rebuilding global fisheries', *Science* 325 (2009): 578–85; T. A. Branch, 'Not all fisheries will be collapsed in 2048', *Marine Policy* 32 (2008): 38–39; T. A. Branch, O. P. Jensen, D. Ricard, Y. Ye and R. Hilborn, 'Contrasting global trends in marine fishery status obtained from catches and from stock assessments', *Conservation Biology* 25 (2011): 777–86; N. Daan, H. Gislason,

J. G. Pope and J. C. Rice, 'Apocalypse in world fisheries?: The reports of their death are greatly exaggerated', *ICES Journal of Marine Science* 68 (2011): 1375–78.

34. Jackson, 'Ecological extinction and evolution in the brave new ocean'.

35. CMFRI, 'Annual Report 2006–2007' (Cochin: Central Marine Fisheries Research Institute, 2007).

Two

RESTORING THE GANGA FOR ITS FAUNA AND FISHERIES

Nachiket Kelkar and Jagdish Krishnaswamy

Blind Dolphins and Murky Waters

Across the Gangetic floodplains in North India, local people are familiar with the folklore of the mysterious 'Soons', a dark creature that materialises from the murky river and disappears instantly. Everyone knows it is not a fish, but very few know that it is a river dolphin, a mammal. This animal is the oldest cetacean species alive in evolutionary time, representing an ancient lineage of dolphin-like creatures living in the Tethys Sea, later uplifted during the formation of the Himalayan mountain range. Two species of 'true' river dolphins, today found only in the Amazon and the Indus-Ganges-Brahmaputra systems, are unique freshwater mammals entirely dependent on river habitats for their survival. Of these, the Ganges river dolphin[1] (*Platanista gangetica*—including its subspecies, the Indus river dolphin, *P. g. minor*) is found in India, Nepal, Pakistan and Bangladesh. Owing to millions of years of evolutionary adaptation in the murky, sediment-loaded Indo-Gangetic river systems, Ganges river dolphins are almost totally blind, having lost their eyes to disuse. With only rudimentary pores for eyes, completely lacking a crystalline lens, they navigate in the turbid waters with the aid of highly effective echolocation.[2]

Freshwater biodiversity and riverine ecosystem services are highly threatened.[3] The rivers that the endangered Ganges river dolphin occurs in happen to be among the most severely human impacted freshwater ecosystems in the world. Conservation of unique riverine species is thus an urgent need and also a major challenge in the face of declining resources, water diversion, excessive pollution and over-exploitation.

Despite this, the Gangetic basin feeds over 500 million people even today. The Ganga was declared India's national river in 2008 and the Ganges river dolphin made India's national aquatic animal.[4] Such concern about conduct with living creatures is not new even if this particular kind of conservation consciousness is a phenomenon of the modern era. Imperial protection for the animals of the Ganges river (including some fish species) was an important aspect of Emperor Asoka's wider policy of *Dhamma* (third century BCE), which made an attempt to define sensitive conduct even towards common species that would not be eaten or used otherwise, as revealed in Pillar Edict V.[5] The significance of this regulation is undeniable, as it extended from total prohibition of hunting or slaughter to imposing temporal bans on the exploitation and sacrifice of several common species. Asoka's policy remains resoundingly relevant, especially as we assess the current state of the Gangetic basin and its wildlife.

The river dolphin has become a prime candidate for conservation efforts in recent times.[6] First, it has the enigma and charisma associated with dolphins in general. Second, it is locally common and identified easily by many inhabitants of the riverbanks, but is perceived as a threat by almost nobody. Third and perhaps most important, the river dolphin's ecology and future is strongly connected with that of the people of the Ganges in many ways.

Dolphins cannot be seen in isolation from their riverine landscape, the complex texture of which is knit together from different social, political, economic, geological, hydrological, historical and ethical strands. Be it inside the river or on the banks, the world of the endangered Ganges river dolphin is a complex, diverse aggregation of social and ecological collisions and conflicts. The species is thus more than a symbol of the river: its presence in healthy populations could be considered an index of the ecological integrity of the river system as a whole. More immediately, the species could also be a rallying symbol for an approach to conservation that goes beyond the mere protection of individual animals to a more holistic set of arrangements that ensures that human use (or rather abuse) does not endanger the integrity of the riverine system and freshwater ecology. How does one save an iconic endangered species and aquatic emblem in such an iconic river? Here, there is a bitter irony. The Ganga is perhaps the most intensively used river in the world, and sadly, the most abused as well. Conservationists often argue for the ideal of 'coexistence' of wildlife and human needs that depend extensively on biodiversity and ecosystem services.[7] But how can we rise to the challenge of reconciling the diverse needs of millions of people with socially just conservation in a fractured society? These are the larger questions we hope to unpack. For now, it is best to start with the river itself.

Sanctuary for the Ganga?

This journey can begin with a boat ride on the Ganga. Ochre-buff agricultural floodplains with remnants of tamarisk scrub, industrial belts and brick kilns stretch as far as the eye can see. Boats overloaded with people, bales of hay, cattle, motorbikes and metal trunks noisily dash across the river. The grey waters glare and gradually fall silent again. Dolphins sense the boats through the opaque grey curtains and swim away, turning and surfacing again. They are effectively blind and must rely on sound to evade an array of fine-meshed gill nets successfully. Untreated sewage flows into the river from the ghats. Suddenly there are gunshots in the distance, and fisher folk, staging a protest march, run helter skelter.

The scene described here was and is an adequate sketch of any river stretch in the Gangetic floodplains and depicts the daily life of an imperiled freshwater cetacean species, and the precarious human condition around it.

A good place to find answers to the riddle of coexistence is the Vikramshila Gangetic Dolphin Sanctuary (VGDS) in Bhagalpur, Bihar, the only existing sanctuary specially designated to protect the Ganges river dolphin. Named after an ancient Buddhist university, it was notified in 1991 due to the high abundance of river dolphins in a 60–67 km long stretch of the Ganga between the towns of Sultanganj and Kahalgaon.[8] The sanctuary riverscape has a diversity of riverine habitats such as meanders, countercurrent pools, sandbars and imposing granite outcrops in deep channels. In many reaches, the river course changes year to year, often shifting northward over large distances, a consequence of sediment loads from the Himalayas. This region is unique in having an almost intact assemblage of India's riverine vertebrate megafauna, including dolphins, smooth-coated otters, turtles, the occasional gharial or mugger, fish and numerous resident and migratory bird species. This makes it a unique aquatic equivalent of well known reserves of surviving terrestrial megafauna, no less important than Kaziranga in Assam or Bandipur in Karnataka. That it is not as well known is evidence of the marginality of aquatic ecology and wildlife among the general public, policy-makers and even ecologists. Terrestrial systems, even now, get the lion's share of conservationists' attention. The Vikramshila sanctuary has largely been without monitoring or management interventions by concerned government departments. After the dolphin became the national aquatic animal awareness has increased, but this has not translated into much significant on-ground action.

Shifting Boundaries

Vikramshila may well be designated a Protected Area, but even here, there seems no respite for the dolphin. A fundamental need of conservation planning is the presence of a fixed spatial or temporal domain within which interactions, whether of conflict or of cooperation, may be expected to take place. Limits to resource exploitation can be realistic only as per the clear definition of boundaries, ownership and tenures. Terrestrial Protected Areas or protected lakes have definite boundaries that need enforcement and maintenance for effective conservation. In open access, linear and highly dynamic systems such as rivers, conservation often has to be achieved through cultural or behavioural fences on human conduct and regulated use—rather than guns, well defined physical boundaries and fences.[9]

And therein lies the problem, for riverine Protected Areas *cannot* be fenced by boundaries.[10] It is not that fences do not work or are porous: they are simply not feasible. These imaginary, symbolic fences may only wobble around the central tendency of the river's dynamic and ever changing course. They pose every difficulty of definition: boundaries, rights of usage, management authorities.

Immediately after the declaration of the Vikramshila sanctuary, the fisheries department came into conflict with the directives of the forest department. The fisheries department still recognises fishing as a legitimate activity, whereas forest and wildlife protection laws do not. So the former department refused to 'recognise' the sanctuary and continued to provide permits and identity cards for 'free-for-all' fishing. Such interdepartmental conflict left fisher folk highly confused and many readily, and obviously, disregarded the existence of either the sanctuary or the nationwide hunting ban on species such as river dolphins. Many fishers regularly hunted river dolphins for oil from their blubber, commonly used as bait to catch a species of catfish. Both authorities, ignorant of each other's priorities and situations, played blame games, neither managing fisheries well nor protecting river dolphins. Given a difficult law and order situation (the area was susceptible to dacoit gangs patrolling the *diara* (islands formed between a main river and its tributaries) lands and maintaining territorial boundaries through fights to protect their villages as well as other criminal gangs running illegal operations for powerful politicians and erstwhile zamindars), the forest department never dared to step inside the river's open, fluid, flooding, receding boundaries much less monitor the river stretch or bring turtle and dolphin poachers or bird hunters to book. It is, therefore, easy to understand why, for most of its initial years, the sanctuary existed only on paper. The neglect was compounded by policy choices, as the state governments of the 1990s seem to have largely ignored the issue in Bhagalpur District where the sanctuary is located. It is commonplace to label this as the absence of political will. The law and order situation worsened over this period, leading to the Vikramshila sanctuary becoming a 'punishment posting' for forest officials, compared to other lucrative opportunities in the state. Until very recently, Bhagalpur was not even a separate Forest Division (lacking a Conservator of Forests posting), and the sanctuary's headquarters were in the deciduous forest-dominated district of Banka. The problems were compounded by the inadequacy of the forest department, which was more familiar with forests and plantations than with rivers and their ecosystems. The usual tool kit: silviculture, pug mark counts, fire control and cutting game trails was of little relevance on the water front.

Conservation Efforts

There are several fisher families in this region, living in extremely poor socioeconomic conditions and all heavily dependent on the river. Although fishing was technically illegal in the sanctuary, it formed the main, and often the only, livelihood for thousands of marginalised fisher folk. In 1999, a significant civil society initiative led by Professor Sunil Choudhary through a small team called the Vikramshila Biodiversity Research and Education Centre (VBREC) launched a mass awareness campaign for fishers in the region. Believing that protecting river dolphins while also sustaining the fishers' livelihood needs was crucial to obtaining support of local fishers for river conservation, the team worked hard to put a stop to the intentional killing of river dolphins in the sanctuary area. In 2001, the Patna high court directed both the Union and Bihar state governments to allocate funds to support river dolphin conservation in the state.[11] This intervention helped, and the team's continued presence and persistent monitoring of threats to dolphins and other wildlife, socioeconomic surveys and awareness campaigns, resulted in a considerable reduction in the killing of dolphins in Vikramshila. The team developed a network with key fishers to get reports of accidental entanglement of dolphins and illegal activities in the sanctuary area. They also chose local spokespersons for dolphin conservation from among the fishers, using the community's respect for their traditional knowledge. Preserving an open attitude to integrated research, the team has successfully collaborated with local fisher folk, river dolphin conservationists, sociologists, wildlife scientists, cetacean experts, filmmakers and fisheries biologists across the world to enhance the conservation focus on this riverscape.

The Vikramshila sanctuary and the surrounding riverscape today has the highest known density of Ganges river dolphins across their distribution range.[12] As dolphin hunting is negligible here, the place offers an excellent platform for robust conservation biology research to estimate effects of other threats to dolphin abundance and distribution. Together with the VBREC team, we have been conducting ecological research on dolphins for improving population sampling methods and assessing long-term distribution of river dolphins in the sanctuary with the background theme of river dolphin-fisheries interactions at multiple scales. We have been trying to identify in detail the ecological factors and mechanisms to help estimate the extent and the nature of conflict and competition between dolphins and fishermen.

Knowing the River Dolphin Better

Over the years there has been intense and increasing competition for use of foraging space and for fish prey, aggravated both by local fishing practices and landscape-level factors, such as flow reduction in tributaries from upstream diversion of water for irrigation.[13] As a result, by May 2008, the seasonal flow significantly reduced with the progress of the dry season, much of it attributable not to natural flow dynamics but clearly to impacts via human agency. Due to reduction in flows, the dolphins tend to concentrate in the main channel of the river in the peak of summer. The depleted flow leads to congregation of both fishers and dolphins in the main channel, causing intense competition over the concentrated fish resources at specific locations. The high spatial and temporal overlap has led to an increased fatal risk of accidental entanglement of dolphins in gillnets.[14] It is easy to wrongly interpret the observed spatial and temporal overlap of dolphins and humans as 'harmonious coexistence'. It is actually the outcome of a shared resource or ecological function that attracts both wild species and humans, drawing them into severe competition and negatively affecting both entities. Further, loss of fish prey from preferred areas caused by excessive fishing pressure in more productive river reaches might force dolphins to forage in suboptimal habitats. Based on our quantification of overlap and impact of fishing on river dolphins, it may be possible to clearly identify reference sites for dolphin-fisher coexistence and to maintain both dolphins and fishers in mutually tolerable states. Our prolonged observations in the sanctuary have revealed long-term persistence of Ganges river dolphin populations at certain specific areas or hotspots. The persistence of such habitats despite changes in river morphology each year suggests the need for creation of 'no-fishing zones' at these sites, with buffer areas where fishers can be allowed to fish in compliance with some regulations, including dolphin-friendly use of fishing gear, thereby causing low disturbance or danger to local dolphin populations.[15]

With respect to robust scientific research, many areas in river dolphin ecology need to be investigated in detail. Unfortunately, in most river dolphin projects in India, research activity does not go beyond the initial documentation of threats and routine, crude, count-based surveys.[16] Modern techniques of estimating dolphin abundance, such as independent double-observer surveys, need to be improved and made suitable for having robust estimates with associated uncertainty, using statistical sampling and modeling to avoid undercounting of dolphins due to their diving behavior. There are many interesting questions about the trophic and behavioural ecology of dolphins that could be tied strongly to their conservation. These include, in particular, research on dolphin acoustics from an ecological point of view, dolphin mating systems, site fidelity and distributional dynamics in relation to riverine productivity patterns, dolphins' trophic position in river food webs, prey selection and strategies of foraging and feeding.[17] Many new interfaces of such research are being explored in the Vikramshila sanctuary through diverse scientific collaborations by the VBREC. These ongoing research studies show a lot of promise for enriching understanding of the elusive Ganges river dolphin in the coming years.

Despite these contributions, the full realisation of Vikramshila as a meaningful sanctuary is still far off in the future. The Ganges river dolphins and the fisher folk of the sanctuary both continue to be victims of much larger problems. Going deeper, one finds that conflicting relationships have been shaped by diverse local and landscape-level social dynamics, the complex textures of which often cannot enter any statistical models as parameters in explaining the causes of endangerment of dolphins directly. A detailed analysis of social, economic and historical changes that have affected the riverscape becomes imperative.

Beyond Ecology: Social, Economic and Historical Aspects

The feudal *panidari* (Jalkar) system of river fishing contracts prevalent in this region was abolished between the years 1987 and 1991. Panidari was the riverine counterpart of the oppressive zamindari system, where powerful *panidar*s or waterlords laid claim to stretches of the Ganga river and 'owned' all fishing and ferry movement rights within that stretch,[18] thereby grabbing a large chunk of whatever fishers would fish there and demanding that they pay tax. Needless to say, the panidars would harass, beat up, or even kill, fishermen and their families who refused to work on the Jalkar contracts in this area (from Sultanganj downstream to Pirpainti) or pay up the fish tax.

For the Bihar state governments between the period from the fall of the Karpoori Thakur government (1979) and the reign of Lalu Prasad Yadav (1990–2005), freeing all rivers, or 'flowing water bodies', from the panidari for everyone to fish in was a major political advantage to the socialist ruling party.[19] But the abolition also meant that fishing in the river now became free for all. After the abolition, criminal gangs came in and illegally continued to extort fish catch from these fishermen at gunpoint, killing anyone who refused or defied them. A fishing mafia ring soon developed, illegally seeking monopoly over fishing areas through force and brutality. They continue to use highly destructive fishing practices to capture the smallest of fish in the river to cater to the huge market for small fish at Siliguri in northern West Bengal. Mosquito nets (*kapda jal*) and beach seines (*kachaal jal*) are excessively operated by criminals in the vicinity of highly productive confluence habitats and in floodplain wetlands marginally connected to the main river channel. These highly destructive nets set off longstanding conflicts channel. These highly destructive nets set off longstanding conflicts between traditional fishermen and the fishing mafia. Criminals and local fishers often spar with each other over the issue of ownership and fishing rights for confluence channels (*kol*) and floodplain wetlands (*dhab*). The problem stems from ambiguous definition in the Fishing Act: the dhab is cut off from the main river in the dry season and the kol 'may or may not' get cut off. The dhab may be leased out to private contractors, but not the kol if it is wider than 100 m at the confluence. On the ground, such a definition is difficult to make sense of. There have been shootouts, murders and even organised massacres of fishers over fishing territories and rights to fishing areas. Furthermore, multiple traditionally non-fishing castes have also plunged into the free-for-all fishing, from dominant classes of landholders such as Bhumihars and Rajputs to marginalised people such as Gangotas or Muslims. In a state where caste plays an important role in determining almost any action, free fishing has thus led to serious caste based conflicts. Interestingly, our recent surveys show that fishing villages 'outside' the sanctuary (upstream of the river at Sultanganj) are mentioning that they seldom fish inside the Protected Area, for criminal activity is higher inside than outside. This validates impacts of historically contested claims over ill defined rules and rights, which is a failure of fisheries management.

Confluence habitats are highly preferred by both fishers and river dolphins, owing to the aggregation of fish in these areas. Destructive netting practices (such as barricading of confluences with mosquito nets) cause mass mortality of larval and juvenile fishes, reducing recruitment to the main river and suppressing viability of fish populations. Indiscriminate destruction of fish stocks by criminals along with social threats has ousted both traditional fishermen and river dolphins from their preferred fishing locations. Strict enforcement is needed to ban such destructive fishing practices.[20] But who will control them? There has been no real change with regards to riverfront protection, despite a general perception of improved administrative efficiency in the state of Bihar, especially with reduction in road and highway robbery, murder rate and theft. According to local fishers, regular patrolling and the mere 'presence' of police along riverbanks can control fishing mafia activity. With severely diminishing returns even from fishing of small fry, the current status of the fisheries is also endangered and on the verge of large scale collapse. The change in institutional control, from the formal tender-based private contract system with inbuilt exploitation to an open access free-for-all situation of harassment and lawlessness, has now forced fishers to rethink. Recent surveys indicate that many fishers, lacking knowledge of any other system, now perceive even the days of Jalkars as better than the present state, and mention that the panidari at least afforded some protection to them because of 'bonded' labor. This vicious cycle reveals that both private and open access arrangements have failed to work, and opens doors to consideration of co-management of common pool resources.[21]

The Decay of a Socio-ecological System

Kahalgaon is the central site of the fisher folk movement against the administration, the fishing mafia, and also the sanctuary. Their outcry against the oppression of criminal gangs and mafia is genuine. However, the fishers' own use of resources also needs critical scrutiny. The Ganga Mukti Andolan, a fisher community-led movement, is agitating for the denotification of the sanctuary, which it alleges has blocked access of traditional fishers to the river's resources. People dependent on Protected Areas for their livelihoods often seek denotification of these areas because of both restricted access and criminalisation of their means of livelihood. But in reality, no stretch of the sanctuary is devoid of fishermen or fishing activity. Even after the declaration of the sanctuary, fishers have continued to fish in whatever way and at whatever magnitude they like, using old identity cards issued by the fisheries department to fish freely anywhere in the Ganga river and the lack of monitoring by the forest department as an escape route. Legally, the very legitimacy of 'traditional fishing rights' is questionable, as the tradition itself has a dubious existence now. These traditional fishermen worked as labourers in the panidari jalkars for several generations.

Even if a claim for fishing rights in the name of tradition[22] is entertained, the negative ecological impacts of existing fishing practices, even the relatively non-destructive techniques, are very high, not just on dolphins but on the fishery itself. The Andolan's persistent claim is that fishers have always lived in harmony with river dolphins and other wildlife, blaming all illegal killing and poaching on criminals. But the evidence paints a different picture. Some Kahalgaon fishers continue to kill turtles in a clandestine fashion, sometimes hunt dolphins for oil, kill the occasional gharial and predate on wild birds. The fisheries department rules specify that fishing with gillnets less than 40 mm in diameter is illegal anywhere in the Ganga's main channel, even outside the sanctuary. Thus, almost eighty per cent of the existing fishing in the sanctuary is illegal and destructive to river dolphins and fish populations, be it by the mafia or traditional fishermen. Irrespective of who fishes, current levels of fishing activity can seriously aggravate resource depletion rates. This is a qualitatively new situation and may not have past precedent: so harking back to 'traditional' practices, however laudable a goal, does not have an ecologically sound basis.

In the Shadow of Farakka

It is true that these fishers are a highly marginalised people, affected not just by degraded socioeconomic conditions but also by ecological destruction. But the sanctuary is clearly not the sole or even major reason for their marginalisation. In fact, the Protected Area holds the promise of being a worthwhile venture for securing their interests. It is part of a relatively more productive segment than many other river stretches in the Ganga. Still, the mesh sizes of fishers have kept shrinking year after year, with many already much below the lower restricted limit. But overfishing, pollution, local factors, and poverty explain only a small fraction of this decline. There are larger, landscape-level historical reasons for the severely depleted state of the entire floodplain river system.

The proverbial rug has been pulled from under our feet by the successive river engineering projects that have adversely affected riverine ecosystems.[23] The Farakka Barrage built in 1972–73 almost entirely destroyed the commercial hilsa (*Tenualosa ilisha*) fishery in the upstream reaches of the river, within which Vikramshila is situated.[24] The hilsa is an anadromous fish that migrates upriver at the start of the monsoons to breed and then returns to the estuary and sea for its adult life. The barrage physically obstructed the species, along with many others, from migrating to reproduce, causing its extinction further upriver, and leading to cascading declines downstream as well. The hilsa, highly valued across the region (which bears a significant imprint of Bengali culture, where hilsa is a culinary cultural symbol) for its taste and as a seasonal delicacy, had been an important commercial resource for the fisher populations and a crucial seasonal prey-base for wildlife. But today, the fish can be regarded extinct in this region, playing hardly any ecological or commercial function. Studies have estimated ninety-nine per cent reductions in availability of hilsa upriver, since the barrage was built.[25] This decline is a shocking example of the collapse of an important fishery of India's inland waters. Many other economically valued fish species have also met with the same fate: *Anguilla benghalensis*, a once common catadromous eel, the freshwater stingray *Pastinachus sephen*, and a bagrid catfish *Mystus menoda* have also disappeared.

Barriers to movement imposed by dams, pollutant loads, degradation of spawning habitat and overfishing have led to declines in other native commercial carp species (such as rohu and katla), and catches are gradually being replaced by 'trash' species, mainly small catfish, barbs and gobies.[26] Average fish sizes available and caught in fishing in these reaches indicate the presence of mostly juveniles and small-sized adults, which is another stark indication of ecosystem-level fisheries collapse.[27] Fishermen lift up their empty nets to find only tiny fish caught after over fourteen hours of painstaking effort. The resource base of the Ganga is so degraded today that fishermen are scrounging for scraps. Fishing has also shifted to shallower areas. Owing to their feeding morphology, river dolphins tend to forage in shallow river areas and feed mostly on small schooling fish. As fishers are now compelled to target only small fish, resource competition and conflict with dolphins has likely intensified over the years. This is evident in the increased cases of accidental entanglement and death of dolphins in small mesh gill nets.[28] It is an example of the far reaching, negative landscape-level impacts of large barrages: in many ways the ecological and economic consequences of such projects intensify fisher-dolphin conflicts.

India, China and Mindless River Development

India's record on rivers does not show any deeper appreciation of the immediate, painful lessons to learn from other Asian nation states. In China, the Yangtze River dolphin or baiji was declared extinct in 2006. It was deemed the first human-caused extinction of a cetacean species.[29] The species was not actively targeted or hunted out, but was 'accidentally' killed by destructive fishing techniques (rolling hooks) and extensive degradation of its habitat. The story of the baiji's demise, poignantly told by Samuel Turvey,[30] could well be repeated in the Indian subcontinent as a result of large scale water development projects and resource exploitation practices.[31] The baiji was lost recently and several unique and endemic species in the highly diverse Yangtze ecosystem are also extinct already, or critically endangered or alive only in captivity: the Yangtze Softshell Turtle, Chinese Alligator, Paddlefish and Chinese Sturgeon.[32] The health of the people dependent on the Yangtze has been declining and all indicators of river health are already critical. The Yangtze is sometimes called the largest open sewer in the world but are India's rivers far behind?[33] While there is increasing awareness and appreciation of the threats to river species in India, macroeconomic developmental forces, such as industrial demand on rivers have become drivers in many a 'developing country' or emerging economy. Such secular trends seem to prevail despite significant political differences and 'nature tolerant' Asian cultural and social values, reflecting in the massive depletion of river production systems (fisheries, farming) in China and India alike.

Economic cost-benefit analyses suggest that large river development projects are highly unsustainable and often ecologically destructive.[34] They are based on profound belief in technologically grand design but not on ecological reason. A few voluntary organisations may not be able to do much to question this dominant paradigm when ideas such as river interlinking still hold fast with India's educated middleclass.[35] Large-scale public opinion is a must at all levels (as in the case of urban forests taken up by Agarwal, this volume),[36] to critically consider the potential impacts of river interlinking and associated water developments.

Declines and irregularities in river flows have wiped out many species from large reaches. Dolphins and gharials have undergone substantial range reductions in most of the upper Ganges, Yamuna, Chambal and the Ken-Betwa-Sone rivers.[37] In addition, large dams might have genetically isolated river dolphin populations within the Ganges basin.[38] Rivers originating in the peninsula, which are not fed by snowmelt and are further exploited by dams and irrigation projects have been receiving less and less water each year. Most rivers in the distribution range of the dolphin have heavily altered flow regimes, degrading river habitats and reduced fish abundance.[39] Even the Brahmaputra river system is under threat from a series of major run-of-the-river dam projects, and from seismic surveys for oil exploration. Several towns on the Ganges do not have efficient working treatment systems for sewage and solid wastes. Interlinking and dam projects, diversions, embankments, irrigation projects, agricultural land use changes and sand mining are extremely serious emerging challenges to ecologically sustainable use of water resources. The extent of degradation in some sites is of concern for both biodiversity and fisheries, if inaction continues alongside reckless technological interventions.[40]

The quest for meaningful, achievable coexistence means that scientific criteria, and socio-ecological realities must inform tradeoff decisions in order to benefit wildlife conservation and human welfare. Our work illustrates the many challenges that ecologists and wildlife biologists, elected representatives, administrators and social scientists face in evolving a framework for coexistence. This is especially complex where species conservation has to be achieved in human-dominated landscapes. The dominant conservation (or rather, preservation) paradigms that stress exclusion of humans are of little relevance here.[41] Coexistence essentially implies the sustainability of different levels and kinds of human extraction and activities if viable populations of endangered species are also to be conserved, for the sake of the entire ecosystem. What, then, is the basis for coexistence, when the river itself has become ecologically impoverished?

Alternatives for Overcoming Destitution

It is tragic that Bihar, a land of three large fertile floodplains, has to import more than seventy-five per cent of its fish from pond culture farms in Andhra Pradesh today. Moreover, these imports virtually sustain fish market economic turnover, according to local fishers. This unfortunate state of affairs reminds us that immediate and strong steps are urgently needed. It is important to enforce strict bans on destructive fishing techniques used by fishing mafia and 'traditional' fishers alike. Ecological restoration of all major and minor rivers in India needs to be undertaken urgently to ensure natural and adequate flow regimes, multi-objective habitat maintenance, protection of hydrological dynamics and services, natural flooding regimes and pollution control.[42] Dam reoperations to ensure adequate flows and variability in river discharge remain a neglected aspect of river management in most regions today.[43] Regulated and non-destructive fishing sustained over a long term could itself lead to restoration of collapsed fish stocks and needs to be the foremost goal for the management of the Ganges basin fisheries. The restoration should lead to improved health, numbers and availability of native commercial carps and preponderance of larger fish sizes through improved juvenile recruitment. Despite being regulated, restorations will enhance and not depress fisher livelihoods. Large scale scientific monitoring programs for fisheries need to be instituted to assess restoration programs critically.[44] The material dignity of fishers and the restoration of the river system are closely interlinked. There have been episodes of mass exodus of fisher families from the Gangetic plains (as high as forty to eighty per cent of the male workforce) to work as construction laborers in cities, because 'nothing is left to fish' and the perennial threat of criminal gangs. Given the failure of market-oriented private control systems and subsistence-oriented free fishing, cooperatively managed alternative livelihoods from common pool resources hold promise to achieving the twin ends of river dolphin conservation and enhancement of commercial gains for fishers.[45] However, the current state in which cooperatives exist is abysmal.[46] If carried out with ecologically sensitive and sound methods, even co-managed commerce may not be antithetical to dolphin conservation.[47] Alternative fisheries could be developed, providing small-scale, species-specific gear that could be 'dolphin-friendly' in terms of reduced entanglement and sizes caught.[48] While reducing pressure on the already depleted river fish resource base, these options could also improve the local economy through involvement of fishers' knowledge and enterprise. An example that has been gathering positive reviews for its income generation potential across rural Andhra Pradesh, Assam and West Bengal is the creation of community-based, lease owned pond carp aquaculture through fishing cooperatives.[49] Fisher compliance towards biodiversity conservation also needs to be ensured in the process,[50] so that fishers who own leased ponds can also monitor adjoining river stretches and help sanctuary authorities in regulating illegal, destructive fishing. The recent Food Security Act and rural labour programs could enhance both nutrition and wage rates of fishers, providing some protection to livelihoods without adverse impacts on fisheries.

Bringing Back Dignity to the River

Recent political changes in Bihar have led to some improvements in governance, and these can help secure such conservation initiatives. Improved social security could help create opportunities for involving fishers in small-scale ecotourism around the Vikramshila Sanctuary, making them important stakeholders in sanctuary management. The sanctuary's proximity to Kolkata offers a good opportunity for such initiatives. River dolphin tourism has started in a few locations along the Chambal River on a small scale. Planning ecotourism ventures in Vikramshila would also require assessing their benefits to fishers as against other commercial interests, as well as critically evaluating the ecological impacts of tourism itself. But if well planned, these measures can help conservation efforts, as they utilise and preserve traditional skills and ecological knowledge for conservation. The Mahatma Gandhi National Rural Employment Guarantee Scheme (MNREGS) too can be effectively used towards this end, on a cooperative, open and equal footing. The importance of sustained monitoring and action in all these initiatives cannot be overemphasised: for river dolphins, for fisher folk, and for the river itself.[51]

After the dolphin was declared the national aquatic animal, Bihar has taken some measures, such as the appointment of 'dolphin *mitras* (friends)' from among local fishermen who will monitor illegal fishing and intentional killing of dolphins. However, this has the danger of becoming reduced to symbolic cash incentives and may not be enough, particularly in the absence of sustained funding and governmental interest. In fact, fishers themselves never took to the scheme because of these uncertainties.[52] Nevertheless, the scheme can, if well supported, inculcate a sense of goodwill about dolphins among local fishers, and could be developed into a means of conservation, through economic gains to complying fishers. Enlisting local fishers as informers of harmful fishing and poaching activities in the river could be an important community-based monitoring initiative that bestows honour and responsibility to local partners and resource users.

Vikramshila sanctuary, with its multivariate creases offers a mirror to the conjugated futures of dolphins and people. It provides the best juxtaposition of situations and can be a foundry for interdisciplinary ecological research, where ideas may be tested right in the river. With virtual, fuzzy and often abstract boundaries of definition, spatiotemporal changes of the river's course, ambiguous tenure and uncertainty, this riverscape defies many existing ideas of managing nature. Amidst this, Vikramshila still offers hope and holds the promise of evolving into a 'true' sanctuary for dolphins. As at the same time, it illustrates the prospect of rivers such as the Ganga regaining their true meaning as sanctuaries for humankind and for fellow creatures that share the riverscape adjacent to age-old centres of human occupation and use.

Rivers in India—or elsewhere for that matter—are living, organic and dynamic entities, with their flow and flood, their feed and seed, worshipped and feared by humanity for what they give and what they can take away. They are the strong threads to which the pulse of our lives is inextricably tied: the baselines of civilisation. Yet today, they represent one of the biggest tragedies of our culture and ecology: many have been choked, depleted, poisoned and interrupted by dams. The biophysical nature of a river that flows from the mountains and hills to the sea, transporting water, sediment, nutrients and sustaining diverse ecosystems and communities, has been now thwarted severely by human activities. In many rivers, the entire dry season flow is diverted for agriculture, industrial and urban use until the river itself ceases to exist. Despite the demonstrated folly of not allowing rivers to flow unbounded from headwaters to estuaries and deltas, technocratic policy and public discourse is still dominated by an idiom of 'rivers flowing wastefully into the sea.' Belatedly, the National Water Policy has made a token, last priority mention of 'minimum environmental flows' to be maintained in a river, although this itself is an obsolete concept and needs to be replaced with 'ecological flow regimes.' The biogeochemical and physical functions and ecosystem services it provides, especially for downstream coastal ecosystems and dependent communities, are largely ignored. The dominant existing paradigms of water resource development are also socially unjust apart from being ecologically shortsighted. Rivers have become muted, sad metaphors to the erosion of our ecological wisdom. Reducing water consumption and pollution by agricultural and urban sectors, cooperative floodplain pond-based fisheries, alternative livelihoods and restoration of fish stocks can enable rivers to sustain biodiversity, local communities and ecosystem services. Keeping rivers alive with their natural flows,[53] productivity and dynamism will ultimately support coexistence of fisheries with river dolphin conservation. One way forward could be to modify operations of existing dam reservoirs to maintain flow regimes that cause minimal levels of risk to endangered fauna and fisheries during critical periods, as demonstrated in some recent research on gharials in the Sone River.[54] Conserving these together will also

Acknowledgements

We thank Professor Sunil Choudhary, Sushant Dey and Subhashish Dey of the VBREC, Bhagalpur, for introducing us to, and helping understand the Vikramshila sanctuary, its wildlife, people and challenges to conservation. We also thank Professor Upinder Singh, Shri M. B. Chitampalli and Meera Vishwanathan for their expert inputs on Emperor Asoka's edicts. We would also like to thank the volume editors, Professor Mahesh Rangarajan, M. D. Madhusudan and Ghazala Shahabuddin, as well as the anonymous reviewers from Orient BlackSwan for providing critical comments on this manuscript.

Notes

1. Also sometimes known as the South Asian river dolphin. The other species, found in the Amazon river system, is the Amazon River Dolphin or Boto *Inia geoffrensis*. Another species, the Chinese River Dolphin or Baiji *Lipotes vexillifer*, is thought to have become extinct in the last decade. A few other dolphin species, though mostly marine, have a few populations occurring in rivers and estuaries.

2. B. D. Smith and G. T. Braulik, '*Platanista gangetica*' in *IUCN Red List of Threatened Species*, version 2013.2. Available at http://www.iucnredlist.org (accessed 30 December 2013).

3. B. Collen, L. McRae, G. Kothari, R. Mellor, O. Daniel, A. Greenwood, R. Amin, S. Holbrook and J. Baillie, *Living Planet Index 2010 and Beyond: Rising to the biodiversity challenge* (Gland, Switzerland: World Wildlife Fund, 2008).

4. Notification No. 521, registered no. 33004/99 (New Delhi: Ministry of Environment and Forests, Government of India, 2009).

5. The 'Gangapuputaka' mentioned in Pillar Edict V is not the Ganges river dolphin, contrary to popular belief, but most likely the Red Junglefowl (see M. B. Chitampalli, *Nisargavachan* [Marathi], Nagpur: Sahitya Prasar Kendra, 2007). This seems the most valid translation. We thank Professor Upinder Singh, M. B. Chitampalli and Meera Vishwanathan for their help in this matter.

6. Many conservationists have argued that the critically endangered gharial should have been made the National Aquatic Animal, as it needs much more protection today, and requires undisturbed (or 'pristine') stretches of rivers and sand banks for nesting, free of human disturbance (see, J. Lenin, 'The song of the Ganges gharial: Reorienting conservation', *Seminar* 577 [2007]; and T. Nair, *Ecological and Anthropogenic Covariates Influencing Gharial* Gavialis gangeticus *Distribution and Habitat Use in Chambal River, India* [Mumbai: Tata Institute of Fundamental Research, 2010]). On the other hand, the river dolphin is a highly resilient river predator that seems to persist even in ecologically degraded rivers (see N. Kelkar,

gharial: Reorienting conservation', *Seminar* 577 [2007]; and T. Nair, *Ecological and Anthropogenic Covariates Influencing Gharial* Gavialis gangeticus *Distribution and Habitat Use in Chambal River, India* [Mumbai: Tata Institute of Fundamental Research, 2010]). On the other hand, the river dolphin is a highly resilient river predator that seems to persist even in ecologically degraded rivers (see N. Kelkar, J. Krishnaswamy, S. Choudhary and D. Sutaria, 'Coexistence of fisheries with river dolphin conservation', *Conservation Biology* 24 [2010]: 1130–40).

7. F. Madden, 'Creating coexistence between humans and wildlife: Global perspectives on local efforts to address human–wildlife conflict', *Human Dimensions of Wildlife* 9 (2004): 247–57.

8. S. K. Choudhary, B. D. Smith, S. Dey, S. Dey and S. Prakash, 'Conservation and biomonitoring in the Vikramshila Gangetic Dolphin Sanctuary, Bihar, India', *Oryx* 40 (2006): 189–97.

9. J. Bengtsson, P. Angelstam, T. Elmqvist, U. Emanuelsson, C. Folke, M. Ihse, F. Moberg and M. Nyström, 'Reserves, resilience and dynamic landscapes', *Ambio: A Journal of the Human Environment* 32 (2003): 389–96; T. P. Moulton, 'Defying water's end: Do we need different conservation strategies for aquatic systems compared with terrestrial?', *Aquatic Conservation: Marine and Freshwater Ecosystems* 19 (2009): 1–3.

10. D. L. Saunders, J. J. Meeuwig and A. C. J. Vincent, 'Freshwater Protected Areas: Strategies for conservation', *Conservation Biology* 16 (2002): 30–41.

11. S. K. Choudhary, et al., 'Conservation and biomonitoring in the Vikramshila Gangetic Dolphin Sanctuary'.

12. Kelkar, et al., 'Coexistence of fisheries'.

13. Kelkar, et al., 'Coexistence of fisheries'.

14. Kelkar, et al., 'Coexistence of fisheries'.

15. Kelkar, et al., 'Coexistence of fisheries'.

16. A. M. Smith and B. D. Smith, 'Review of status and threats to river cetaceans and recommendations for their conservation', *Environmental Reviews* 6 (1998): 189–206; R. Sinha, B. Smith, G. Sharma, G. Prasad, B. C. Choudhury, K. Sapkota, R. K. Sharma and S. K. Behera, 'Status and distribution of the Ganges susu (*Platanista gangetica*) in the Ganges River system of India and Nepal', *Occasional Paper in IUCN Species Survival Communication* 23 (2000): 54–61.

17. R. S. Lal Mohan and N. Kelkar, 'The Ganges River dolphin' in A. J. T. Johnsingh and N. Manjrekar (eds), *Mammals of South Asia*, (Hyderabad; Universities Press, 2014).

18. P. D. Reeves, 'Inland waters and freshwater fisheries: Issues of control, access and conservation in Colonial India' in D. Arnold and R. Guha (eds), Nature, Culture, imperialism (New Delhi: Oxford University Press, 1995): pp. 260–92.

19. C. Gupta, 'Unshackling the Ganga', *Down to Earth* 2 (1993): 22–24.

20. Kelkar, et al., 'Coexistence of fisheries'.

23. D. Dudgeon, 'Large-scale hydrological changes in tropical Asia: Prospects for riverine biodiversity', *Bioscience* 50 (2000): 793–806.

24. M. Banerjee, 'A report on the impact of Farakka barrage on the human fabric', (New Delhi, South Asia Network on Dams, Rivers and People, 1999).

25. A. I. Payne and S. A. Temple, *River and Floodplain Fisheries in the Ganges Basin* (London: Marine Resources Assessment Group Limited, Overseas Development Administration, 1996).

26. Choudhary, et al., 'Conservation and biomonitoring'; K. K. Vass, S. K. Mondal, S. Samanta, V. R. Suresh and P. K. Katiha, 'The environment and fishery status of the River Ganges', *Aquatic Ecosystem Health and Management* 13 (2010): 385–94.

27. Kelkar, et al., 'Coexistence of fisheries'.

28. Kelkar, et al., 'Coexistence of fisheries'.

29. S. Xie, Z. Li, J. Liu, S. Xie, H. Wang and B. R. Murphy, 'Fisheries of the Yangtze River show immediate impacts of the Three Gorges Dam', *Fisheries* 32 (2007): 343–44.

30. S. Turvey, *Witness to Extinction: How we failed to save the Yangtze River dolphin* (Oxford: Oxford University Press, 2008).

31. Turvey, *Witness to Extinction*.

32. D. Dudgeon, 'Large-scale hydrological changes'; Xie, et al., 'Fisheries of the Yangtze River'.

33. Turvey, *Witness to Extinction*.

34. J. Bandyopadhyay and S. Perveen, *The Interlinking of Indian Rivers: Some questions on the scientific, economic and environmental dimensions of the proposal* (London: SOAS Water Issues Study Group, School of Oriental and African Studies, King's College, 2004).

35. A. K. Biyani and S. K. Gupta, 'River Inter Linking', *Current Science* 87 (2004): 277–78.

36. R. Agarwal, 'Fight for a Forest', *Seminar* 638, no. 613 (2010): 48–52.

37. S. Choudhary, S. Dey, S. Dey, V. Sagar, T. Nair and N. Kelkar, 'River dolphin distribution in regulated river systems: Implications for dry-season flow regimes in the Gangetic basin', *Aquatic Conservation: Marine and Freshwater Ecosystems* 22 (2012): 11–25.

38. Smith and Smith, 'Review of status'.

39. B. D. Smith, A. K. M. A. Haque, M. S. Hossain and A. Khan, 'River dolphins in Bangladesh: Conservation and the effects of water development', *Environmental Management* 22 (1998): 323–35; S. E. Bunn and A. H. Arthington, 'Basic principles and ecological consequences of altered flow regimes for aquatic biodiversity', *Environmental Management* 30 (2002): 492–507.

40. Vass, et al., 'The environment and fishery status'.

41. K. S. G. Sundar, 'Cranes, cultivators and conservation', *Seminar* 638 (2010): 34–37.

'Basic principles and ecological consequences of altered flow regimes for aquatic biodiversity', *Environmental Management* 30 (2002): 492–507.

40. Vass, et al., 'The environment and fishery status'.

41. K. S. G. Sundar, 'Cranes, cultivators and conservation', *Seminar* 638 (2010): 34–37.

42. Dudgeon, 'Large-scale hydrological changes'; D. Dudgeon, 'River rehabilitation for conservation of fish biodiversity in monsoonal Asia', *Ecology and Society* 10 (2005): 15.

43. B. D. Richter and G. A. Thomas, 'Restoring environmental flows by modifying dam operations', *Ecology and Society* 12 (2007): 12.

44. Dudgeon, 'River rehabilitation'.

45. Castro and Nielson, 'Indigenous people'.

46. M. Sharma, *Landscapes and Lives* (New Delhi: Oxford University Press, 2006).

47. D. Soto, J. Aguilar-Manjarrez, J. Bermudez, C. Brugere, D. Angel, C. Bailey, K. Black, P. Edwards, B. Coste-Pierce, T. Chopin, S. Deudero, S. Freeman, J. Hambrey, N. Hishamunda, D. Knowler, W. Silvert, N. Marba, S. Mathe, R. Norambuena, F. Simard, P. Tett, M. Troell and A. Wainberg, 'Applying an ecosystem-based approach to aquaculture: Principles, scales, and some management measures', FAO/Universitatde les Illes Balears Expert Workshop Palma de Mallorca, Spain. In D. Soto, J. Aguilar-Manjarrez and N Hishamunda (eds), *Building an Ecosystem Approach to Aquaculture* (Rome: FAO Fisheries and Aquaculture Proceedings, UN, 2007), pp. 15–35.

48. Soto, et al., 'Applying an ecosystem-based approach'; S. K. Das, 'Small-scale rural aquaculture in Assam, India: A case study', *NAGA: World Fish Center Quarterly* 29 (2006): 42–47.

49. Das, 'Small-scale rural aquaculture'; T. J. Abraham, S. K. Sil and P. Vineetha, 'A comparative study on the aquaculture practices adopted by fish farmers in Andhra Pradesh and West Bengal', *Indian Journal of Fisheries* 57 (2010): 41–48; M. C. Nandeesha, 'Farmers as scientists: Andhra Pradesh fish farmers go into revolutionary carp research', *Aquaculture Asia* 6 (2001): 29–32.

50. R. Ramakrishna, 'Kolleru carp culture in India: An aquaplosion and an explosion', *Aquaculture Asia Magazine* 25 (2007): 12–18; M. E. Lam and D. Pauly, 'Who is right to fish?: Evolving a social contract for ethical fisheries', *Ecology and Society* 15 (2010): 16.

51. Kelkar, et al., 'Coexistence of fisheries'; Choudhary, et al., 'Conservation and biomonitoring'.

52. Personal communication with S. Dey.

53. B. D. Richter, R. Mathews, D. L. Harrison and R. Wigington, 'Ecologically sustainable water management: Managing river flows for ecological integrity', *Ecological Applications* 13 (2003), 206–24.

54. J. Krishnaswamy, 'Saving India's rivers and riverine ecosystems'. *Fundamatics* 2015, December 10.

Three

SARUS CRANES, CULTIVATORS AND CONSERVATION

K. S. Gopi Sundar

In mid-1998, after an unbearably hot night in a small hotel in Etawah town that had no electricity, I stood between a bright white stretch of alkaline wastelands and a drying lake in Mainpuri District in southwestern Uttar Pradesh, North India. Croplands and villages dotted the landscape as far as the eye could see, and the steady chugging sound of motors pumping up ground water was carried by the hot *loo* or summer winds. Even the smallest towns I had passed by had thousands of people, many milling about *chai* shops, buying sticky sweet *jalebi*s that attracted bright yellow wasps, apparently unaffected by the blistering heat. Conversations spanned from new guns that their school-going son had asked for, to the caste of the new bureaucrat at the district headquarters. A well used bus crammed full with people blew up fine dust as the driver attempted in vain to negotiate the deep potholes in the road. The bus was literally stopped in its tracks for half an hour by a kilometre-long herd of cattle that meandered calmly through the town, herded by Rajasthani men sporting lavish moustaches, colourful turbans and easy wrinkled smiles. I stood on the bridge beside the village Sauj peering through binoculars into the Sauj lake as the drying lotus leaves fluttered in the wind. This was the very spot where Allan Octavian Hume (British administrator and later, founder of the Indian National Congress) perhaps stood in the 1830s, and from where the American crane specialist Ron Sauey searched for the Siberian cranes in the 1970s. The nearly dried out lake was the only source of water for kilometres, and was maintained by the village to grow lotuses and harvest fish. In the shallow water amid lazing water buffaloes and pigs stood the largest flock I had ever seen of the world's tallest flying bird, the Sarus crane. Nearly 300 majestic cranes crowded the safe shallows, many of them sleeping in the hot afternoon with their beaks tucked away below their wings. A watchful crane on the edge preened itself and shook free a small white down feather that caught the sunlight as it sailed away. Thus began a fascinating discovery of cranes, crops and cultivation that continues to this day.

Conventional ideas of wildlife conjure up images of misty forests, species new to science, poisonous snakes and predators that stalk herbivores. In India, such forests are minuscule in extent relative to its cultivated landscapes, and most are maintained as protected wildlife reserves. At most, they cover just about six per cent of the country's landmass. These national parks and wildlife sanctuaries are responsible for the preservation of the diversity of life in the country and form the backbone of the conservation movement. Not surprisingly, the major part of the effort for wildlife conservation, including research, is focused on the forested Protected Areas, particularly in ecological 'hotspots' that retain a relatively higher number of species than elsewhere. Maintaining such hotspots as human-free areas for wildlife amidst an expanding economy and a growing human population remains a continuing challenge in India. This is true despite about half the country's land area already being under the plough, with most cultivable areas already having been cleared, and population growth rates having fallen from an all time high of 2.1 per cent in the 1970s to 1.7 per cent a year in 2011. My focus will be on this mostly treeless, human-dominated agricultural landscape which, in all but the permafrost areas of Earth, is the dominant land use and is considered the single largest threat to biodiversity, largely due to destruction of natural habitats.[1]

The attempt to understand how to maintain agricultural areas as potential wildlife habitats is not a new idea, but has been slow to gain traction in South Asia. Studies in croplands from across the globe have provided two important findings that underscore why conservationists need to pay more attention to these areas. First, the list of species that use agricultural landscapes as either refugia or primary habitats is not small, and is growing rapidly. For many of these species, the major fraction of their population resides in these unlikely non-forested habitats. The list goes well beyond insects, small mammals and snakes, and includes large predators like leopards, hyenas and jackals.[2] Second, and perhaps more importantly, agricultural lands will continue to increase the world over at the cost of natural habitats, particularly in the current scenario of globalisation and rapid increase of the human population. Apart from the primary effect of immediate loss of habitat, secondary effects of farming due to pesticides, fertilisers and soil erosion will also pose significant challenges to wildlife conservation. The importance of understanding how to engage with wildlife conservation in agricultural landscapes, therefore, cannot be emphasised enough.

One group of animals that has received a disproportionately large amount of interest in farmed areas are birds, due to the relatively large number of species that are able to persist in croplands and their utility as indicator species.[3] In this essay, I focus on recent studies on a six-foot tall bird, the Sarus crane. This is a globally threatened species found largely in the rice-wheat landscape of the Gangetic floodplains in North India. Using this species as a case study, I explore two major questions relevant to developing meaningful conservation interventions: Is conservation of birds in intensively farmed areas possible in India, and are our conservation policies and paradigms sufficiently developed to include these species and areas? What conditions can maximise the ability of farmlands to maintain high species diversity in India? In a sense, these questions are as significant as those that arise from forest conservation but they deserve much more sustained attention and action.

Sarus Cranes in Uttar Pradesh and Elsewhere

The largest global population of Sarus cranes currently occurs in Uttar Pradesh that has over 199 million people with a density of over 800 people per square km, and 57 million livestock, all of whom use virtually every inch of the land, resulting in a heavily human-dominated landscape.[4] Formal cultivation of rice here—progressing from seasonal gathering to storing of grains for planting—can be dated to at least 8,360 years ago, possibly being the first ever formal cultivation of rice worldwide.[5] The natural vegetation was likely wet grassland and deciduous forest; explorations and clearing of the land may have been hastened (though not initiated) by the use of iron, steadily leading to the landscape dominated by smallholder farmers. This river valley has been the demographic centre of gravity of South Asia for two millennia and human-nature relations here deserve a closer look.[6] Today, Uttar Pradesh is one of four of the most intensively human-modified and cultivated locations in the world, sharing top spots with Europe, the midwestern United States and southern China.[7] A miniscule proportion of the landscape constitutes woodlands, grasslands and wetlands—shallow, low lying areas that are flooded either by the monsoon or by overflows of the excellent network of irrigation canals. These are a few hectares each in size, scattered amidst private fields forming very tiny non-cultivated pockets. A very small number of the larger wetlands are designated Protected Areas, such as Soor Sarovar in Agra and Saman in Mainpuri, and are maintained as deep water bodies to attract wintering water birds. An even smaller extent of large woodland areas remains, largely as Reserved Forest, less often as sanctuaries. Nearly all of the non-crop lands are panchayat lands retained for common use. The non-protected uncultivated areas are heavily used by people to graze cattle, or extract natural resources such as timber, lotus stems and leaves, clay, reeds and water. The degree of use of wetlands and the variety of uses they have here is poorly understood.

Under the prevailing conservation emphasis on undisturbed Protected Areas, Uttar Pradesh's cultivated landscape would not therefore feature in the list of areas important for wildlife. The landscape here, however, is perfect for Sarus cranes partly due to the birds' ecology and behaviour, and in part due to the farmers and what they do.[8] In fact, the maintenance of the landscape by people appears to make the region conducive for the cranes. Crane breeding pairs maintain territories that they defend assiduously from other pairs. Each requires a small patch of wetland to make nests, and the current situation with several scattered wetlands makes it possible for a large number of pairs to breed amid crop fields. Non-breeding cranes, which comprise young birds that are yet to find partners or those that have not yet found territories of their own, live in flocks. These flocks require medium to large wetlands, and the community wetlands especially in southwestern Uttar Pradesh are perfect for the purpose. Being wetland birds, Sarus cranes do well in areas with flooded rice paddies where the landscape resembles a wetland during their breeding season. When small wetland patches are not available, cranes use the rice stalks to make their nests and incubate eggs in the rice fields. Two aspects of farmer behaviour are critically important to allow cranes to survive here—their practice of retaining wetland patches of all sizes, and positive attitudes towards the cranes that disallow killing them. Major threats to Sarus cranes are mortality incurred due to flying into power lines (especially new lines that are as yet unfamiliar to resident cranes), increase in egg and chick mortality due to proliferation of crow and feral dog populations in rural areas, decline in the numbers of small and large wetland patches, conversion of croplands to townships, and changes in cropping patterns from wet crops like rice to drier crops like corn and soyabean.[9]

In other parts of the world that have Sarus cranes, human use of the landscape has provided mixed benefits for the species. In South East Asia, Sarus cranes are rare due to conversions of large extents of undisturbed wetlands to farmlands, and a high degree of hunting and egg removal in areas accessible to locals, which has necessitated setting up paid guards at nests to improve breeding success.[10] In northeastern Australia, Sarus cranes seem to breed primarily in areas where woodlands have been cleared for cattle rearing. Artificial control of predators and keeping grasslands free of trees here seem to be enabling their persistence. Sarus cranes are therefore strongly affected by human modifications of the landscape across their entire distribution range. People's attitudes seem to favour them in Australia, but are not conducive in South East Asia. Observations from North India have given rise to suggestions that religion is a strong determinant of local value systems, but this appears not to be valid everywhere. Local and sub-regional cultures are more important than mere religious affiliation and further study is needed to know why cranes and cultivators go so well together in Uttar Pradesh.

Crops, Cropping and Attitudes

Sarus cranes appear to do well in areas like southwestern and central Uttar Pradesh that have flooded rice paddies during the monsoon and relatively moist wheat fields during the winter. The network of irrigation canals that supports the rice-wheat cropping cycle here creates artificial patches of wetlands due to leakages, thus providing additional areas that cranes can use. This is more evident in semi-arid regions like Rajasthan where the best breeding populations of Sarus crane occur alongside irrigation canals, and the cranes are reputed to be travelling along canals radiating out from the relatively new dams on the Narmada river.[11] Hitherto dry regions with unsuitable conditions are becoming wet, prompting cranes to expand their range. In areas with drier crops like sugarcane and soyabean, cranes practically disappear from the landscape. Ironically, the high human densities in Uttar Pradesh disallow large land holdings, and therefore mechanisation. Cultivation is almost entirely manual. Tractors and harvesters can cause severe disruption over wide swathes of land and are not conducive for bird survival. This is a bonus for cranes and the other bird species that persist here. The relatively small land holdings also ensure considerable staggering in the planting times. This ensures that the birds generally have some suitable fields to move into while the farmers are working in others.

Nesting begins with the first planting of rice, and chicks hatch when the rice is a couple of feet high allowing them to hide in the crop for two months when they begin to fly. Farmers here use tall rice varieties suited for flooded conditions, and this ensures that Sarus chicks can hide well in them. Chicks from late nesting pairs, however, stand the risk of being exposed before they have grown enough to fly due to the rice harvest. The mortality of such chicks is high, and only pairs with wetlands in their territories manage to successfully raise chicks when they hatch late in the season. Wetland vegetation gives the chicks the cover they need.

Panchayats or elected village councils in southwestern Uttar Pradesh appear to have done better at retaining wetland patches as common lands. Retaining these wetlands has inadvertently allowed the largest Sarus crane population in the entire world to occur here, and their population here appears to have been stable for the last half century.[12] Sarus cranes are revered for their supposed lifelong pair bond, and farmers tolerate crop damage, even allowing birds to nest inside rice fields. Notwithstanding these adjustments by cranes, however, farmer tolerance is vital for their continued survival. While western Uttar Pradesh has crane-tolerant farmers and plenty of the birds, crane numbers decline eastwards and eventually disappear in the eastern districts of Uttar Pradesh. Cranes have been extinct in Bihar and West Bengal for a few decades at the least. This contrast in numbers appears to be a result of varying attitudes of farmers and little else, though a specific study to document this is not yet available. Cranes have had a considerable period of time to adjust their behaviours to cropping patterns, and farmers have retained reverence for the birds in many parts of the state. Ironically and accidentally, the large human population (disallowing large land holdings) and village politics (allowing retention of wetlands and cropping patterns) provide perfect conditions for Sarus cranes here. We now know that flooded rice crops in the Indian subcontinent are used by over 350 species of birds—possibly the highest number of species using any single crop in the South Asian region.[13] Mechanisms that allow for this persistence and coexistence are only just being looked into, and it appears that a closer look at rice fields in terms of their avian diversity will provide rich fodder for learning.

Conservation in Farmlands

Clearly, farmed areas are worthy of conservation efforts. Are current policies and conservation paradigms in India adequate to accommodate both farming and water birds? And what will it take to keep some of the bird friendly landscapes the way they are?

Policies are woefully deficient in recognising the importance of agricultural areas for biodiversity conservation. Reserved forests, national parks and wildlife sanctuaries are seen as synonymous with wildlife or with ecological integrity and biological diversity. It is only very recently that appreciation for the high degree of species persistence in agricultural areas has begun to exist. There has not been adequate interest or time for wildlife-related policies to incorporate and explicitly include species of the farmlands. Similarly, farming policies are developed almost entirely independent of ecological considerations. Wetlands are well recognised for their values such as their capability to recharge ground water. Notwithstanding their use by wildlife, this is an important function for agriculture but is largely ignored by departments that focus on increasing crop production. Currently, wetlands are classified as a category of 'wastelands', and are managed by the Department of Rural Development whose mandate is to increase cultivated areas.[14] This mindset and ethos has largely been responsible for wetland attrition in India.[15] Unfortunately, the extent of wetland decline and areas facing the most rapid declines remain poorly documented, though improvements in remote sensing technology are beginning to provide descriptive information on the complexities inherent in studying wetlands.[16] Finally, human use and extraction of products from wetlands and other community lands is an activity and practice that spans centuries, and is the reason for the continued persistence of wetlands, despite the burgeoning human population. Corruption and governmental focus on increasing cultivated area have combined to accelerate conversions of such lands to agriculture and other exclusive uses, depriving a significant section of the farming community of their utility. Recently, this resulted in a public interest litigation by farmers who demanded conservation and restoration of community lands. The Supreme Court of India provided a strong directive to state governments to ensure that community lands would not be converted, and that converted ones would be restored notwithstanding the cost of the development project undertaken.[17] This is the best available legal recourse available to prevent the decline of community wetlands with potentially far reaching ecological consequences, but is much less known relative to the cases under the Forest Conservation Act. However, wildlife does not figure in the language of these departments except perhaps as pests that cause crop damage and require removal from the landscape.

The primary driver of successful conservation of birds in farmlands in other countries is economics. In the 'set aside' scheme of the United States originating in the 1930s, farmers were provided a subsidy to maintain small chunks of natural habitat like wetlands amid their fields. These small units were actively managed through federal funding to maximise their utility for birds. Since economics was the motive behind these schemes, habitats that were set aside were rapidly lost when farming corn for methanol become more profitable.[18] The capability of federal funding to keep up with the finances required to persuade farmers to retain these natural areas diminished greatly, and most of the land set aside for conservation has since been converted to croplands. In Europe, similar agri-environment schemes were implemented, from practices encouraging farmers to maintain hedges and even small pockets of trees and grasslands, to very focused interventions such as payments to ensure that during mechanised seed planting, one row was deliberately missed, thus allowing very small but incredibly important strips of land to become available inside the crop for nesting birds.[19] Few such projects were, however, able to provide evidence of improvements of avian populations at the national level, making it impossible to assess the impacts of such federally funded schemes on biodiversity.[20] Occasionally, farmers collaborate with scientists to actively benefit birds that use farmed areas. In California, for example, when burning straw after rice harvest became illegal due to the Rice Straw Burning Act, fields were kept flooded allowing the decomposition of straw, and benefitted enormous numbers of wintering water birds.[21] Finally, viewing wildlife as beneficial to agriculture—e.g., in the form of pollination, as pest controlling agents, etc.—is a growing theme in the agriculture conservation culture, particularly in areas where wooded plants continue to dominate farmed landscapes.[22]

Economic interventions for farmland birds in the Indian context have not been attempted. However, these may not be pertinent or successful in Uttar Pradesh. Many farmers are currently tolerant due to deep rooted belief systems, and economic compensation programs would likely corrode and dismantle these nature friendly attitudes. Land holdings are too small to allow a set aside programme, and farmer density is too high to allow maintaining a large number of new wetland patches. At least one small wetland patch is required to help the breeding success of one pair of Sarus cranes, suggesting the low practicality of undertaking either formal protection of wetland sites or paying for them to aid species conservation. Commonly executed strategies like fencing wetland areas may prove to be damaging as nesting cranes are known to abandon fenced areas due to the human activity. Also, the level of knowledge on the requirements of bird species that use farmed areas and the areas where natural wetland patches would be most beneficial for birds are very poorly understood. Viewing landscapes like Uttar Pradesh under the 'beneficial to agriculture' ethos would cover few species, and would in fact exclude species like cranes that do crop damage.

Planning for the Future

What then would be the most advisable strategy for Sarus crane conservation in Indian conditions? And how (and via whom) would it be actualised on the ground? First and foremost, the landscape requires being looked at in its entirety and not as a set of small and disconnected wetland sites. The farmers, their practices, the crops they use and their ancient attitudes require as much attention, if not more, as the cranes and the wetlands themselves. Preliminary discussions with panchayat leaders in Uttar Pradesh have provided three important aspects that together have important implications on how to structure conservation interventions. First, wetlands are maintained primarily for the utility they offer, and much less for the religious or cultural values they retain. Further, wetlands are valued primarily for their use as grazing grounds and for retaining water, and any other additional services they may provide (such as silt and fish) are ancillary at best. Finally, wetlands are most valued in areas where they have declined greatly (e.g., eastern Uttar Pradesh) where prospects for their restoration are minimal (due to very high human population density). Not surprisingly, biodiversity did not feature in these conversations, which aimed to understand how farmers value the non-crop features of the landscape. These findings help underscore why a purely biodiversity-centric or a preservationist approach to wetland conservation would be highly ineffective in these areas. Effectively modifying approaches to maximise wetland utility for farmers, for example, by providing an understanding of how to maximise growth of vegetation for grazing, will instead be required. These approaches will have much wider ramifications in strengthening continued coexistence of food production and biodiversity conservation. These conservation interventions are not new given that retention of community lands is a practice with a long history. Though the region has long attracted scholarly attention of historians and sociologists, these dimensions call for study and reflection. Linking these practices with biodiversity conservation on landscapes not previously considered important for species conservation is the novel addition.

To enable the most parsimonious and least sanctimonious marriage of the two elements—ancient community practices and conservation of biodiversity—I argue that understanding the pulse of the land through farmers would give us our most cost effective conservation strategy. Understanding this in any detail currently eludes us. That many wetlands and cranes still persist despite intensification of cultivation and increase of human population in Uttar Pradesh is a clear message. The farmers appear to recognise and preserve the multiple values of the landscape, rendering it useful as an enormous production system while also retaining species of conservation interest. This is distinctly different from farmland areas in some countries where farmers have negative attitudes towards wetlands and/or wildlife, thereby reducing the potential of conservation efforts.[23] Maximising access to persisting natural areas for common use will include interventions such as grazing, fire, episodes of dryness, and removal of weeds like reeds that may be necessary to maintain tropical floodplain wetlands.[24] Such human use is usually excluded from protected wetlands to the detriment of many habitats while also causing an immense degree of antagonism among the people reliant on these systems.[25] The ethos of open use of habitat to benefit wildlife is both ironic and an antithesis to dominant paradigms of conservation thought in this part of the world, but is clearly an effective direction to undertake wildlife conservation with minimal compromise of human use of the landscape. Large water birds and the productive agricultural landscapes they occur in are still below the radar of most conservationists. Multidisciplinary research to understand the intricacies of cropland-wildlife systems, and to enable meaningful inputs into policy is urgently required. Increased discourse that assists in explicitly including wildlife in decisions pertaining to farmed landscapes is the need of the hour.

Notes

1. D. Tilman, J. Fargione, B. Wolff, C. D'Antonio, A. Dobson, R. Howarth, Schindler, W. H. Schlesinger, D. Simberloff, D. Swackhamer, 'Forecasting agriculturally driven global environmental change', *Science* 292 (2001): 281–84; R. E. Green, S. J. Cornell, J. P. W. Scharlemann and A. Balmford, 'Farming and the fate of wild nature', *Science* 307 (2005): 550–55; N. C. Saxena, *Eucalytpus in India: The God that Failed* (New Delhi: Sage, 1995).

2. Athreya, et al., 'Big cats in our backyards'; M. J. Novacek and E. E. Cleland, 'The current biodiversity extinction event: Scenarios for mitigation and recovery', *Proceedings of the National Academy of Sciences (USA)* 98 (2001): 5466–70.

3. An indicator species is a species whose life history and population parameters relate to (or 'indicate') changes in its habitat and requirements. For wetland species, an indicator species could help indicate decline or improvement in wetland quality. See BirdLife International, *State of the World's Birds 2004: Indicators for our changing world* (Cambridge: BirdLife International, 2004) and W. van der Weijden, P. Terwan and A. Guldemond, *Farmland Birds Across the World* (Barcelona: Lynx Edicions, 2004).

4. Anonymous, 'Agricultural statistics at a glance 2010'. Available at http://eands.dacnet.nic.in/Advance_Estimate-2010.htm (accessed 22 April 2014); Office of the Registrar General of India, 'Population of States/Union Territories by sex and percentage share of population in total population: 2011'. Available at http://www.censusindia.gov.in/2011-prov-results/DATA_FILES/Final PPT 2011_12.PDF.

5. A. Saxena, V. Prasad, I. B. Singh, M. S. Chauhan and R. Hasan, 'On the Holocene record of phytoliths of wild and cultivated rice from Ganga plain: Evidence for rice-based agriculture', *Current Science* 90 (2006): 1547–52; T. T. Chang, 'The origin, evolution, cultivation, dissemination, and diversification

of Asian and African rices', *Euphytica* 25 (1976): 425–41; I. Habib and F. Habib, *The Atlas of Ancient India* (New Delhi: Oxford University Press, 2012).

6. S. Sharma, M. Joachimski, M. Sharma, H. J. Tobschall, I. B. Singh, C. Sharma, M. S. Chauhan, and G. Morgenroth, 'Late glacial and Holocene environmental changes in Ganga plain, Northern India', *Quaternary Science Reviews* 23 (2004): 145–59; V. N. Misra, 'Prehistoric Human Colonization of India', *Journal of Biosciences* 26 (2001): 491–531.

7. N. Ramankutty and J. A. Foley, 'Characterizing patterns of global land use: An analysis of global croplands data', *Global Biogeochemical Cycles* 12 (1998): 667–85; P. S. Thenkabail, M. Schull and H. Turral, 'Ganges and Indus river basin land use/land cover (LULC) and irrigated area mapping using continuous streams of MODIS data', *Remote Sensing of Environment* 95 (2005): 317–41.

8. G. W. Archibald, K. S. G. Sundar and J. Barzen, 'A review of the three subspecies of Sarus Cranes (*Grus antigone*)', *Journal of Ecological Society* 16 (2003): 5–15; K. S. G. Sundar, 'Effectiveness of road transects and wetland visits for surveying Black-necked Storks *Ephippiorhynchus asiaticus* and Sarus Cranes *Grus antigone* in India', *Forktail* 21 (2005): 27; K. S. G. Sundar and B. C. Choudhury, 'Conservation of the Sarus Crane *Grus antigone* in Uttar Pradesh, India', *Journal of the Bombay Natural History Society* 103 (2006): 182–90; K. S. G. Sundar, 'Are rice paddies suboptimal breeding habitat for Sarus Cranes in Uttar Pradesh, India?', *The Condor* 111 (2009): 611–23.

9. Sundar, 'Are rice paddies suboptimal'; K. S. G. Sundar and B. C. Choudhury, 'Mortality of sarus cranes (*Grus antigone*) due to electricity wires in Uttar Pradesh, India', *Environmental Conservation* 32 (2005): 260–69; K. S. G. Sundar, 'Agricultural intensification, rainfall patterns, and large waterbird breeding success in the extensively cultivated landscape of Uttar Pradesh, India', *Biological Conservation* 144 (2011): 3055–63.

10. M. Handschuh, V. Rours and H. Rainey, 'Clutch size of Sarus Crane *Grus antigone* in the Northern Plains of Cambodia and incidence of clutches with three eggs', *Cambodian Journal of Natural History* 103 (2010).

11. J. Kaur and K. Kathju, personal communication.

12. Archibald, Sundar and Barzen, 'A review of the three subspecies'.

13. K. S. G. Sundar and S. Subramanya, 'Bird use of rice fields in the Indian subcontinent', *Waterbirds* 33 (2010): 44–70.

14. Ministry of Rural Development, *Wastelands Atlas of India* (New Delhi: Department of Land Resources, Ministry of Rural Development, 2005).

15. B. Gopal, 'Does inland aquatic biodiversity have a future in Asian developing countries?', *Hydrobiologia* 542 (2005): 69–75.

16. S. Panigrahy, T. V. R. Murthy, J. G. Patel and T. S. Singh, 'Wetlands of India: Inventory and assessment at 1:50,000 scale using geospatial techniques', *Current Science* 102 (2012): 852–56.

17. *Jagpal Singh vs State of Punjab*, Judgement for civil appeal no. 1132/2011 in SLP (C) no. 3109/2011 (New Delhi: Supreme Court of India, 2011).

18. J. R. Hetkert, 'Response of bird populations to farmland set-aside programs', *Conservation Biology* 23 (2009): 1036–40; S. Secchi and B. A. Babcock, *Impact of High Crop Prices on Environmental Quality: A case of Iowa and the Conservation Reserve Program* (Ames, Iowa: Center for Agricultural and Rural Development, Iowa State University, Ames, IA, 2007).

19. W. J. Sutherland, 'A blueprint for the countryside', *Ibis* 146 (2004): 230–38.

20. D. Kleijn, M. Rundlöf, J. Scheper, H. G. Smith and T. Tscharntke, 'Does conservation on farmland contribute to halting the biodiversity decline?', *Trends in Ecology and Evolution* 26 (2011): 474–81.

21. C. S. Elphick and L. W. Oring, 'Conservation implications of flooding rice fields on winter waterbird communities', *Agriculture, Ecosystems and Environment* 94 (2003): 17–29.

22. J. E. Banks, 'Divided culture: Integrating agriculture and conservation biology', *Frontiers in Ecology and the Environment* 2 (2004): 537–45.

23. M. Pyrovetsi and G. Daoutopoulos, 'Contrasts in conservation attitudes and agricultural practices between farmers operating in wetlands and a plain in Macedonia, Greece', *Environmental Conservation* 24 (1997): 76–82; I. Herzon and M. Mikk, 'Farmers' perceptions of biodiversity and their willingness to enhance it through agri-environment schemes: A comparative study from Estonia and Finland', *Journal for Nature Conservation* 15 (2007): 10–25.

24. M. M. Douglas, S. E. Bunn, R. J. W. Pidgeon, P. M. Davies, P. Barrow, R. O'Connor and M. Winning, 'Weed management and the biodiversity and ecological processes of tropical wetlands', Draft final report, National Wetlands R & D Program, Environment Australia and Land and Water Australia, 2001; P. N. Reeves and P. D. Champion, 'Effects of livestock grazing on wetlands: Literature review', NIWA Client Report: HAM 2004–059 (New Zealand: National Institute of Water and Atmospheric Research Limited, 2004); W. J. Mitsch and J. G. Gosselink, *Wetlands* (New Jersey: John Wiley and Sons, 2007).

25. M. Lewis, 'Cattle and conservation at Bharatpur: A case study in science and advocacy', *Conservation and Society* 1 (2003): 1–21.

Four

CITIZEN ACTION AND LAKE RESTORATION IN BENGALURU

Harini Nagendra, Ramesh Sivaraman and S. Subramanya

Urbanisation is emerging as one of the most significant drivers of global environmental change.[1] The impacts of city growth are especially noticeable in India, where urban landscapes have rapidly expanded over the last two decades. The country still has a predominantly rural population, but its ecological profile, as much as its economic milieu, is dominated by dwellers of both town and country. Bengaluru, India's third largest city with a population of over six million and a decadal growth rate of thirty-eight per cent between 1991 and 2001,[2] is a case in point, providing a characteristic example of rapid expansion at the expense of natural ecosystems. It has grown much faster than cities at the pan-Indian level, and a closer look at not only the environmental challenges but also the opportunities in the metropolis may help chart ways of making spaces for nature in the Indian city.

While Bengaluru has undoubtedly experienced an explosion in growth in recent decades, it has a long, complex and multi-layered past. The settlements around the city have a recorded history that dates a millenium and a half, at least as far back as the fifth century CE.[3] Urban settlements made their first appearance, however, only in the sixteenth century CE when it was established as the capital of the local king Kempe Gowda's kingdom.[4] These settlements, along with the surrounding agricultural landscape that sustained their presence, required the availability of a continuous supply of fresh water. Unlike many other old settlements, however, the city of Bengaluru was located in the rain shadow of the Deccan hills, and lacked the presence of a large river to provide fresh water. The absence of perennial fresh water from a free flowing river was a limiting factor for growth and required ingenious working solutions.[5] The undulating topography of this region gives rise to a number of small streams, which were dammed to form multiple series of tanks throughout the larger region.[6] Inscriptions found near lakes indicate that some of these lakes date at least as far back as the fifth century CE.[7] It is worth noting that even a thousand year old city like Delhi, which had the river Yamuna, also until very recently used streams from the Aravalis as active water sources.[8] The use of topography and gradients for water capture was evidently known to many town builders and is corrective to modern planners who imagine the past as a tabula rasa.

Lakes were an important feature, in fact, the key artifact of the landscape of Bengaluru. Indeed, for those of us living in concrete dominated city environments today, the network of lakes in the Bengaluru area would have unimaginably dense. In 1830, for instance, a mindboggling 19,800 lakes were recorded in the region surrounding Mysore.[9] The surface water provided by these lakes earlier constituted over fifty per cent of the water supply of Bengaluru.[10] Yet now this lake network lies disrupted and in decay, with many lakes converted to urban land uses, and others polluted and choking with waste, or completely dry and weed infested. There is logic to this process of physical decay and biological death of these closed water bodies. The original network of lakes in Bengaluru was created by checking the flow of rainwater through earthen embankments along a topographic gradient such that the outflow of water from a lake at a higher level supplied water to the lakes at a lower level through canals.[11] Lakes were linked through a web of canals or *kaluves*, connected to the surrounding agricultural-wetland landscape. They ranged in size from small ponds (*kuntes* or *donnes*), of less than a hectare, used for cattle washing and drinking, to extensive large lakes (*keres*) hundreds of hectares in area, used for agriculture, fishing, drinking water and domestic uses.[12] All were rain fed. The small and medium tanks were seasonal; only large tanks were perennial.

Lake ecologies were connected to and maintained by human management in a closely linked socio-ecological system. The ways in which capital was invested and labour deployed, or the many cultural and social meanings embedded in these waterscapes lie beyond the scope of this essay but these do require more sustained analyses.[13] Wetlands, orchards and agricultural fields surrounded the lake, and these were irrigated by water from open wells that were dependent on the ground water table recharged by nearby lakes. Water was used for drinking, for domestic purposes such as washing, and for replenishing the ground water table. In the monsoon, rain water overflowed from lakes into adjacent wetlands, and was used for agriculture, principally to irrigate the rice crop. When water levels began to recede, cattle grazed on the wetlands, which were largely designated as *gomala*—common property wetlands where community grazing and seasonal agriculture took place. There was extensive fishing in the wetlands and lakes. Idols were immersed in the tanks during festivals.[14]

The wetland-agricultural-grazing-orchard landscape surrounding the lake acted as a natural catchment to recharge the lake with fresh precipitation. Since most lakes were seasonal, and pollution levels were low, siltation was easy to control. The silt was extracted annually in the smaller lakes, and every few years for the large lakes in the dry season, and the fertile silt was used by cultivators as inputs into agriculture.[15] Some of these lakes also constituted important sacred spaces, and many important local religious festivals were initiated or concluded at local lakes. Critical for conservation, lakes also supported a range of important local flora and fauna, including a rich diversity of birds, insects and fish.

As the city began to import piped water from the Cauvery river in the early twentieth century, lakes lost their importance as suppliers of fresh water, and instead became blamed for a host of ills such as flooding and malaria. Many of the city's lakes were drained and converted to other land uses, including bus stands, golf courses, malls and residential areas.[16] With urbanisation, much of the wetland-agricultural landscape around lakes has been converted to impervious concrete-covered surfaces. Instead of rainwater precipitation, sewage and effluents fill the few lakes that remain, converting them from seasonal to perennial ecosystems and drastically altering their ecology and biodiversity. Most surviving lakes are heavily polluted with sewage and industrial waste, and have significantly reduced water levels. Due to the disruption and transformation of this previously well planned and maintained extensive network into a few isolated and disconnected lakes, significant flooding is often reported in the monsoon season.[17]

The change from agrarian to urban land use has moved in parallel with changes in lake management and administration. Historically, lakes were managed by the village communities living adjacent to the lake, sometimes with financial support from the rulers. The community structure, while deeply hierarchical and exclusive, still invested considerably both in symbolic and substantive terms in maintaining the lakes.[18] Specific families and communities were designated to maintain lake canals, bunds, and desilting, and specific groups were given permissions to use the lake for fishing, collection of fodder, agriculture and the washing of clothes. These specialised, locally varying and adaptive roles played by different communities were gradually replaced or supplemented by formal governance structures imposed by the Mysore princely state and British government agencies.[19] Later, a bewildering array of government departments became involved with aspects of lake management, with overlapping jurisdictions. These included the Department of Minor Irrigations, Department of Fisheries, Ecology and Environment Department, Karnataka State Forest Department, Lake Development Authority, Karnataka State Pollution Control Board, the Bangalore Development Authority[20] and the Bengaluru Municipality (Bruhat Bengaluru Mahanagara Palike or BBMP). And this list of eight government agencies is by no means a comprehensive one!

In 1983, in response to increased public concern about the condition of lakes in the city, the Karnataka state government constituted an expert committee to investigate this issue. The recommendations of this committee, popularly known as the Laxman Rao committee, resulted in the transfer of administration of most of the city's lakes to the Karnataka State Forest Department.[21] While this resulted in the survey, fencing and protection of several of the city's lakes, the situation continued to deteriorate. The department secured the perimeters of the water bodies in most cases but stopped short of doing anything more at a time when other threats to their integrity had become equally significant. In 2002, the Lake Development Authority was constituted as an autonomous body responsible for the maintenance and restoration of lakes in Bengaluru.[22] The authority attempted to implement new public-private-partnership (PPP) approaches to lake management, which met with widespread resistance from civil society, environmentalists and activist groups, and resulted in a number of public interest litigations which have arrested this process for the time being. Currently, lake governance is in the process of being consolidated, with the BBMP and Bangalore Development Agency assuming responsibility for the maintenance of the majority of the lakes within the city limits, along with the Lake Development Authority and other authorities, which continue to manage a small number of lakes.

Currently, there are about 210 lakes located within the administrative boundary of greater Bengaluru.[23] Given the abysmal condition that most of these lakes are in, the municipal and city development authorities plan to conduct large scale restoration and rejuvenation programs. These need to be carefully designed. Although these lakes are of human origin, over centuries they have acquired natural characteristics and have become nature preserves or nature zones. Yet, their transformation into urban landscaped spaces is perhaps the most significant change in their recent history. While these lakes are undoubtedly critical sources of water supply, and important nature preserves, they also form vital social spaces in a cramped, concrete-dominated city environment. Given the high levels of socioeconomic, cultural and linguistic diversity in the city, lakes can become contested public spaces, especially Bengaluru's lakes whose historic use and design have changed over time. For instance, for many of the earlier inhabitants of the city, lakes continue to have a significant role in religious and sacred rituals,[24] but with increasing urbanisation they also play a new role as urban recreational spaces, and locations for reconnecting with 'nature' in the city.[25]

Although lake restoration programs have been conducted in the past, they have been expensive and lake conditions have deteriorated soon after in many lakes. Restoration has been piecemeal—one lake is treated, but the upstream and downstream lakes remain polluted, and kaluves continue to be blocked, so that in a few years the lake returns to its original polluted condition, as has happened with several of Bengaluru's lakes in the past.[26] Lake dredging is largely conducted based on considerations of engineering and cost without taking into account principles of ecological design. There is no acknowledgement of the need to treat each lake as a unique individual entity with its own appropriate method of restoration based on its social and ecological context.

A number of urban researchers, naturalists and concerned citizens have engaged in extensive discussions with the BBMP since 2007, seeking to develop guiding principles for lake restoration and management that are geared towards conservation in urban environments, while paying attention to the need for urban recreation, social inclusion, maintenance of cultural diversity, and providing space for traditional livelihoods and for the urban poor. Given the diversity and disparity in the city, such common efforts that bring together the middle classes and the under classes are especially important. Such inclusive approaches do not and cannot level differences but an open, transparent process can at least be a step towards a better future. It is important that the initiative of the legally constituted authority has enabled the process to move forward.[27]

A Resident Motivated Restoration: The Case of Kaikondanahalli Lake

The process described may sound fine in the abstract but the path is a difficult, even thorny, one. How the process works and what the serious challenges are can be best understood by looking at one instance in some detail. The case in point is a highly degraded site where the initiative came from residents of the lands adjacent to the lake. Once heavily polluted with sewage from nearby residential areas, the Kaikondanahalli Lake located in the southeastern corner of Bengaluru has now been restored, witnessing huge increases in bird, insect, amphibian and snake diversity, as well as extensive recreational use by local residents. This was based on a process that included carefully dredging the lakebed to remove silt, diverting sewage, restoring the bund and planting a rich diversity of native trees and shrubs around the periphery. Based on inputs from an association formed by a group of residents, working with the local body that represents many of the original farmers, the lake waterspread area has been maintained during rejuvenation to the maximum possible extent without uprooting existing trees. A walkway has been created around the lake which avoids the marshy, biodiversity rich southern end.

Taking into account the requirements of cattle owning households from the nearby peri-urban villages, a separate path has been created to allow cattle to approach the lake, for a cattle wash. At the western end, bathroom facilities have been designed in a location adjacent to a nearby school for children from less wealthy, peripheral city areas. These associated facilities will serve a dual purpose, allowing the children from the school and migrant labour in nearby sheds to utilise it during weekdays, while enabling access to lake visitors during mornings, evenings and weekends. There is also an aim to make some provision for the washing of clothes and cattle in a confined upstream enclosure without polluting the lake. This is especially essential as there is a large population of poor migrant workers living just adjacent to the lake who regularly use the restored lake to wash clothes. While this should not (and probably cannot) be completely banned, it should be confined to certain areas to prevent widespread pollution of the lake. Controlled harvesting of grass for grazing is also being permitted at the marshy end of the lake in order to provide fodder for consumption by local cattle as well as to prevent overgrowth of grass in the lake during the dry season.

This lake provides an example of conservation in urban settings, which requires concerted, committed action from a number of sectors. Here, goals of recreation and access to greenery and ecological principles are as important as considerations of technical and economic feasibility. The requirements of citizens from diverse socioeconomic and cultural backgrounds are incorporated into the decision-making process. Collective action by a number of sectors, including the government, local citizens, researchers, nongovernmental organisations and businesses is required to make effective progress towards sustainable ecological and environmental planning. The task of lake restoration brings together citizens on a common platform. The fact that it is a government sanctioned initiative and many discussions are in Kannada opens up spaces for many. Yet, even a working consensus is hard to achieve in the context of life in an urban environment. Social, cultural and linguistic heterogeneity, coupled with economic inequalities, make it particularly challenging to create social capital and facilitate collective action.

Elinor Ostrom formulated a Social Ecological Systems framework that indicates conditions that can facilitate successful collective management of natural resources.[28] Social barriers to restoration that are relevant to Bengaluru's lakes include the exclusion of specific socioeconomic groups, lack of leadership and/or low social capital.[29] Such barriers to restoration and maintenance are relatively low in Kaikondanahalli, where the diversity of actors is moderate, there is minimal exclusion of groups and social capital is particularly strong with good leadership, following the recent process of lake restoration through community involvement. In addition, dependence on the lake provides a strong motivation for collective action. The peri-urban area surrounding Kaikondanahalli Lake has witnessed rapid urban growth in recent years with a severe scarcity of ground water, on which these communities are dependent. There has been tremendous recognition of the need for healthy, functioning lakes for ground water recharge, in addition to the need for lakes as urban spaces for exercise, recreation, and communion with nature in otherwise busy and crowded urban settings.

Further, it is critical to have functional community rules that manage the types of activities permitted in the lake. Such rules and norms were in place during earlier times when the local communities had greater control over lake management. Following restoration, the community association maintaining the lake has developed an informal and evolving set of operational community rules as well as informal norms of lake monitoring. The community has also been particularly successful in networking with government agencies, specifically with the BBMP Lakes Division over the past five years for lake restoration and maintenance, forming a trust that manages the lake with approval from the BBMP.

The time has come to really begin to pay attention to urban commons, and challenges of the commons are central to the question of urban governance. Urban commons generate benefits to a particular region, ranging from natural resources such as lakes or small parks to infrastructure such as streets. When the commons are in good condition, everyone in the neighbourhood benefits, but when conditions seriously erode, a tragedy of the commons may occur, with urban communities frequently failing to be sufficiently organised to provide the level of collective action as well as networking with the government that is required to deal with these challenges.[30]

Yet, the experiences in Bengaluru indicate that sustained engagement by citizens can result in change. While the progress achieved may not be optimum or ideal, it does represent a step forward, and the social capital and potential for collective action that has been built can be capitalised on for future urban conservation initiatives. After many decades of neglect, lake management in Bengaluru shows some signs of hope. If the citizens of Bengaluru can mobilise the administrative and political will to sustain these programs at a larger scale, then there is truly some hope for a green urban future.

The Scope for Collective Restoration in the Urban Context

A small but increasing number of lakes in Bengaluru have been cleaned up and restored with the help of innovative collaborations between local communities and government agencies. Thus, collective action by a diversity of local actors seems to be making headway in providing pressure to influence the plethora of administrative agencies involved in lake maintenance to take some action.

Local communities, because of their presence near the lake, are well situated to undertake challenges of monitoring to identify problems such as land encroachment, blocked water channels, and the dumping of solid waste or inflow of sewage and industrial effluents. Yet, it is well beyond the scope of citizen groups to tackle these problems unaided. In contrast, government agencies have the legal authority to prevent unwanted activities and harmful use of the lake but rarely have the required information about what is going on at different locations. Thus, monitoring and maintenance of urban lakes requires the collaboration of local groups and government agencies. An illustrative example of this is an instance from Kaikondanahalli Lake, where repeated inflows of sewage by workers in a neighbouring apartment under construction were unattended to despite a number of complaints to the builder, but eventually addressed because of action by the government, which eventually acted under pressure from local citizens.

Further, when local actors and government agencies cooperate, the chances of long-term success of lake rejuvenation are also greater. Understaffed government agencies now routinely contract out the task of developing lake restoration project reports to consultancy agencies, and unfortunately such agencies mostly provide identical, shoddily prepared proposals for rejuvenation that fail to take into account the unique socio-ecological context and requirements of each lake. Citizen groups, on the other hand, have the local knowledge of social needs, and can work closely with technical ecological and engineering experts to draft restoration plans for each lake, taking into account their specific requirements.[31] Yet, concerns of equity remain important, and some research indicates that citizen groups that organise activities such as lake restoration can often exclude practitioners of traditional livelihoods such as fishers and fodder collectors and restrict use of the lake for washing clothes, which may be extremely difficult for the urban poor, many of whom depend on lakes for daily domestic activities.[32] Concerns of equity are important across all Indian cities, and similar issues of exclusion of the poor around fresh water ecosystems have been observed in Delhi, on the banks of the Yamuna.[33] These deserve much greater attention from planners, activists, the judiciary and citizen movements than is currently the case, and constitute one area where upper to middle class citizen movements have largely failed in Indian cities. While it is too early to say that the Bengaluru lake restoration efforts are a success, they have helped shed light on innovative approaches to reconcile environmental repair and renewal with knowledge-based intervention and citizen partnership with government. They are also significant in a larger sense. Making spaces for nature in the city requires thinking in new ways far removed from the 'parks and fences' approach. The vibrant civic life of India's cities is under challenge from sprawl as also from exclusivist ways of protecting water bodies and green spaces. Perhaps, these small steps in Bengaluru are part of a new emerging fabric that gives nature its due but does so in a manner where all, not just a few, citizens can aspire to be equals and partners.

Acknowledgements

The authors greatly appreciate inputs provided by the BBMP Chief Engineer (Lakes) B. V. Satish and his team, the Chief Conservator of Forests (Urban) Brijesh Kumar, Ashwin Mahesh, M. B. Krishna, Gladwin Joseph, Rohan D'Souza, Priya Ramasubban and Vinay Sreenivasa during multiple discussions on Bengaluru's lakes. We acknowledge research funding provided by a Ramanujan Fellowship from the Department of Science and Technology to Harini Nagendra.

Notes

1. N. B. Grimm, S. H. Faeth, N. E. Golubiewski, C. L. Redman, J. Wu, X. Bai and J. M. Briggs, 'Global change and the ecology of cities', *Science* 319 (2008): 756–60.

2. H. S. Sudhira, T. V. Ramachandra and B. H. S. Subrahmanya, 'City profile: Bangalore', *Cities* 24 (2007): 379–90.

3. B. L. Rice, *Epigraphica Carnatica Volume IX: Inscriptions in the Bangalore District* (Bangalore: Mysore Government Central Press, 1905).

4. B. L. Rice, *Mysore: A gazetteer compiled for government* (Westminister: Archibald Constable and Company, 1897).

5. Rice, *Mysore*; Srinivas, *Landscapes of Urban Memory*.

6. Rice, *Mysore*.

7. Rice, *Epigraphica Carnatica*; T. V. Annaswamy, *Bengaluru to Bangalore: Urban history of Bangalore from the pre-historic period to the end of the 18th century* (Bangalore: Vengadam Publications, 2003).

8. See Ravi Agarwal, this volume.

9. R. B. N. Sundara, *Bengalurina itihasa (A History of Bangalore)* (Bangalore: Vasanta Sahitya Granthamala, 1985).

10. S. U. Kamath, *Karnataka State Gazetteer: Bangalore district* (Bangalore: Lotus Printers, 1990).

11. Rice, *Mysore*.

12. F. Buchanan, *A Journey from Madras through the Countries of Mysore, Canara, and Malabar* (New Delhi: Asian Educational Services, 1807).

13. See Srinivas, *Landscapes of Urban Memory*.

14. Srinivas, *Landscapes of Urban Memory*.

15. Buchanan, *A Journey from Madras*; Bruhat Bangalore Mahanagara Palike (BBMP), *Namma Bengaluru Nisarga: An action plan for development of Bangalore's lakes* (Bangalore: BBMP, 2010).

16. K. Gowda and M.V. Sridhara, 'Conservation of tanks/lakes in the Bangalore metropolitan area', *Management of Environmental Quality* 18 (2007): 137–51; BBMP, *Namma Bengaluru Nisarga*.

17. BBMP, *Namma Bengaluru Nisarga*.

18. Rice, *Mysore*.

19. Kamath, *Karnataka State Gazetteer*.

20. Gowda and Sridhara, 'Conservation of tanks'.

21. Gowda and Sridhara, 'Conservation of tanks'.

22. Gowda and Sridhara, 'Conservation of tanks'.

23. BBMP, *Namma Bengaluru Nisarga*.

24. Srinivas, *Landscapes*.

25. Nair, *The promise of the Metropolis*.

26. R. D'Souza and H. Nagendra, 'Changes in public commons as a consequence of urbanization', *Environmental Management* 47, no. 5 (2011): 840.

27. H. Nagendra, R. Sivaram and S. Subramanya, 'Lakes of Mahadevpura Constituency, Bangalore: Current status, changes in distribution, and recommendations for restoration' (Bengaluru: BBMP, 2011).

28. E. Ostrom, 'A general framework for analyzing sustainability of social-ecological systems', *Science* 325 (2009): 419–22.

29. H. Nagendra and E. Ostrom, 'Applying the social-ecological systems framework to the diagnoses of urban commons' *Ecology and Society* (forthcoming).

30. Nagendra and Ostrom, 'Applying the social-ecological systems'.

31. See Nagendra, Sivaram and Subramanya, 'Lakes of Mahadevpura'.

32. J. Sundaresan, 'Planning as commoning: Transformation of a Bangalore lake', *Economic and Political Weekly* 46 (2011): 71–79.

33. A. Baviskar, 'What the eye does not see: The Yamuna in the imagination of Delhi', *Economic and Political Weekly* 46 (2011): 45.

Five

THE FIGHT FOR AN URBAN FOREST

The Delhi Ridge

Ravi Agarwal

सबज़ा-ओ-गुल कहाँ से आये हैं?
अब्र क्या चीज़ है, हवा क्या है?
(Whence come the greenery and flowers?
What are clouds? What is the air?)

—Mirza Ghalib

The Fragile Forest

The battle to protect Delhi's largest urban forest, the Delhi Ridge, has been intense and is an ongoing one. The Delhi Ridge is quite unique, lying in the heart of the metropolis, and has been part of the city's multilayered and complex history, even though large parts of it have been built upon today. Like many natural green areas in cities around the world, it is struggling to survive rapacious urbanisation, as well as to maintain its forest character.

The now global city was once contained within a cusp formed by the tail of the 1.5 billion year old, 800 km long Aravali mountain range which peters off at the river Yamuna. The hilly spur, known as the Delhi Ridge, once occupied almost fifteen per cent of the city's land, though now much of it has been flattened. In the past, the elevation of the Ridge offered a perhaps unrivalled view over the northern plains of the Punjab, providing the city ecological as well as military security. In fact the *Delhi Gazetteer* (1883–84) states, 'The hills of Delhi, though not attractive in themselves, give a pleasant view across the Jamuna and in the clear weather allows, it is said, even a glimpse of the Himalayas'.[1] The dry deciduous and scrub forests of the Ridge form a fascinating ecosystem which has been critical for the city's ecological health in terms of air quality, biodiversity and water systems. Though citizen action has managed to spur legal protection[2] to about 7,800 hectares of the forest, the fight for saving it, led by citizens' groups and the courts, is far from over. It is worth noting that large parts of the Ridge as defined in topographical and ecological terms still remain beyond the ken of legal protection. Its future is contested and marked by deep uncertainty.

Land is scarce, and increasingly expensive in Delhi (National Capital Territory or NCT),[3] which already hosts over seventeen million people, with a population density of over 10,500 people per square km. The city has in recent times spilled over into the adjacent peri-urban areas. The now densely urbanised peripheral townships of Gurgaon and Faridabad also partly lie on the Ridge spur as it enters the capital city. The combined population of the area, known as the National Capital Region (NCR),[4] now exceeds twenty-five million.[5] Here, new high technology businesses, special economic zones,[6] glitzy upmarket malls and residential colonies have drawn people into these 'new dream destinations'. This immense, almost seamless urbanisation has placed a massive demand on the forest leading to stone quarrying, ground water over extraction, and the conversion of forest land for housing, industry and transport corridors. The ecological impact of such development has been cumulative, cutting across political boundaries. Yet most of the successes in protecting the Ridge have been mainly in New Delhi, the capital city, and not in the surrounding region at large. This serves to demonstrate the specific political dynamics[7] of the city.

But first, a quick overview of the Ridge's basic topography and ecology is in order. The Aravali range enters Delhi (where it is called the 'Ridge') through its southwest boundary (Haryana), and immediately splits into two spurs. One arm heads a short distance eastwards, before tapering off at Tuglaqabad, while the other forks westwards to end forty kilometres away in the north, at the river.

These arms of the hilly plateau had enclosed the various cities of Delhi built over 900 years. Many historic structures still exist here, like the ruins of the city built by the rulers of the Delhi Sultanate in the thirteenth and fourteenth centuries and the towering Qutub Minar. However, it was in independent India that the boundaries of the Ridge were transgressed and hillocks blasted to make space for hundreds of thousands of refugees and migrants who arrived after Partition in 1947. Unfortunately, the trend of urbanisation in the Ridge has continued unabated to this day, making it unrecognisable compared to its pre-Partition avatar. Large residential colonies, several religious institutions, universities and security force camps (which were allotted temporary land but have stayed on permanently) are present here. The four isolated but legally 'notified' forest patches which remain today were once a contiguous forest tract. These are the Asola Wildlife Sanctuary (6,200 hectares, Southern Ridge), Sanjay Van (633 hectares, South Central Ridge), the Central Ridge (864 hectares, behind Rashtrapati Bhavan) and the Northern Ridge (87 hectares, Delhi University).[8] Since other Ridge areas have not received the same legal status, though they are geomorphologically identical, they are constantly being 'developed'. This has given rise to citizens' protests and led to long legal battles.

A large forest in the midst of a dense, highly urbanised and growing city is a very unusual blessing. Its ecological functions are probably more needed today than ever before. The Ridge forest not only acts like a 'green lung' and carbon sink for the city, it also lowers ambient temperature within the city, acts as a noise buffer, and protects the city from desert sands blowing in from Rajasthan in the south. Once rich in animal and plant life, it has records of leopards, foxes, porcupines, chinkara and blackbuck, though now mainly nilgai and smaller animals like hares can be seen. Even lion hunts were known in the eighteenth century, whilst later porcupine and jackal were trapped and killed as vermin in the British period.[9] The bird life is still rich and the forest abounds in avifauna, with elusive birds of prey like the shikra, seasonal migrants, and more than 150 other resident species.[10]

Most importantly, the Ridge forest once supported a complex, even intricate network of water channels, critical in a chronically water scarce region. Several of these have now been lost or are now highly fragmented or even dysfunctional. The mesh of water flows helped recharge the groundwater and the wells via the fractured and porous quartzite rocks. The channels fed into a large number of wells, stepwells, natural and manmade lakes, reservoirs and *nahars* (streams) that fed the river Yamuna. Also, the water collected in its deep natural depressions to form *jheels* (lakes) or was stored in human-made *hauz* or storage ponds. In fact many places in the city were (and still are) named after these water landmarks.[11] Today, criss-crossing roads and housing have interrupted the natural drainage of the water, blocking flows to large water catchments such as the Najafgarh Jheel, or the Hauz Khas Jheel, which have turned dry. Many nahars have become open sewers, and are now being covered up to make roads, while the wells have disappeared.[12]

Re-naturing the Ridge

The Ridge has a quirky history of afforestation. Till the fourteenth century, the rocky outcrop had dense subtropical flora which was then cleared in some areas for security reasons, being replaced by orchards.[13] The afforestation of the Ridge was probably begun in the fourteenth century by Firoz Shah Tuglaq, who used it for hunting, and then later by the British foresters.[14] However, much of the plantation was of an exotic weed-like tree, the 'vilayati keekar' (*Prosopis juliflora*), which gradually overwhelmed much of the diverse native vegetation.[15] After 1911, when Delhi was made the new capital of British India, afforestation was carried out in the Northern Ridge and both this and the Southern Ridge were fenced to allow natural regeneration.[16] Pradeep Krishen, the historian of Delhi's trees writes, 'Afforestation work on the New Delhi Ridge began in 1914 on an experimental plot of land only 202 acres in an area in (what is now) Chanakyapuri. By 1929 this had grown to over 1000 acres.'[17] As if in acknowledgement of the aesthetic quality of the forest, there were even plans (ultimately discarded) to build the Viceroy's residence on it, and declare the surrounding forest as reserved.[18] Krishen adds, 'The New Delhi or Central Ridge (it was called southern Ridge, at first), framed the city to the west and barely figured in initial plans until Viceroy Hardinge had the impulse to place the Viceroy's residence on its highest eminence'.[19] Hardinge later 'backed down and the Viceroy's house (now Rashtrapati Bhavan) was eventually built on top of a decapitated hill at Raisina'.[20]

Over time there were several orders issued by the British to protect the forest. The complete list of notifications declaring various portions of the Delhi Ridge land as 'forest' under forest laws, are hard to find.[21] From available records, it appears that as early as in 1878, parts of the Ridge were declared as a Reserved Forest under the then Indian Forest Act (IFA), 1878. Later, between 1913 and 1948, additional areas on the Northern and Central Ridge received protection. Setting aside of the Ridge and subsequent afforestation was integral to creating the new imperial capital.

In 1980, twenty sites in the Northern, Southern and Central Ridge were declared as Protected Forests, now under the new IFA of 1927.[22] In 1986, the Lieutenant Governor of Delhi declared 1,880 hectares of forest in the Southern Ridge as the Asola Wildlife Sanctuary.[23] By 1991, an additional 840 hectares of the Bhatti Mines area were brought under the Asola sanctuary (where till the mid-1970s large scale stone quarrying took place before being banned by the courts, though it still continues in the border state of Haryana). Though many of these earlier notifications had technically never been withdrawn, their current validity had become uncertain, especially since many land markers have disappeared over time.

After India became independent, a new institution, the Delhi Development Authority (DDA),[24] was formed through an Act of Parliament in 1957, with the objective of developing centralised master plans (MPD, Master Plan of Delhi) especially for housing. Most non-forest land automatically came under its control. The master plan, however, only recognised the Ridge Forest as a 'Regional Park,' with no mention of any Protected Forest status, thus ignoring earlier notifications. In the midst of this confusing and unclear situation, the earmarking of major chunks of the Ridge forest for 'development' in 1992 raised alarm amongst some public minded citizens. The cluster, indeed thicket, of notifications, rules and enactments, though vital for protection, also leaves ample scope for ambiguity.

The Campaign to 'Save the Delhi Ridge'

The fight to protect the Ridge forest began in the 1979–80, led by student groups like Kalpavriksh and others, who stopped tree felling and land allocation for schools, through a series of protests and petitions,[25] even prompting intervention by Prime Minister Indira Gandhi.[26] Earlier still, the latter had halted construction of transmission towers in the Ridge. Such actions were significant as they entailed a direct union government role. But it was only in the wake of the 1992 order that affairs came to a head. For those who had grown up walking in the forest or birdwatching, the new 'development plan' was both a death knell and a call to action. The moment converted ordinary citizens into activists. Voluntary organisations and citizens came together under the banner of the 'Joint NGO Forum to Save the Delhi Ridge' with prominent nongovernmental organisations like the World Wide Fund for Nature (WWF), Kalpavriksh and Srishti spearheading the action. It was truly a moment of passion. School children marched through the streets of Delhi, carrying banners they had painted, residents organised colony meetings, activists devised new slogans, gathered supporters and confronted politicians, as the media carried the story day in and day out, even airing 'Save the Ridge' spots during prime time news. Eminent citizens signed petitions and wrote letters supporting the idea of the Delhi Ridge forests being the 'green lungs' of the city, especially when a new influx of motor vehicles was causing massive air pollution. It was a timely campaign which quickly hit home.[27]

A major thrust of the campaign was to retain the forest as a natural area, rejecting plans of various horticulture departments in the city. The latter aimed to make it a landscape park. There were fundamental differences in how the idea of the 'green' as a forest, as distinct from a park, was understood. A forest was linked with 'wildness' and chaos, while the park represented safety and control. The DDA saw the Ridge as a 'Regional Park,' manicured, with fountains, pathways and picnic cottages like the already named Buddha Jayanti and Mahavir Jayanti Parks which had been laid out on the Central Ridge. The forest had been landscaped and replaced with a park. Horticulturists now argued that citizens benefitted by using the green areas and needed jogging tracks, benches and grass which was not long and wild and also 'clear of snakes', and that protecting the Ridge like a 'wild' forest would harbour antisocial elements. Many citizens, on the other hand, made a case for the forest as an ecosystem whose diverse biodiversity could only survive in a natural forest, where the grasses, shrubs and trees were left for animals, birds and insects to feed and nest in. They said that parks, of which Delhi already had over 12,000, needed water, manure and labour, while a forest merely had to be left to itself. It was not only a qualitatively distinct and more complete ecosystem but also a place where the ecological functions of the Ridge were more completely fulfilled. The forest after all could serve as an open air laboratory to study plants and soil, fauna and the water cycle. Transcending merely aesthetic functions, it could be a great open air library of science for the city, especially its younger citizens. At issue and in contention were two competing visions of 'green'. One was nature-centric, while the other was more human-centric. One saw value in an open interdependent ecosystem, the other in an intricately redone park landscape. It is fortunate that the 'forest' view has prevailed over that of the 'park', given that the former clearly performs a more natural role.

However the associated legal and land ownership issues surrounding the Ridge areas were complex and institutionally intertwined (and still are). For example, while the DDA and the forest department owned Sanjay Van (South Central Ridge) and the Northern Ridge, the Central Ridge was under the Central Public Works Department (CPWD), the Delhi Administration, and the Land and Development Office (L&DO) while the forest department owned the Asola sanctuary land. No agency wanted to relinquish control and it was clear that only a higher level action could resolve the issue of the Ridge forest as a whole.

Given the public outcry and the complexity of the issues involved, the Delhi government appointed a ten member committee headed by eminent former civil servant Lovraj Kumar (then member, Planning Commission) in April 1993 to frame a management plan for the Delhi Ridge. Four members from nongovernmental organisations (Srishti, Kalpavriksh, WWF and Indian National Trust for Arts and Cultural Heritage [INTACH]) were part of the committee along with officials. On the basis of plans provided by the DDA, the committee recommended that four of the areas be notified as Reserved Forests, and that the forest character of the area be maintained irrespective of which agency managed the land.[28] This has remained unfortunately a lacuna ever since, as agencies like the DDA have horticultural departments with no expertise or interest in managing forests and the areas they control are often crowded with ornamental plants. Further, and surprisingly, no ground survey was carried out to confirm if there were other forested areas on the Ridge. Nevertheless, the committee's recommendation was very significant and on 24 May 1994 the specified areas were duly notified as Reserved Forest under Section 4 of the Indian Forest Act, 1927.[29] The rationale for excluding areas other than the specified 7,777 hectares was never made clear, and continues to haunt the city to this day. The decision taken was a welcome step but an incomplete one.

For the moment the well meaning, persistent and conservation-minded middle class citizens[30] had won the day. They had been amply supported by the media and the courts who supported their view of nature and its association with 'quality of life.' But the poor and under classes, who lived in and around the forest, had been excluded from the debate. Many of the latter soon faced eviction, displacement and relocation from the Ridge. Notably, this imagination (of a Ridge sans poorer inhabitants) was shared by elected decision-makers, who feared that land left undeveloped or unprotected would ultimately lead to it being squatted upon by slum dwellers. The unprecedented decision to protect such a large area of urban land from development was perhaps early evidence of the new imagination of a 'global' city and the increasing power of the middle class. On the positive side, it brought forth the important idea of preserving nature in the city, which led to other new urban conservation laws to check unfettered construction, new campaign possibilities, and setting aside land for projects like the Aravali Biodiversity Park on the Ridge.[31]

After the Notification: The Early Years

After the notification the mandatory settlement of forest rights began under Section 4 of the Indian Forests Act, 1927, but was immediately mired in controversy since it was obviously discriminatory. For example, amongst the first to be asked to leave were the ragpickers and shanty dwellers on Central Ridge, who lived adjacent to a large police camp. Meanwhile a Gurdwara and a well known charitable hospital also on the Ridge were left untouched, and the President's bodyguard owned a polo club on Ridge forest behind the Rashtrapati Bhavan itself. When citizens protested, the President, rather than face public ire, temporarily shut down the club. It was relocated elsewhere on the Ridge, only to lead to another legal battle subsequently (see the section on Army Polo Ground in this essay). The club however reopened at the same place some years later and is still operational.

Another similar controversy, which illustrated the bias in land use, concerned the three settlements around the Bhatti Mines, which lay within the bounds of notified forest on the southern boundary of the city. An affidavit was filed in the Supreme Court by the Chief Secretary of Delhi. The court was then examining the case for removing all illegal encroachments from the forest. It now categorised 30,000 residents living in three colonies adjacent to the Asola Wildlife Sanctuary, as 'encroachers'. In contrast, adjoining farmhouses were left untouched. Critics argued that such choices demonstrated a class bias against the poor. In any case, the court ordered them to relocate in 1996.[32] Most people living in these houses were from the Ouds nomadic tribes, who are traditional mud diggers specialising in the construction of ponds and canals. They had been employed in the now closed Bhatti Bajri mines, where they had quarried red gravel used for construction (1975–92). Through political connections and perhaps some patronage,[33] two of the colonies have managed to stay on to date, though their fate continually hangs in balance. Neither have they secured their rights nor is it clear what will happen next.[34] Several other significant and sometimes unsuccessful court battles have since ensued, and these exemplify the difficulties in protecting the Ridge land from being diverted for other land use. Most of them concern demands made by state actors or government agencies. One of the early battles (1997) dealt with the shifting of the President's Polo Ground from the Central Ridge to another location westwards known as Nicolson's Range, without the mandatory tree felling or land diversion clearance. In an attempt to stop this, Srishti and other groups approached the Delhi high court. The case made headline news, since the court had served notice to the Chief of Army Staff himself. However, there was little or no help forthcoming from the forest department to argue a case against such a major institution, not even for the purpose of providing boundary maps of the notified Ridge. Consequently the court let the Army off with a mere warning.[35]

The problem is fundamentally an issue of administration. Delhi is administered by a multiplicity of land development agencies, transport authorities, civic service providers and security agencies, which often work in isolation from each other. For example, land, which can be urbanised or developed, is controlled by several agencies, including DDA, Municipal Corporation of Delhi (MCD), New Delhi Municipal Corporation (NDMC), CPWD, L&DO, Delhi government, the Cantonment Board (Defence), etc. These multiple authorities often seem to make their development plans in isolation from each other, resulting in confusion. However, land such as the notified Ridge forest, is designated as 'forest' under forest laws, and legally outside the purview of such urbanisation plans. On the other hand, these various agencies often view this land as 'unused,' or 'wasted,' and believe it should be made 'productive'. Separately but simultaneously, they issue demands to bring it back to the 'urbanisation' pool. Under such constant onslaught and pressure, making the case for keeping the forest, has become increasingly difficult.[36] The forest is seen as unused, as waste, as land that can and should be made productive.

Unfortunately, as mentioned earlier, several Ridge areas were excluded from the 1994 notification. Many parts of these tracts have been subsequently built upon. The DDA, which controlled land use for non-forested land, started treating remaining areas as fair game for 'development' under the master plan; even though many were well forested and earlier notifications still granted them a status of Reserved or Protected Forests. This led to more controversy and conflict. Amongst the most important contests was the one concerning 650 hectares of the Vasant Kunj Ridge, half of which was controlled by the Indian Army. In 1997, the DDA proposed building thirteen five star hotels (International Hotels Complex) in the area, despite the existence of a lush forest and many small and large water bodies in the same location. This forest had an even more hilly and rocky character than the Central and Northern Ridge forest. Here, the water bodies were lodged in deep rock cracks and structures, some of which are still relatively undisturbed and harbour a variety of bird life. An NGO, the Citizens for Lake and Quarry Wilderness (CLQW), along with others, approached the Supreme Court to stop these plans.[37] After long hearings, the Court eventually rejected the project, but left the Army area untouched and exempted 92 hectares of the remaining area, allowing the construction of one hotel. Subsequently, in 2006, the DDA, unwilling as ever to give up, again proposed new constructions of private institutions and shopping malls in the area without obtaining any of the mandatory environmental clearances. The matter promptly came before the Supreme Court. This time, the lapses were condoned and construction cleared in another long drawn and futile court battle. The area now houses some of the most expensive shopping malls in the city, catering to a select few, even as the functions of the Ridge for the benefit of millions of Delhi's citizens are lost forever.

Ongoing Issues

The inability to precisely define the boundaries of the Ridge has continued to cause many legal conflicts over the years. These have only worsened as the pressure on land has increased. The Master Plan of Delhi, 2001, (MPD–2001) clearly and unambiguously states, 'The Aravali Ridge in the NCT of Delhi comprises the rocky outcrop stretching from the University in the North to the NCT (National Capital Territory) in the South, and sizeable areas of the same have been designated as such', but this has been of limited help.

The whole rocky outcrop was set aside as a regional park,[38] which *became* the Ridge. This was done even though there were other similar forests, such as on the Vasant Kunj Ridge, which were not notified. There was and is no clarity on ground about delineating boundaries, making it difficult to detect or establish violations of protection. The anomalies between the 'notified' areas on paper, and the actual forest land on the ground, have become apparent over time, raising contentions about the land being 'forest' or open for development. Anomalies abound, with sharp differences over when and which land was or was not notified as forest.

A case in point will illustrate the consequences. In an October 2010 case, the Delhi high court upheld the DDA's proposal to make 750 premium housing structures on a forested Ridge area. This had been opposed by the forest department, which claimed this to be part of the 'geomorphological Ridge',[39] though it was not 'notified'. The court, however, held that if the landowning agency (DDA), as the authority that prepares the master plan, 'clearly and categorically' states that the land is not in the Ridge area; other authorities have 'no locus to raise any objection'. The order gave supremacy to the master plan over forest claims. The case is under appeal in the Supreme Court. Taking a contrary view on an earlier occasion, the Supreme Court had struck down the building of hotels on the Vasant Kunj Ridge by the DDA, relying on its expert committee's report which denoted the area in question as 'similar to Ridge area', since there was 'no statutory definition of the Ridge'.[40]

In addition, even on many parts of the notified Ridge the boundaries have not been marked on the ground, as a result of which there is constant evidence of new encroachments on forestland. A survey carried out by Srishti in Sanjay Van,[41] for example, reveals the presence of unauthorised playing fields, garbage dumps and expanding religious structures in the forest. In other parts too there have been encroachments by religious trusts, residents of adjoining colonies and others. The forest is being encroached upon both from the outside as well inside, as the boundary is permeable and unclear.

The question of whether to keep the ecological integrity of the forest intact or divert it hangs over the Ridge like the sword of Damocles. Does the Ridge serve the city better as a forest or should it be used for other needs, like roads and landfills? In 2001, the MCD proposed to use three unused quarry pits in Bhatti Mines as garbage landfills, unmindful of the fact that this would result in converting the forest into the dump yard of the city. Upon being rejected by the Ridge Management Board (hereafter, Ridge Board) they directly approached the Supreme Court (subsequently the case was transferred to the Delhi high court in 2009). They pleaded that they were facing a garbage crisis while bypassing all procedures as laid down in the Forest Conservation Act of having an approved Environmental Impact Assessment, conducting a public hearing or approaching the National Board of Wildlife. It was only after the intervention of a voluntary organisation that the court rejected their plea in April 2011, after ten years.[42] No one has found a place to dispose of the garbage in an environmentally sound manner yet. The search continues.

In a city which is highly water stressed,[43] the role of the Ridge in recharging ground water is being increasingly recognised, even though not strongly enough to make a case for its conservation solely on these grounds. When the issue of allowing a hotel to be built on the Vasant Kunj Ridge came up, the Environmental Pollution Control Authority (EPCA), on directions from the Supreme Court, evaluated the impact such a move would have on the 315 acres of the Vasant Kunj Ridge. It stated that the nearly 7,00,000 kiloliters of water required by the hotel annually was four and a half times the *total* water recharge capacity of that portion of the Ridge,[44] and recommended that the hotel be disallowed. The hotel was however permitted despite this observation. Its impact on the ground water hydrology will clearly entail long-term adverse consequences.

The question of groundwater reserves came up in case of the landfills in the Bhatti Mines Ridge area. The Environment Impact Assessment report cautioned against the landfills as they would have an impact on surface water as well as ground water. The assessment stated, 'During monsoon and post monsoon seasons some adjoining pits get surface runoff, which is generally held stagnant for 3–4 months within the pits. Water containment may be affected by the construction and operation activities of the project' and that 'the groundwater will further go down where the pits are used as SLF (sanitary landfill facility) ...'[45] Though the landfill was disallowed, it was halted since it contravened forest laws rather than for reasons linked to water conservation.

Various citizens and voluntary organisations have also taken up the water issue. Residents of houses and apartments around a natural lake on South Central Ridge, Neela Hauz, which was destroyed owing to a new bridge being built for the Commonwealth Games, started a campaign to restore the lake. They successfully appealed to the Delhi high court to have it restored.[46] A voluntary organisation, Tapas,[47] also approached the Delhi high court to have natural water bodies enumerated and a committee was set up for their restoration. Many of these are on the Ridge. In yet another ongoing case in the Delhi high court, citizens are attempting to protect what is left of the Ridge as an important ground water recharge zone,[48] with an estimated recharge potential of 60 million cubic meters annually.[49]

The ground water tables between Delhi and adjoining Haryana are interlinked and often contiguous. Despite the Aravali hills having been declared as an Eco Sensitive Zone,[50] the past decade has witnessed prime fresh water lakes like Badkal, Suraj Kund and Dumduma, which were once popular tourist spots in the vicinity of Delhi, drying up completely. Rampant mining, overdrawal of groundwater and loss of catchment areas to urbanisation are the main causes of this situation. New and often illegal high rise colonies have sprung up, made by private builders, often without requisite site clearances. More than 200 mines have been operating in Haryana and Rajasthan, both illegal and quasi-legal, devastating the Ridge outcrop and the vegetation on it. Over the past decade there have been a string of court cases, filed in an attempt to stop the rampage. Various governmental bodies like the Ridge Management Board (RMB) and the EPCA have asked the mining to be stopped since it impacts ground water in Delhi.[51] The Bhatti Mines landfill

EIA too noted that that the ground water sloped in two directions and thus had a 'strong hydraulic gradient' both towards Haryana as well as towards Delhi. Any contamination from the mines would affect ground water in both states.[52] The Supreme Court has passed various stringent orders from time to time; the latest issued in May 2009 banned all mining in the area.[53] However, only time will tell if these strictures are effective in the face of population and developmental pressures.[54]

Institutional Mechanisms

As is evident by now, some of the most powerful institutions in the land have been concerned with the conservation of the Ridge and its forest. The only (non-statutory) body, which has been exclusively entrusted with the task to protect and restore the Ridge forest, is the Ridge Management Board (RMB), constituted in October 1995, which reports to the Supreme Court.[55] Heavily loaded with governmental functionaries, the board is chaired by the Chief Secretary of Delhi, with high-ranking members such as the Vice Chairman of the DDA, along with four civil society members. Two of the civil society representatives were appointed at the time of the inception of the RMB, while the other two were inducted in 2001, evidently owing to their long involvement in Ridge issues. However there is no clear criterion for such appointment, and some members have never attended a single meeting for several years in a row! In spite of these shortcomings, the RMB is probably a singular example of a high powered body, which exists to protect a specific urban forest. Along with the Central Empowered Committee (CEC),[56] appointed by the Supreme Court, the RMB has become the nodal body for allowing any diversion of land for non-forest use on the Ridge. But one fact is inescapable. The prime designated function of restoration and protection of the forest is on the back burner.

As per the orders of the Supreme Court, any diversion of land not only from the notified Ridge forest, but also from the areas surrounding it—the 'geomorphological Ridge'—needs clearance both by the RMB as well as the CEC. Unfortunately, in most instances, it is governmental bodies that have made requests for forest land diversion. The board has to play a conflicting role of adjudicating among various institutions of the state. Requests are made on grounds of 'security installations,' 'public transport,' or 'nationally important events' like the Commonwealth Games, citing a larger public purpose. Invariably, such requests have been granted in one form or another, while in almost all cases requests made by private parties, such as access roads for schools, have been denied.

In recent years some of the clearance demands have included those from the Army for security installations communications infrastructure and housing, the municipality for landfills, the Delhi Metro Rail Corporation for metro links, the Delhi Jal Board for building water tanks, the DDA for pathways, the erstwhile Delhi Electricity Supply Undertaking for laying transmission lines, the Commonwealth Games Authority for stadiums and parking lots, the Delhi Police for building police stations.

The numerous governmental agencies that have violated the Ridge forest, have not faced any punitive action for doing so. One example is of the CPWD which was allegedly illegally building a parking lot and public toilets in the Mahavir Jayanti Park under instructions from the Minister for Urban Development in 2002 without any mandatory clearance from the board. Though the CPWD was forced to reverse this action, no punitive action has ever been taken.The incident came to light due to alert citizens, but no one was held accountable. Similarly the DDA was found to have made a road in Central Ridge without permission, even though they are represented on the board. Only a court action in 2004 put a stop to this. On another occasion in 2004, 5,000 metric tonnes of rubble was dumped on the Ridge by the DDA, and again though this was later removed, no action was ever initiated.The CPWD has dumped rubble from a road bridge project into the Neela Hauz, a water body on the Southern Ridge, and citizens have gone to court to have this removed. However, it got away scot free in 2009. More recently in 2011, the Army was pulled up by the Delhi high court for illegally constructing housing in the geomorphological Ridge. No action was taken against them. In many cases, clearances or violations by state bodies like the Army have been condoned by the CEC by merely imposing a monetary fine. However, in no case have the violations been reversed.[57] It is clear that there are limits to which any such protection can go, especially if the government itself is not dispassionate in its judgement. Suggestions for protection by the RMB remain a nonstarter.

Many other pending issues remain unresolved as well. For example, plans for restoring the original vegetation have never been drawn up. This will entail debates and choices on what we mean by native, local or indigenous. For the purpose of this essay, it will be trees, shrubs and plants indigenous to the Delhi region. Restoration work of the sort done for the wetlands of Delhi by the Centre for Environmental Management of Degraded Ecosystems may well show the way forward. Also many structures remain within the Ridge area whose future is uncertain, and the tendency to convert the forest into a horticultural park continues.

Future Horizons

The idea of a forest as 'pure' nature in an urban space is under constant challenge. Today it seems inconceivable that such a large area in a megalopolis could be kept out of a 'development zone' when the demand for land is astronomically high. Till now a series of citizens' actions, government policy, administrative innovations and the Supreme Court's hawk eye has helped keep this large forest alive. Though fragmented, this forest is far larger than other city forests like Guindy in Chennai, and still has remnants of forest native to this region. Those, too, are under intense pressure, especially for land for construction: the value of the land has escalated as cites have grown and the law is but a fragile fence. Yet its continued existence hangs on a 'soft' utility it offers in terms of health, water, recreation, aesthetics or even biodiversity. Each time these compete with more 'urgent' uses (such as roads, establishments and security) a part of it is sacrificed.

Most people in Delhi have not seen the Ridge forest or have done so in a picture postcard manner with little grasp of its ecological value and multifaceted environmental roles. Its role in history in the battles of 1857–58 are better known than before but its topographical features and settlement history, the way it was afforested and the fact that it is now a biodiverse zone are all of incalculable value for citizens. Herein lies a challenge. The heterogeneous and shifting communities surrounding the Ridge forest do not necessarily see it as valuable ecological space to be protected but as land to be used and occupied. Imaginative and creative use of its paths can make it accessible and educationally rich in a way many urban forests are elsewhere in the world. It is distressing that many citizens have scant respect for the forest and even dump garbage in it. For it to survive over time, it will need more than legal protection, and other actions, which involve people at large, need to be initiated urgently. Wider awareness and better marking of boundaries is imperative but we need to ask how to make the border meaningful to ensure the Ridge survives as intact biological entity. Educating residents and institutions, especially those who border the forest, and providing them a role in protecting it, including the Ridge in the curriculum of Delhi schools with field visits,[58] creating nature trails and walks, encouraging university-based research projects on it and involving citizens' groups in reforesting and playing a watchdog role are some measures which will help reclaim the forest for the city, rather than isolate it as an issue for administrators and courts alone.[59] Further, institutions which have been already built on the Ridge should have a special responsibility and plans to preserve the area.[60] Such community-based measures will enable people not only experience the diversity of the forest first hand, but also help inculcate a coexistence ethos which respects all forms of life and which is necessary for a sustainable future. Classroom projects in schools, university led research, creative work by artists, film makers and photographers.[61] The Ridge can be arena, site and platform for all these and much more. Such measures will inculcate respect for the land. Careful conservation and science led ecological restoration with community involvement can keep the Ridge forest not only alive as an entity but also enrich it as a mosaic of life. Some of the approaches taken up in Bengaluru to revive lakes and city forests[62] may be of relevance, but at this moment it is unclear who will be the prime mover in Delhi.

However it needs to be recognised that many of these suggested measures are from a middle class perspective. In a diverse urban space such as Delhi, there needs to be a wider study carried out to suggest ways to involve citizens across the spectrum. An important constituency in this regard are the poorer people living in and around the Ridge who depend on it for fuel wood and other basic necessities such as simply toilet space. Such communities need to be as much part of the decisions made about the use of the Ridge, as the elite and middle classes who wish to conserve it for its ecological services and research values.

Ironically, it is the metro rail, a contemporary symbol of equitable urban development, which in traversing over the fabulous green canopy of the Ridge, provides a spectacular bird's eye view of its expanse. One can only hope that this may provide a new impetus for citizens to protect a unique natural urban heritage, which is critical to the wellbeing of the city and whose future can hardly be taken for granted. Careful conservation and science led restoration with broad community involvement can help keep the Ridge forest alive as a living entity and enrich it as a mosaic of life. By doing so, the ecological integrity of the Ridge and the remaking of city life in more holistic, equitable way can proceed together.

Notes

1. *A Gazetteer of Delhi District, 1883–84*. Reprint (Gurgaon, Haryana: Vintage Books, 1988), p. 2. Originally published by the Punjab government.

2. The area concerned was declared as a Reserved Forest under Section 4 of the Indian Forest Act, 1924, in 1994.

3. The NCT consists of approximately 1400 square kilometres of Delhi state.

4. The National Capital Region (NCR) consists of the state of Delhi and parts of Haryana and Uttar Pradesh. This concept has been formalised by the NCR Planning Body, a high level interstate body for making regional plans that is headed by the prime minister. It has been largely ineffectual in implementing these plans so far. See www.ncrpb.nic.in for more information (accessed 24 April 2014).

5. See Anonymous, *City Development Plan Delhi, for the Department of Urban Development* (New Delhi: Government of India, IL&FS Ecosmart Ltd., 2006),

pp. 2–9. Available at http://jnnurm.nic.in/nurmudweb/toolkit/CDP_Delhi.pdf (accessed 5 February 2014).

6. Special economic zones have been created to foster industrial growth and urbanisation through government-private partnerships or purely private ownership. They change agricultural land into commercial use and will put pressure on natural resources like water.

7. For a recent ongoing campaign to protect Mangar Bani forest which is part of the Ridge just outside of Delhi, see http://savearravali.wordpress.com/ and http://www.tehelka.com/story_main52.asp?filename=Ne070412Delhi.asp (accessed 24 April 2014).

8. Government of NCT of Delhi, 'Recorded Forests'. Available at http://www.delhi.gov.in/wps/wcm/connect/doit_forest/Forest/Home/Forests+of+Delhi/Recorded+Forest (accessed 13 May 2014).

9. Pradeep Krishen writes about porcupines being killed for protecting plantations and eliminating animals which destroyed seedlings, and jackals being shot to eliminate them, so that the viceroy's and viceriene's sleep would not be disturbed by their howling at night. See P. Krishen, 'Realising the ridge', *India Today, Delhi Special*, 2012, pp. 46–47.

10. For a detailed description of the biodiversity see Anonymous, *The Delhi Ridge Forest: Decline and Conservation* (Delhi: Kalpavriksh, 1991); Krishen, *Trees of Delhi,* pp. 24–25; U. Ganguli, *A Guide to the Birds of the Delhi Area* (New Delhi: Indian Council of Agricultural Research, 1975), p. 11; and *A Gazetteer of Delhi District*, pp. 20–21.

11. For a detailed description of the water systems, see Sohail Hashmi, 'Death of a river', *Kafila*, February 2011. Available at http://kafila.org/2011/02/04/death-of-a-river-yamuna-jamuna-delhi (accessed 12 April 2014); Narayani Gupta, 'Delhi's history as reflected in its toponymy' in Maya Dayal (ed.), *Celebrating Delhi* (New Delhi: Viking Books, 2010), pp. 96–97; and *A Gazetteer of Delhi District.*

12. Manoj Mishra, 'Dreaming of a blue Yamuna' in Bharati Chaturvedi (ed.), *Finding Delhi: Loss and renewal in a megacity* (New Delhi: Viking Books, 2010), p. 74.

13. For a detailed discussion, see Jaweed Ashraf, *Studies in Historical Ecology of India* (New Delhi: Sunrise Publications, 2004), pp. xiii, 21–22.

14. For a detailed discussion, see Michael Mann and Samiksha Sehrawat, 'A city with a view: The afforestation of the Delhi Ridge, 1883–1913', *Modern Asian Studies* 43 (2009): 543–70.

15. Pradip Krishen reports on a small 100 hectare area called Mangar Bani, protected as a sacred grove on the border of Delhi, which 'is like a little outdoor museum of what parts of Delhi Ridge might have looked like.' The rocky outcrop supports trees like dhau, hingot, khair, kumttha, dhak, phulai and kareel. See Krishen, *Trees of Delhi*, pp. 24–25.

16. For a detailed description see Ganguli, *A Guide to the Birds of the Delhi Area,* pp. 9–10.

17. Krishnan, *Trees of Delhi.*

18. Kishen, 'Realising the Ridge'.

19. Krishen, 'Realising the Ridge'; Krishen, *Trees of Delhi*.

20. Krishen, *Trees of Delhi*.

21. See Srishti, 'The Delhi Ridge, Issues and Perspective—a paper' (New Delhi: Srishti, 1994); Anonymous, *The Delhi Ridge Forest*, pp. 26–27.

22. 'Reserved Forest' and 'Protected Forest' are categories of protection under the Indian Forest Act, 1927, which differ in their measure of stringency in defining what activities are allowed or disallowed in these areas. The Indian Forest Act, 1927, resulted from amendments of the earlier Act of 1878 though the changes were minimal.

23. Under the Wildlife (Protection) Act, 1972, the central or state governments can notify areas as national parks or sanctuaries, offering a very high level of protection. Such areas cannot be denotified by the state government. Denotification requires permission from the National Board of Wildlife headed by the prime minister.

24. The Delhi Development (Provisional) Authority (DDPA) was constituted through a Delhi (Control of Building Operations) Ordinance, 1955, which was replaced by the Delhi Development Act, 1957, with the primary objective of ensuring the development of Delhi in accordance with a Master Plan. The DDA, in effect, has complete control of designating land use in the city and has a poor record of protecting natural green areas.

25. Kalpavriksh first petitioned the chief of the Metropolitan Council of Delhi, Kedar Nath Saini, in September 1979, and then Prime Minister Indira Gandhi in March 1980. As a consequence, Lt Governor Jagmohan notified part of the forest a Protected Forest under the Indian Forest Act, 1927, and subsequently stalled the 'clearing' of Kushak Nallah grassland and scrub jungle after a student protest in September 1981. See Anonymous, *The Delhi Ridge Forest*, p. 31.

26. Mahesh Rangarajan writes that Indira Gandhi 'took steps to secure the city forest in the summer of 1980, when petitioned by a student group. What the group was unaware of was her central role a few years earlier in getting key Indian Air Force installation modified to preserve the skyline as well as the integrity of the forest.' See Mahesh Rangarajan, 'Striving for a balance: Nature, power, science and India's Indira Gandhi, 1917–1984' *Conservation & Society* 7, no. 4 (2009): 299–312.

27. For the details of the campaign, see Srishti, *Saving the Delhi Ridge, One Year of Conservation Action* (New Delhi: Srishti, 1994).

28. Government of National Capital Territory of Delhi (NCTD), 'Report of the committee to recommend the pattern of management of the Delhi Ridge' (New Delhi: Government of NCTD, 2004).

29. See Delhi Gazette, *Notification No. F.10 (42)-I/PA/DCF/93/2012-17(1)* (New Delhi: Development Department, Government of NCTD, 1994). A Reserved Forest cannot be easily denotified and has to follow certain regulations involving the state and central governments. In the case of the Ridge, it would in addition need a clearance from the Ridge Management Board, the Central Empowered Committee and the Supreme Court of India.

30. Amita Baviskar critiques 'bourgeois environmentalism' led by middle class groups to 'examine issues of political legitimacy and the ability (of the urban poor) to make claims in the public sphere.' For a detailed discussion, see A. Baviskar, 'The Politics of the City', *Seminar* 516 (2002). Available at http://www.india-seminar.com/2002/516/516%20amita%20baviskar.htm (accessed 10 February 2012).

31. Other laws and assessments have followed, such as the Delhi Preservation of Trees Act, 1994, (available at http://forest.delhigovt.nic.in/act/chap1.html, accessed 24 April 2014), environmental impact assessment for large urban projects, and the setting up of Yamuna and Aravali biodiversity parks (available at http://www.dda.org.in/greens/biodiv/aravalli-biodiversity-park.html, accessed on 10 July 2012).

32. *M. C. Mehta vs Union of India*, WP(C) 4677/1985, orders of 9 April 1996 and 9 May 1996, Supreme Court of India, Delhi.

33. A senior leader of a major political party belonging to the same community has apparently lent them his support (personal communication with community activist Chanderpal, June 2008).

34. For more details, see also *Civil Society Magazine*, 'Bhatti's odds in legal dilemma', New Delhi, August 2009. Available at http://www.civilsocietyonline.com/aug07/aug079.asp (accessed 21 March 2012)

35. *Srishti and Ors vs Govt. of NCT of Delhi, Chief of Army Staff and Ors*, WP(C), 1996, high court of Delhi, Delhi.

36. In 1998, there was a curious proposal for the rehabilitation of captured 'dancing bears' in the Asola Wildlife Sanctuary. The Delhi government after giving the go ahead to the project withdrew it after experts declared the area inhospitable for the animal due to lack of water and green cover. However, since 2011, rhesus macaques trapped from the city are being released in the Asola-Bhatti Ridge, under orders from the Delhi high court.

37. *T. N. Godavarman Thirumulpad vs Union of India*, Writ Petition (civil) 202 of 1995, and *Unison Hotels Ltd. vs DDA and Ors*, SLP (Civil) No 8960/97, Supreme Court of India, Delhi, judgments of 13 September 1996, 19 August 1997 and 8 March 2004.

38. *The Master Plan of Delhi*, 1962, and the *Plan* for 2020 designates the Ridge forest as a Regional Park.

39. *Kenneth Builders & Developers Ltd vs Union of India and Ors*, WP(C) 10647/2009, judgment of 30 July 2010. Available at http://www.indiankanoon.org/doc/146778/ (accessed 24 April 2014).

40. For more details on this issue, see the report 'Constraint Area and M/s Unison Hotels Ltd, Vasant Kunj' (Delhi: Environmental Pollution [Prevention and Control] Authority for the National Capital Region, 2000), p. 24; *T. N. Godavanman Thiumulpad vs Union of India and Ors*, judgment of 17 October 2006, in WP (Civil) 202/1995, Supreme Court of India.

41. See Srishti and Toxics Link, *Delhi Ridge Under Threat: Community conservation of Sanjay Van report* (New Delhi: Srishti and Toxics Link, 2011). Available at http://toxicslink.org/delhiridge/studies-and-reports/

delhi-ridge-under-threat-community-conservation-of-sanjay-van-report/ (accessed 24 April 2014).

42. See *Almitra Patel and another vs Union of India and Ors*, IA by NGO Forum for the NCR (WPC 5236/2010), judgment of 26 May 2011. Available at http://toxicslink.org/delhiridge/wp-content/uploads/Landfill_Order_Dated_26.05.pdf (accessed 24 April 2014). Also see K. Kohli, 'Landfill is minefield for MCD', *Civil Society Magazine* (2011): 31–35.

43. According to a report on groundwater by the NCR planning board, the water table in Delhi is dipping by two metres a year. It says that the city draws 0.47 billion cubic metres (bcm) of water from the ground every year while only 0.28 bcm gets recharged. As a result, Delhi loses a whopping 0.19 bcm of groundwater in a year. See National Capital Region Planning Board, 'Functional plan for recharge of groundwater in NCR', 2010. Available at http://www.ncrpb.nic.in/Consolidate_pre_document.pdf (accessed 25 April 2014).

44. Anonymous, 'Report on Constraint Area and M/s Unison Hotels Ltd, Vasant Kunj' (New Delhi: Environment Pollution (Prevention and Control) Authority For the National Capital Region, 2000), p. 10.

45. Anonymous, 'Environmental impact assessment study for proposed landfill facility at Bhatti Mines, Delhi', final report carried out for the Municipal Corporation of Delhi by Consulting Engineering Services (India) Pvt. Ltd (New Delhi, 2005), pp. 4–18, 20.

46. The residents of the area formed the Neela Hauz Citizen's Group to further their campaign. See www.neelahauz.in (accessed 25 April 2014).

47. Tapas NGO's website is available at http://ngotapas.org/ (accessed 25 April 2014).

48. *Ramesh Chopra and Ors vs Union of India and Ors*, WP (civil) 11884–87/2006 in high court of Delhi, Delhi.

49. Vikram Soni, 'Three waters: An evaluation of urban groundwater resource in Delhi', *Current Science* 93, no. 6 (2007).

50. Gazette Notification of Ministry of Environment & Forests dated 7 May 1992.

51. Filed by the Delhi Ridge Management Board in the Supreme Court of India under I.A. No. 1785/01, *M. C. Mehta vs Union of India*, asking that the government of Haryana be directed to stop all mining activities and pumping of groundwater in and from area up to 5 km from the Delhi-Haryana border in the Haryana side of the Ridge, inter alia, stating that in the larger interest of maintaining the ecological balance of the environment and protecting the Asola Bhatti Wildlife Sanctuary and the Ridge located in Delhi and adjoining Haryana, it was necessary to stop mining.

52. Anonymous, *Environmental Impact Assessment Study for Proposed Landfill Facility at Bhatti Mines*, pp. 4–38.

53. The three member bench said the 'time has now come to suspend all mining in the above area on Sustainable Development Principle which is part of

Articles 21, 48A and 51A (g) of the Constitution.' *M. C. Mehta vs Union of India*, I.A. No. 1785/01, judgment of 8 May 2009.

54. Several reports show that mining continues. For some examples, see http://www.indiaenvironmentportal.org.in/taxonomy/term/116?page=5 (accessed 25 April 2014).

55. Office of the Development Commissioner, Constitution of Ridge Management Board, Office of the Development Commissioner, Government of NCT, No F.56 (225)/95/Dev./No/5596–5612.

56. The six member Central Empowered Committee (CEC) was set up by the Supreme Court of India on 9 May 2006. It has played a key role in technically examining forest-related cases all over the country, which are referred to it for assistance by the Supreme Court. Its term was recently extended, in May 2011.

57. The Metro (Delhi Metro Railway Corporation) was granted permission to make an overhead track over the Southern Ridge after a five per cent cost was imposed. In another case the Army was granted post-facto clearance to a housing project on three acres of the Ridge. They had refused to stop work despite orders by the CEC, and only approached the RMB after a private citizen took them to the Delhi high court. See Anonymous, 'Court stops Defense construction on Delhi ridge', *Indo Asian News Service*, 5 December 2011. Available at http://in.news.yahoo.com/court-stops-defence-construction-delhi-ridge-095855978.html (accessed 25 April 2014).

58. The Asola Bhatti Sanctuary (Southern Ridge) does have a Conservation Education Centre run by the Delhi government, but it is rarely visited.

59. Examples of such approaches can be found for example in the protection of the Bengaluru lakes. See Harini Nagendra, 'Maps, lakes and citizens', *Seminar* 613 (2010). Available at http://www.india-seminar.com/2010/613/613_harini_nagendra.htm (accessed 10 July 2012). Also see Nagendra, et al. this volume.

60. For example, Jawaharlal Nehru University (JNU) has large forested areas. Hospitals as well as new malls and hotels can be involved in creating special programmes. The new Ambedkar University of Delhi has a School of Human Ecology that could help study and monitor bird and flora populations.

61. A recent initiative by Toxics Link is one such attempt. Available at https://www.facebook.com/SanjayVanDelhiRidge (accessed 10 July 2014).

62. See Nagendra, et al., this volume.

Six

BLACK SHEEP AND GREY WOLVES

Pastoralism in the Deccan

Nitya Sambamurti Ghotge and Sagari R. Ramdas

The Deccan plateau of South Central India, which includes considerable parts of Maharashtra, Andhra Pradesh and Karnataka, consists of large uncultivated stretches of grasslands.[1] The grasslands of the Deccan are not verdant open pastures stretching far and distant as imagined in the mind's eye. Instead, they are an ancient geographic formation of molten basaltic rock formed thousands of years ago and consist of vast scrub plains and grasslands which have borne the ravages of time—droughts and floods, conquests and raids, cycles of famines and abundance. Massive bare boulders and rocky outcrops with small streams that flow through valleys dot this varying landscape. Southern tropical thorn scrub forests, along with patches of tropical dry deciduous forests, are believed to be the 'original' vegetation, though what this means in a landscape where the human presence dates many millennia is itself increasingly open to question. The former consists of open, low vegetation characterised by thorny trees such as different *Acacia* species, with short trunks and low branching crowns that rarely meet to form a closed canopy.[2] The understorey is poorly developed and consists of spiny and xerophytic species, mostly shrubs. During the brief southwest monsoon season, an ill defined herbaceous layer can be discerned.

The Deccan plateau is home to a major predator, the Indian wolf *Canis lupus pallipes*, which is a subspecies of the grey wolf. The Indian wolf occupies the southernmost range of wolves worldwide, and is commonly found in semi-arid habitats consisting of agro-pastoral lands, scrub forests and grasslands.[3] It is much smaller in size than the Eurasian wolf.[4] The Indian wolf is now the apex surviving carnivore species of the Indian open plains.[5] The other major carnivore of these lands, the cheetah, has been extinct in India since the late 1960s. Wolves share this space with the great Indian bustard, the Jerdon's courser, blackbuck, chinkara, nilgai, jackal, caracal and jungle cat.[6] Estimated to number a possible 2,000–3,000, the Indian wolf is considered endangered and listed under Schedule 1 of the Indian Wildlife (Protection) Act, 1972[7]. The International Union for the Conservation of Nature and Natural Resources (IUCN) Canid Specialist Group concurs with its endangered status.[8]

Where there are wolves, often there are sheep. This is true not only of the Deccan. In the Trans-himalaya and Himalayas, the Tibetan wolf (another subspecies of the Indian wolf) plays the same kind of ecological role with the wild urial, the mouflon and domesticated sheep, which are herded by nomadic pastoral communities. Across the steppes of Europe, Central Asia, the vast grasslands of Mongolia sweeping down to South Asia, wolves, sheep and pastoral communities have shared the same space over centuries. The Deccan plateau of India is home to traditional shepherding communities—the Dhangars, Kurumas, Gollas and Kurubas. The sheep have contributed food, fibre and manure for humans as well as served as a food source for wild predators.

This landscape and its people, habitats and species perhaps typify a large part of India's ecology, given that four-tenths of the country is semi-arid, but this fact is marginal in the consciousness of both the communities that support conservation and those that support development. Despite mentions in conservation literature and early ecological anthropology, and its association with keystone species like the blackbuck or bustard, the grassland has been a neglected biome in conservation studies.[9] It is extant but rendered 'invisible' in much of the literature, scholarly and popular, in policy works. This is paralleled by the general indifference evident in development literature to animal rearing itinerant groups, such as the shepherds of the Deccan. Historical and sociological research have filled the gap to an extent but there is a long way to go in terms of science based critiques of existing conservation and development policies for the grassland habitat, its associated wildlife and the peoples' livelihoods that it supports.[10] In this essay, we explore the intrinsic linkages and interactions between pastoral livelihoods and conservation in the context of the grasslands of the Deccan. We suggest that the transhumant livestock livelihoods of pastoral peoples, who share the same habitat as the Indian wolf, are critical for sustaining and conserving the complex biological diversity of the grasslands and its endangered apex species. This points towards new approaches to conservation which walk a line between letting things be in a free for all on the one hand and strict statist exclusion of local livelihoods from conserved landscapes on the other.

Pastoralists, Herding and Habitats

Studies drawing upon archaeological evidence, ancient and more recent texts, hero stones combined with oral traditions and cults of pastoral communities, point to the presence of sheep pastoral systems in the semi-arid regions of the southern Deccan plausibly going back to the Neolithic-Chalcolithic period c. 3000 BCE.[11] The belief systems of the communities today deserve mention. Shepherds of the region generally believe that they were specially created by the gods for the explicit task of rearing sheep—specifically the black Deccani. The shepherds of the Deccan are an ancient hunting warrior tribe and their favourite god is Khandoba also known as Malanna. Legend has it that Khandoba's second wife Banai or Banu was a shepherdess and while taking his marriage vows, Khandoba committed to protecting her sheep and all the sheep of the Deccan. Biroba, Beerappa or Beeranna, as he is affectionately known depending on the specific geographic location, is the exclusive god of the pastoral communities of the Deccan and is said to have created both sheep and the shepherding communities.[12] In Maharashtra, the home villages of the Dhangars and other shepherding communities such as the Ramoshis and Matangs are mainly found in the districts which fall in the rain shadow region of the Western Ghats: Pune, Satara, Ahmednagar and Sangli.[13] Pastoralism rather than agriculture has been the preferred occupation in these districts of the Deccan plateau as the annual rainfall is extremely low—often less than 600 mm—and soils are shallow and poor. Large scrub fields known as *mal raan* provide ample grazing for sheep but are unsuitable for agriculture. Hero stones found in the region also indicate a livestock based economy in the past.[14]

The cycles of movement are finely in tune with the seasonal shifts in sub-regional ecological conditions. Shepherds in this region spend the four monsoon months from June to September in their home villages practicing some agriculture and as the rains recede, begin their annual migration or *biraad* towards the Western Ghats and the Konkan Coast in search of grazing lands. Farmers in the Konkan in turn welcome these shepherds as their lateritic soils leached by the heavy and intense monsoon rainfall need to be replenished with the dung and urine of these flocks. It is not unfamiliar even now to see shepherds with their huge colourful turbans negotiating their way through heavy traffic in cities like Pune with their sheep, horses, chickens and dogs. For eight months they graze their sheep in open grasslands, forests, fields, by rivers and streams by day, and camp in temporary shelters by night under the same open sky as the wolves.

In neighbouring Telangana (Medak, Mahabubnagar, Nalgonda, Warangal) and Rayalaseema (Ananthapur, Kurnool, Chittoor) and the coastal regions of Andhra Pradesh, the Kuruma and Golla pastoralists continue to rear sheep and goat under transhumant systems.[15] The seasonally migratory shepherds and their flocks of the Telangana and Rayalaseema regions, return to their villages with the onset of the rains in June and resume migration after Diwali. In the coastal districts, they begin to migrate with the onset of the rains towards the forests of the Eastern Ghats. The geographic location of the shepherds determines traditional migratory routes, either westwards into Maharashtra and Karnataka, or eastwards into the lush forests of the Nallamalai and other parts of the Eastern Ghats. They share an ancient bond with peasants along the migratory tract, penning their animals on farmers' fields, who give them food grains in return for the manure.

Biological diversity is not limited to wild plants and animals but also applies to strains of domesticated animals and cultivars that have been selectively bred for local conditions. The animals that are herded, tended, milked, clipped for wool and sold for meat deserve a closer look as they have been bred to thrive in such lands. Special sheep and goat breeds have evolved in these eco-regions, which are adapted to walking long distances and surviving on limited and diverse fodder and water resources. Perhaps the most popular and widespread amongst these breeds, is the coarse wool black Deccani sheep, which is protected from sun, wind, cold and rain by the wool on its body. It has been selected by the shepherds of the Deccan over several generations of breeders for tolerance to drought, fodder scarcities, its capacity to migrate long distances and an ability to endure the large diurnal temperature range and seasonal variations of these sweeping Deccan landscapes. The tall, heavy and hairy Nellore breed originated further east and is the preferred animal of the Golla pastoralists of the coastal districts.

Endangered Grasslands

Many ecologists believe that the thorn scrub vegetation of the Deccan represents 'a degraded stage' of the tropical dry forests, modified by human and livestock use over hundreds of years. This premise awaits further investigation by archaeo-anthropologists and paleo-ecologists as humans have been part of these landscapes for millennia. Perennial grasses of the Deccan, like *Dicanthium annulatum* have gradually been replaced by less nutritious annuals *Chrysopogon fulvus, Heteropogon contortus*, *Eremopogon foveolatus*, *Aristida setacea*, and *Dactyloctenium spp.*[16] Studies on grass diversity and density in Medak district, Andhra Pradesh, for instance, indicate that perennial grasses continue to be found on sandy loamy and black cotton soils, but annuals such as *Aeschynomene indica*, *Dactylactenium aegyptium* and *Corchorus olitorius* populate the red loamy and rocky soils.[17]

Shrinking grasslands and grazing areas in the Deccan have negatively impacted wildlife and domestic livestock alike, both of which have been critical components of the diversity of these landscapes. The attrition did not happen overnight, and it was probably accelerated in the early nineteenth century when the East India Company government set in motion a host of interrelated processes of change. The surveyors of the company began to map out and measure the Indian landscape as its officials believed that all land had to serve a useful and productive purpose. Following upon and parallel to this, there was large scale enclosure of agricultural lands, forests and pastures.[18] Nomadic or itinerant communities, particularly pastoralists such as the Lambadas and Dhangars of the Deccan, who wandered with their herds and flocks across these lands, became the targets for officials. A tangle of laws, executive practices and punitive measures aimed to sedentarise and settle the pastoralists. This also entailed policing and checking the movement of their herds of cattle and flocks of sheep and goats. Settled people were seen as law abiding, productive and regular payers of rent, while itinerants were labelled lawless and destructive. Prior to the colonial era, people of the Deccan lived in an ecosystem, which historically witnessed sometimes conflictual but often mutually sustaining relationships between agriculture, forest and pastoral zones. While these patterns await further research there was a continuum and interplay that was replaced by more rigid lines on the land.[19] Travelogues by authors who traversed these landscapes in the early part of the nineteenth century record the close relationship that existed between settled agricultural regions, pastoral lands and natural forests. They record how wild animals crossed from one kind of landscape to another, and goats and cattle had grazing areas in the villages. Villages often had a practice of collective regulation of grazing lands.

A closer look at the Hyderabad State, which geographically occupied the central parts of the Deccan plateau, will help clarify the picture. The Nizam's government did not regulate agriculture practices, or restrict the movement of cattle and nomadic communities.[20] It was home to one of the largest cattle populations in India, partly because of the presence of large number of long established cattle rearers such as the Lambadas, who made these regions their permanent home, and largely due to its rich grazing tracts. Such groups were integral to the larger state system of exchanging grain and salt, and extending credit to cultivators and supplies to armies. Enormous uncontrolled expanses of grazing pastures existed all over, where cattle were grazed freely. The colonial state began to police cattle through the use of trespass, market and forest regulation, and under British pressure and influence, the princely rulers of Hyderabad State began to introduce laws and taxes in the latter part of the nineteenth century to regulate cattle movements, cattle markets and cattle grazing. Scientific forestry and state takeover of forest lands shrank the grazing lands quickly and denuded the cattle wealth of Hyderabad State.[21] It resulted in a reduction in fodder and firewood, a deterioration of the soil and health of cattle, destruction of marginal livelihoods and increased pressure on the remaining land.[22] In the adjacent Berar region, the decline of cattle population was due to a mix of factors. Imperial policies that exerted pressure included encouraging the auction of pastures and grazing lands, agrarian extension and reservation of forests. Weakened by fodder scarcity, cattle became susceptible to various diseases and reproductive constraints, and died out. The Khamgaon breed of Berar became extinct after the famine of 1899–1900.[23] Without idealising earlier times in any way, it is possible to aver that factors from the late nineteenth century were to exert new stresses on pastoral activity and livelihoods.

If the colonial rule sought to label itinerant communities as criminal, newly industrialising India after Independence sought to normalise and modernise them. At times, pastoralists were indirectly but adversely affected by policies aimed at redressing inequity. State governments in Andhra Pradesh and Maharashtra broke up village commons and grazing lands to secure plots for Dalits and other landless communities,[24] instead of enforcing the Land Ceiling Act on large land holders, thereby exacerbating the decline of grazing pastures.[25] The village community as a whole, and nomadic pastoralists who were occasional users, were simultaneously dispossessed of their rights to customary grazing lands.

Agriculture, Plantations, Urbanisation

Bringing development to the Deccan has also meant transforming it into a centre of horticulture that exports fruits and flowers.

Canal irrigation has meant that the lands, once left dry and fallow, are cropped for three seasons. Shorter fallows mean less place for the sheep. Earlier, expansion of cotton cultivation had eaten into grazing and forest lands in Berar and Hyderabad regions. These trends continue unabated into the present.[26] Cash crops like onion, chilli, tomato, sugarcane and genetically modified cotton replaced traditional cereals, pulses and oilseeds. Often crops are sprayed with pesticides and treated with chemical fertilisers. All this has serious implications and translates into reduced crop residues and standing crop stubble, both critical forage for domestic animals and wild herbivores alike.[27] Crop residues are also in demand for biomass based energy industries. Foresters often threaten the ecological viability and integrity of grassland ecosystems as they seek to make them into tree covered landscapes. Afforestation projects of the 1970s and 1980s have sought to bring all 'barren' land under tree cover. In the process, these large externally driven processes have eaten away or degraded local ecologies.

As a result, shepherds have had to find alternate grazing grounds. In Maharashtra they now move east to the districts of Latur and Beed in Marathwada; in Telangana they move for extended periods of time into the forests of the Nallamalai and Adilabad, resulting in intensified conflicts with forest dwelling or forest reliant Adivasi communities like the Chenchus and Gonds, and of course contentions with the omnipresent forest guards of the state forest departments. Some shepherds have given up sheep rearing and migrated to cities for jobs.[28] With increase in use of fertilisers, many settled peasants no longer invite the penning of flocks on their fields.[29] The animal husbandry department often aims to upgrade local breeds and replace them with exotics like the Suffolk and Merino. When these fail, attempts are made to introduce hairy mutton breeds like the Red Nellore and the Madgayal.

Further, since the 1990s, the state has been aggressively pursuing neoliberal economic growth policies. The desperate need of developed countries to access new markets in the global South has greatly impacted shepherds and shepherding, and caused huge changes in the composition of their flocks in terms of breed and age.[30]

The wool of the Deccani breed of sheep was once popular in local markets and also sought by the Indian Army as coarse 'barrack' blankets. This collapsed by the mid-1990s, due to the international dumping of wool in the Indian market and the easy availability of cheap synthetic 'shoddy wool' substitutes. The sudden drop in demand for wool meant that it became unprofitable for shepherds to even pay the price for shearing sheep.[31] The indiscriminate introduction of new breeds coupled with larger market forces, have served to threaten the Deccani breed. Today's shepherds are under tremendous pressure within the 'high growth economy' to switch to 'high growth breeds'.[32] New and improved breeds need new and improved fodder, resulting in further stress on the fragile semi-arid grass ecosystem of the Deccan. The grasslands are unable to support these new sheep breeds which have large appetites.

Urban expansion is a more insidious phenomenon. Shepherds and their livestock have to contend with a new emergent landowning class of realtors, and large corporations who fence large tracts of agriculture lands. Open access regimes are giving way to private enclosures. The remaining grasslands and grazing lands of the Deccan are presently wedged between the three rapidly growing metropolises of Hyderabad, Pune and Bangalore. Governments have virtually gifted large chunks of common lands to industry, special economic zones, mines and dams. Social forestry and watershed schemes also cordon off access to pasture. Recent amendments in land laws have driven the explosion of the realty and mining markets, often on private agriculture lands.[33] Fresh threats to these last remaining grazing spaces for wild and domestic animals, appearing in the avatar of biofuel plantations, are being promoted under the country's ambitious Biofuel Mission.

Common property regimes evolved by communities to collectively manage and govern their natural resources have witnessed a significant reduction in area along with a disintegration of the institutional mechanisms.[34] In Andhra Pradesh for instance, lands classified as permanent pastures and grazing lands have halved from 1.17 million hectares in 1955–56 to just over 5,60,000 hectares in 2009–10. While it declined by twenty-eight per cent during the first four decades post-Independence, it shrank rapidly by thirty-six percent post-1990 coinciding with the twenty year period of neoliberal growth.[35] A recent study of the commons in rainfed regions in six Indian states reported a reduction in permanent pastures and grazing lands and lands that are used *de facto* for grazing over a thirty year period from 1981 to 2001. These were mostly arid, semi-arid and sub-humid agro-climatic zones, all critical pastoral area.[36]

Overgrazing of Grasslands

The impacts of domestic stock on grasslands needs to be placed against this wider backdrop of changes in the country. Grazing by livestock is often blamed for the destruction and deterioration of the forests and grasslands by conservationists and foresters. Most analysts are united in their opposition to grazing-based animal husbandry production systems. They single out high stocking rates resulting in high grazing pressure as the primary reason for the elimination of palatable grass species and the proliferation of unpalatable plants.[37] They argue that this results in the out migration of animals that depend on plant cover for food, shelter or nesting. Soil erosion ensues from overgrazing and soils are impacted due to being trampled by the hooves of grazing species. The constant refrain is to cull so called useless and inferior 'scrub' cattle, reduce their numbers and replace them with high producing breeds. Livestock have also been blamed for capturing the grazing spaces of other wild ungulates as they may compete for forage when there is overlap in their diet and habitat. This competition is said to occur when livestock exist in high densities and their consumption limits the forage available for wild herbivores.[38] The outcome is a decline in wild herbivore density, either through reduced fecundity or mortality.

In our opinion, policy decisions on the use and control of land over the last two centuries have in large measure created the crises of reduced availability of grazing spaces today. In addition, severe restriction on mobility of shepherds has aggravated the situation. Seasonal migration cycles such as the system of transhumance, whereby grasslands grow over time and are grazed, rested and reseeded, are becoming harder to sustain. The undermining of local village institutions of decentralised governance such as the panchayats, which are responsible for the management of the commons including grasslands, have added to the crisis. To add to this, grasslands are also being rapidly fragmented into smaller ecologically unviable patches.

Pastoralists and livestock owners reliant on open access systems have responded by changing the species composition of their flocks and herds. There is a clear trend among them of selling and reducing their cattle herds, and shifting to rearing the smaller species of sheep and goats. Recent studies in semi-arid areas, including the three states of the Deccan (Maharashtra, Andhra Pradesh and Karnataka), all point to significant declines in village cattle populations and increase in sheep populations. In response to scarcity, breeders shift to smaller ruminants, which can survive in harsher and less productive environments.[39] Macro figures too convey these massive species changes that have occurred across the Deccan: Andhra Pradesh for instance, witnessed a twenty-five per cent decline in cattle population between 1983 and 2003, and a nearly 200 per cent increase in sheep population during the same period.[40]

Researchers highlight that the compensatory source of grazing, in view of the huge attrition of the resource base, is the availability of pastures in the land category 'current agriculture fallows', which have increased by a considerable amount (twenty-six per cent) from 1981 to 2001. These current fallows support sheep which graze on crop stubble available therein. Crop residue and stubble in semi-arid zones, provide sixty per cent of the fodder requirements of livestock.[41] This also suggests that crop lands, and not grasslands, are the prime source of sustenance of the flocks.

What rarely gets reported are the positive ecological impacts of grazing, even though these are now the subject of extensive research. Well managed livestock grazing has its value in keeping certain landscapes intact. Grazing by livestock keeps woody growth in check and allows for specific kinds of floral biodiversity to thrive. This biodiversity, in fact, is needed for distinct wildlife species to survive, especially those which need open grasslands as opposed to dense forests. Livestock grazing on high standing biomass, makes forage available for small wild herbivores by improving the nutrient quality of forage as well as making quality forage accessible. In the Greater Himalayan National Park, some researchers report that domesticated livestock manure fertilises the pastures and creates greater floral diversity and there does seem to be little competition between domesticated livestock and wildlife herbivores.[42] Unfortunately there are virtually no studies in South Asia that have examined the possible positive interactions in a quantitative manner.[43] There is much evidence that 'pristine landscapes' are actually the products of significant human interventions. These views are echoed by a new generation of environmental historians and archaeologists.[44]

But to return to our own day, a primary reason for the survival of the wolf today, appears, ironically, to be linked back to the existing sheep and goat populations. Today, sheep and goat, rather than wild herbivores, provide sustenance to the last surviving populations of the wolf. In most of the wolf habitats the sheep density was found to be higher than goat and blackbuck, and hence researchers have inferred that sheep and goat are the major prey species of the wolf.[45] Y.V. Jhala reported that sheep were the principal prey of wolves, which attacked sheep flocks at any time of the day or night.[46] Madhusudan and Mishra report that thirty per cent of carnivore diets across India consist of livestock kills.[47] The percentages of losses to wolves are far higher than that. According to the literature, there is hardly any wild prey available for wolves in India besides a few in the small and scattered nature reserves.[48] In Karnataka, the blackbuck was found to be the only major prey species in the distributional range of the wolf, and even here, its density was low except in Rannebenur. Wolves prey on blackbuck, only if they are present in sufficient numbers.[49] According to some estimates,[50] individual packs of four wolves require approximately 75 sq km of land which they mark as their territory. Using these estimates of space, the total area available through the existing chain of reserves/protected areas in the Deccan grasslands (Rehakuri [2.17 sq km], Nanaj [8496.44 sq km], Mayureshwar [5.14 sq km], Rannebennur [119 sq km], Rollapadu [6.14 sq km] and Gudla Brahmeswara [1194 sq km]) is adequate to support a few packs of wolves (130 wolves, to be precise). The official estimate of 2,000–3,000 wolves, when read in conjunction with the reports of wolf sightings by shepherds whilst they graze their flocks points to the strong likelihood of a sizeable proportion of the wolf population surviving and possibly thriving beyond officially Protected Areas. There are possibly parallels with the large carnivores of the upper Himalaya as shown by Bhatnagar and Mishra in this volume.

The forces of development which have shrunk and fragmented these ecosystems and are also virtually squeezing the sheep off their land and with them the shepherds have also spelt the death knell of the wolf of which there are only a few left.[51] Paradoxically, sheep and goats, whose numbers have increased in response to a deteriorating grazing resource base in the semi-arid Deccan, and which have traditionally been viewed and perceived as the bane of conservation, appear to be key species today that are sustaining the survival of the wolf.

Wolves in Legend and Lore

Legends testify to deep ambivalences in the age old relations of sheep, their human owners and their canine predators. Different communities perceive the wolf differently. Among the herders of Mongolia, wolves are venerated despite the paradoxical role they play in their lives both as predator and prey, as defilers of sheep herds and as protectors of the grassland ecology; animals to be feared as well as revered.[52] In Turkey too the wolf is venerated and revered by the pastoralists, as in Japan. The Japanese consider the wolf to be the divine messenger of the mountain deity. However, today the wolf is extinct in Japan, having succumbed to the pressures of bounty hunting, disease and modern development.[53] By contrast, the wolf has been vilified by many European cultures and assumes extremely negative roles in traditional fairy tales, be it 'Little Red Riding Hood', 'The Wolf and The Seven Lambs' or even the famed Russian fable 'Peter and the Wolf'. Legislations enacted in Britain led to its systematic extermination over four centuries ago and today it is regionally extinct in Ireland and Britain.[54] The last wolf in Scotland is said to have been killed in 1743. Even modern novels such as the Harry Potter series portray the wolf negatively, be it as Fenrir Greyback, an ally of the Dark Lord, or as the teacher Remus Lupin, who transforms periodically into a dangerous werewolf. Driven to near extinction in most of western Europe and Scandinavia in the last century, it is slowly making a reappearance, causing panic and confusion among some, and interest and delight among others.

In India, the wolf is only one among many wild predators. It seems to pale in comparison to the tiger, the lion or the leopard. In our complex multi-stratified society, a historian has warned that: 'There were mutually contradictory strands, with the same animal being revered and feared, hunted and worshipped even at the same time. It would be anachronistic to see the past in terms of easy coexistence.'[55] It makes little appearance in the folk and fairy tales of the country with the wily jackal and cunning fox being more popular. This secondary position it holds may paradoxically be a reason for its survival in India today along with the fact that it is small, nocturnal and cohabits with humans not only in rangelands but in the fields with mixed crop and husbandry practices.

Conflicts between Herders and Wild Wolves

It is difficult to assess the impact the slaughter of wolves had during the colonial era on their population, ecology and behaviour. Over 1,00,000 were killed for rewards in British India between 1871 and 1916. As several of the so called wolves killed could have been jackals, the figures are less useful as an index of status than they could have been. But there is little doubt of a decline in some areas. The extermination of wolves remained a priority in the North West Provinces and Awadh, later Uttar Pradesh, right into the 1920s. The Lieutenant Governor singled out the elimination of the wolf as 'the single most important part' of measures for destroying wild animals. In 1875, more people were killed by wolves than by tigers in North India. The North West Provinces and Bihar were among the worst affected by wolf attacks. In 1876, in the North West Provinces, as many as 721 lives were lost to wolves and in turn 2825 wolves were slain for bounties. The loss of lives to wolves was also heavy in Bihar. In 1876, all but a dozen of the 185 deaths were from Patna and Bhagalpur divisions. In turn, they accounted for over half of wolves killed. Among all wolf attacks on humans documented from North India in 1996, seventy-six children were reported injured by wolves of which fifty were reported to be fatal. Direct wolf-human conflicts in the early twentieth-century Deccan were very rare and continue to be rare today. In a recent informal survey conducted in three districts of Maharashtra with over a hundred shepherd families, there were no reports of wolf attacks on humans. Shepherds are also aware that wolves are reservoirs of the rabies virus, which could infect their sheep if bitten. Biologists, on the other hand, have often blamed shepherds of poisoning, shooting, killing and laying traps for wolves or destroying their cubs.

How Pastoralists View Wolves

Although much of conservation literature sees herders and wolves as antagonists, our own field experience and interactions point to the contrary.[56] Shepherds in the Deccan do not perceive the wolf as their biggest threat. Many shepherds we know in fact claim that the presence of the wolf is beneficial to sheep rearing. To understand why this is so, it is important to go beyond a simple profit and loss model and take serious cognisance of their perceptions. The lambs, which are lifted by the wolves, are considered an offering to the gods and many shepherds mention that the presence of wolves in the area ensures they keep constant vigil and take better care of their stock. This point can be best illustrated by reference to a site well known to us. About seventy kilometres due west from Hyderabad, the Kuruma pastoralists of Narsapur, Medak District, have an ancient saying which goes, '*Thodel-Manda Ki Lakshmi Untundi*' or 'a wolf is "Lakshmi" (the goddess of wealth) which brings wealth to the flock'. This stems from a strong belief that the wolf is a harbinger of good luck. If a wolf lifts an animal from a flock the latter is an offering to Beerappa. This loss deters the 'evil eye' from falling upon their flock, which will hence be free of disease and prosper. They attribute expanding agriculture and disappearing grasslands as a primary cause for the wolf disappearing; also a reason for a spurt in sheep diseases. Nor is this an exceptional or unusual case. Further west in Narayankhed, which borders Karnataka and Maharashtra, migratory pastoralists share an identical belief. As they tell us, 'A wolf that enters the flock from one side and leaves the flock at the other, heralds good luck and health for the flock, in turn, bringing wealth, especially if sighted on a Sunday.' Shepherds here frequently sight wolves, wolf dens and wolf pups, particularly during the monsoon months. They are emphatic that they do not attack, kill or smoke out wolves. The reason is very significant: they believe this spells bad luck and disease.[57] Yet, such practices are known in these regions. We surmise that the killing and smoking of cubs reported by many ecologists could largely or wholly be by other communities visiting fields. The matter awaits further investigation and study but there is reason to argue that not all shepherds are uniformly hostile to wolves and some do give coexistence a fair trial. Sheep mortality surveys in stationary and migratory sheep flocks of Medak reveal that diseases and not predators are the major cause of death.[58] The annual losses of sheep to disease and accidents in Ahmednagar were found to be significantly higher than those to wolf predation.[59] Losses were more severe amongst sedentary shepherds as compared to nomadic or migratory ones. A study from Karnataka, however, reported a considerable proportion of sheep loss due to wolves, which again was significantly higher amongst flocks owned by sedentary shepherds as compared to nomadic ones. We tentatively argue that migratory shepherds are better prepared in terms of anti-predator strategies.

Conserving Grasslands with Minimal Conflict

Dominant conservation efforts in the recent past have aimed at conserving nature mainly in wildlife parks and sanctuaries. The expansion of the geographic spread of Protected Areas has been the kernel of preservation policies. Yet, there is just not enough space for such 'people-free wilderness.' Secondly, most approaches are based on studies done in specific locales, often mature tree forests in the Indian case.[60] Much of conservation practice and much (not all) of the biology misses a critical element, which is the people who often live within the landscape. Exclusion of local people from sanctuaries has exacerbated conflicts and also ignores larger landscapes where reconciliation can and should be attempted.[61] This is certainly the case in semi-arid, grassland, desert and open range ecosystems, which make up well over half of the land mass in India.

Both historically and in the present context, the survival of wolves in peninsular India appears to be closely linked to sheep. There is a strong case for sheep rearing in the grasslands and looking beyond Protected Areas towards sustainable management and governance of landscapes, provided there are mechanisms in place to compensate the shepherds for their loss to both disease and wolf predation. In the Deccan, many of the wolf attacks and predation happen in areas outside of Protected Areas. Maharashtra initiated the policy of compensation in 1994. It was the fourth of at least twelve states to do so. Maharashtra's policy is among the most generous. At the urging of the local forest department, in 1999, Maharashtra extended compensation to all livestock listed in 2([18-A]) of the Wildlife (Protection) Act 1972. Lack of knowledge about compensation procedures and schemes and bureaucratic procedures has made it difficult for shepherds to take advantage of and utilise these provisions, although they stand to lose due to wolf attacks.[62] Projects such as the conservation programme for snow leopards[63] and Tibetan wolves, in parts of Himachal Pradesh, have an inbuilt programme for livestock insurance,[64] for instance, which act to deter the shepherds from harming the wild life.

It would appear that the change in landscape and cropping patterns and growing human domination would have driven the wolf away, but studies by wildlife scientists have shown that wolves have in fact adapted to the new situation.[65] Wolves have been seen to adapt and change their diet and resort to scavenging on garbage dumps.[66] Extensive sugarcane plantations in western Maharashtra have proven to be refuges for female wolves for whelping. The eighteen month 'grass' crop which has otherwise been heavily criticised for ruining the environment by lowering the water table has sheltered both leopard cubs and wolf pups. The animals naturally face persecution by sugarcane farmers who smoke their fields prior to cutting the cane, but that happens only occasionally.

Based on scat analysis, an estimated sixty-three per cent of the diet of wolves in North Solapur, Maharashtra, was comprised of livestock, and one hundred per cent in Sangola, Maharashtra, where no wild ungulates remain.[67] Wolves more often feed on goats and sheep than on cattle. Scholars analysed that within livestock, in North Solapur, seventy-one per cent of wolf scats contained goats and sheep, and fourteen per cent cattle. It is evident that within this settled, human-dominated landscape, in the absence of wild herbivores, wolves have almost entirely shifted to domestic herbivores, as a source of sustenance. In fact, predation on livestock has a long history, even though the scale of losses were less in the past. Wolf-sheep interaction is neither new nor novel nor recent but is a long-term structural feature of the Deccan landscape and agro-ecology as it has come to be constituted through a long process of interaction of people, animals and grasslands.

The Forest Rights Act

Inclusive conservancy requires recognition of right holders which was not possible until recently in forest lands. It is here that the newly enacted Scheduled Tribes and Other Traditional Forest Dwellers (Recognition of Forest Rights) Act, 2006 (FRA) allows for synergy.[68] Its relevance to pastoralists is often overlooked due to the centrality of Adivasis and their rights in government forests. This historic legislation recognises the traditional seasonal access of nomadic or pastoralist communities (both settled and transhumant) to graze their animals in forests (Chapter II, Section 3 [1] d). While this legislation does not address the seasonal uses of pastoralists to 'non-forest' lands, it opens up new spaces for pastoralists to negotiate the terms of grazing directly with the settled forest dweller. This can potentially empower both sets of communities to collectively exercise their rights to protect and conserve the forests as spelt out clearly in Chapter III, Section 5 (a, b, c, d) of the FRA:

(a) protect the wildlife, forest and biodiversity
(b) ensure that the adjoining catchment area, water sources and other ecological sensitive areas are adequately protected

(c) ensure that the habitat of forest dwelling Scheduled Tribes and other traditional forest dwellers is protected from any form of destructive practices affecting their cultural and natural heritage

(d) ensure that the decisions taken in the Gram Sabha to regulate access to community, forest resources and stop any activity which adversely affects the wild animals, forest and the biodiversity are complied with

This would be a huge step forward from the prevailing situation where pastoralists are harassed by forest guards, to pay 'arbitrarily imposed grazing fees' or 'bribes,' for permission to graze their animals in the concerned forest. The system of monetary payments in exchange for permission to graze has failed to build a sense of ownership within the community towards protection and sustainable use of forest resources, and does not automatically translate into sustainable use and conservation of forests, livelihoods and wildlife. It also requires that the legislation be used in its broadest sense to be inclusive and respectful of age old customary systems of common use which benefit the larger collective, rather than it being used as a legislation that will restrict access and exclude one group because of the other.

The challenge that presents itself in the governance of these grasslands, is that much of these grasslands no longer exist as distinct and separate 'pristine' geographic spaces and areas, but are spread and scattered across different land categories as defined by the government and as customarily used and identified by local communities. Communities have their own terminologies to identify different village lands which refer to customary landuse (*gautan* lands, *poromboke*, *shikam* lands, *bhanjar* land, *charai zameen*, *patta bhumi*, *cheruvu katta*, *gomala's gayran* and *maal raan*). The government has its own: there are revenue lands (private and public) administered by the revenue department; there are forests, administered by the forest department; and revenue wastelands, which can be public or private. Frequently the people's descriptions and those of the state conflict with one another. The grasslands are interspersed with and scattered across these different land categories—grasslands, agriculture fields, forests, lands near village tanks and canals and lands near streams—and exist like a mosaic or patchwork, one flowing into the other. Somewhere within this patchwork are the Protected Areas, which are few and far between. As discussed earlier, the movement of the wolf in particular, is not restricted and confined by the artificial human-created boundaries of what constitutes an official 'protected grassland zone.' Moreover, the wolf draws its prey from wild and domestic herbivores, particularly the sheep. Given the wide geographic spread of the sheep and their seasonal movements, the wolf too will move. This will need to be factored into the local bodies of rural self-government not only for the sake of wolves but also of sheep. Many of these land categories constitute the commons and are to be governed by the local panchayats or village councils, according to the Panchayat Raj Act. Several panchayats continue to be dominated by powerful land owning communities, who gifted away their village commons for non-livestock/agriculture use to serve their own narrow needs and interests. These decisions severely harmed livestock based livelihoods and the associated grasslands. Pastoralists and shepherds have resisted these in the past, and continue to use their political agency to defend their livelihoods and their identity, even today.[69] In the Deccan, shepherds are organising themselves and leading other communities in the villages to halt the loss of the commons. They are advocating with their gram panchayats to secure their rights of access.[70] In doing so they are in effect fighting for the survival of the last remaining grasslands. As their grazing rights and livelihoods interface with resources that are administered by a range of different government departments, no single law or policy will fully serve to protect their livelihoods or the grasslands. They have to be alert and respond to every policy and legislation that impacts land use, agriculture development, animal husbandry and markets. Where they can use legislations, they are using them. For instance, shepherds in Medak and Chittoor districts of Andhra Pradesh are using the FRA to secure grazing rights in forests.

Along with the FRA, shepherds are bringing pressure on their gram sabhas to operationalise the landmark decision given by the Supreme Court in *Jagpal Singh and Others vs State of Punjab and Others* on 28 January 2011,[71] concerning encroachment of common land, whereby the court gave directions to all the state governments in the country to prepare schemes for eviction of illegal/unauthorised occupants of gram sabha/gram panchayat/*poramboke*/*shamlat* land and to restore these to the gram sabha or gram panchayat for the common use of villagers. FRA provides a framework to foster the synergy between livelihoods and conservation in forest areas, and is a useful starting point to develop a strategy in non-forest regions, which will address both conservation and livelihood challenges. As a welfare state, India has undertaken to look after its human (Article 38 of the Constitution) and wild inhabitants (Article 48) in its Directive Principles of State Policy. Keeping this in mind, it is imperative that the state take all measures and steps to stem the root causes of grassland habitat loss—be they dismantling or denotifying SEZs, restoring natural grassland vegetation as part of government watershed programs, putting a halt to all monoculture plantations, stopping all further diversion of common lands and instituting comprehensive compensation options for shepherds who lose their sheep. This can only happen if we rethink the current model of economic growth and development path that we have embarked on.

The pastoralists struggle to continue their transhumant livelihoods, and their struggle for access to grazing systems is perhaps the most important ally and instrument of conservation today for the Deccan grasslands. If itinerant and peripatetic livelihoods such as transhumance survive, so too will the wolf. Today, the pastoralists are perhaps the only community in the Deccan grasslands, who are advocating that land continue to be retained and used as a grassland, instead of being enclosed and converted into a concrete jungle or a piece of real estate where no wolf would survive.

Conclusion

Wolves and sheep share more than a landscape or a common reliance on the Deccan plateau ecosystems. Pastoralism and wolves, although struggling to survive, have adapted to changing landscapes and agrarian conditions. Pastoralists, in the face of adversity, change migratory routes, expand or shrink their flocks, change their species or the breed composition of their flocks and even graze on new crop residue. The conflicts that shepherds face with the forces of modern development are in fact far larger than those they face with the canine predators of their sheep.

The cheetah has been extinct for decades, though it was once part of the Deccan landscape. What, then, is special about the wolf and why does it need to be preserved? The wolf represents an apex predator in an ecosystem that is often missed or forgotten. It represents a landscape shared with the bustard, Jerdon's courser and blackbuck. As with any apex predator species, there could be long term ecosystem-wide consequences for removing the wolf, such as uneven or explosive growth in certain species and the rapid decline of others. Overpopulation of certain ungulates, leads to the overgrazing of certain grass species, thereby affecting the health and soil of the grassland. This in turn could lead to soil erosion, affecting water quality and the decline of certain critical landscapes.[72]

Both shepherds and wildlife require large tracts of land which are not fragmented. Shepherds and wildlife have coexisted in the past and can continue into the future provided human predation in the guise of development—euphemistically 'the wolf in sheep's clothing'—does not lay waste their land forever.

Notes

1. See http://indiaonline.in/Profile/Geography/PhysiographicRegions/index.aspx (accessed 3 July 2011).

2. World Wildlife Fund and Mark McGinley, 'Deccan thorn scrub forests' in J. Cleveland Cutler (ed.), *Encyclopedia of Earth* (Washington, DC: Environmental Information Coalition, National Council for Science and the Environment). First published in *Encyclopedia of Earth*, 23 September 2008; last revised 21 January 2011. Available at http://www.eoearth.org/view/article/51cbed5f7896bb431f691d38/ (accessed 29 April 2014).

3. Y. V. Jhala, 'Status, ecology and conservation of the Indian wolf *Canis lupus pallipes* (Sykes)', *Journal of the Bombay Natural History Society* 100 (2003): 293–307.

4. D. K. Sharma, J. E. Maldonado, Y. V. Jhala and R. C. Fleischer, 'Ancient wolf lineages in India', *Proceedings of the Royal Society of London. Series B: Biological Sciences*, 271 (2004): S1–S4.

5. M. Singh and H. N. Kumara, 'Distribution, status and conservation of Indian gray wolf (*Canis lupus pallipes*) in Karnataka, India', *Journal of Zoology* 270 (2006): 164–69.

6. Asad Rahmani, 'Conservation outside protected areas'.

7. Sharma, et. al., 'Ancient wolf lineages', p. 4.

8. C. Sillero-Zubiri, M. Hoffmann and D. W. Macdonald (eds), *Canids: Foxes, wolves, jackals and dogs. Status survey and conservation action plan* (Gland, Switzerland and Cambridge, UK: IUCN/SSC Canid Specialist Group, 2004), p. 128.

9. A. Agarwal, R. Chopra and K. Sharma, *The State of India's Environment: A citizens' report* (New Delhi: Centre for Science and Environment, 1982); M. Gadgil, *Ecological Journeys: The science and politics of conservation in India* (Ranikhet: Permanent Black, 2001).

10. Saberwal, *Pastoral Politics*; P. S. Kavoori, *Pastoralism in Expansion: The transhuming herders of Western Rajasthan* (New Delhi: Oxford University Press, 1999).

11. G. D. Sontheimer and M. L. K. Murty, 'Pre-historic background to pastoralism in the Southern Deccan in the light of oral traditions and cults of some pastoral communities' in H. Bruckner, A. Feldhaus, and A. Malik (eds), *Essays on Religion, Literature and Law* (Delhi: Manohar, 2004), p. 161.

12. A. Feldhaus, A. Malik and B. Bruckner, 'Essays on Khandoba' in S. Gunther-Dietz (ed.), *King of Hunters Warriors and Shepherds* (New Delhi: Manohar, 1997), pp. 19–33.

13. Ramoshis are a tribe who were formerly notified as 'Criminal' by the British and today are classified as a Denotified Tribe. The Matang are a Scheduled Caste whose primary occupation was related to making ropes and brooms.

14. A. Dandekar, 'In the name of pastoralism: The early medieval Maharashtra' in S. Ratnagar and R. Heredia (eds), *Mobile and Marginalized Peoples: Perspectives from the past* (New Delhi: Manohar, 2003), pp. 65–88.

15. Golla pastoral communities are also found in the rainfed areas of coastal Andhra Pradesh, where pastoralism has ancient roots and a strong pastoral economy rooted in the past. This is described in detail in A. Murali, 'Whose trees?: Forest practices and local communities in Andhra, 1600–1922' in David Arnold and Ramachandra Guha (eds), *Nature, Culture and Imperialism: Essays on the environmental history of South Asia* (New Delhi: Oxford University Press, 1995), pp. 46–122.

16. World Wildlife Fund, 'Deccan thorn scrub forests', p. 2.

17. Anthra, 'Annual Report 2007–08' (Pune and Hyderabad: Anthra, 2008).

18. B. Bhukya, *Subjugated Nomads: The Lambadas under the rule of the Nizam* (Hyderabad: Orient Blackswan, 2010), pp. 73–116.

19. Murali, 'Whose trees?'

20. Bhukya, *Subjugated Nomads*.

21. Bhukya, *Subjugated Nomads*.

22. Bhukya, *Subjugated Nomads*.

23. D. Satya Laxman, *Ecology, Colonialism and Cattle: Central India in the nineteenth century* (New Delhi: Oxford University Press, 2004), pp. 176–82.

24. The commons, also known as common property resources (CPRs), are regimes evolved by communities to collectively manage and govern their natural resources. In rural India, CPRs generally include community pastures, community forests, wastelands, common threshing and dumping grounds, watershed drainage, tanks, ponds, rivers, rivulets, their banks and beds. See N. S. Jodha, 'Common property resources and the environmental context', *Economic and Political Weekly* 30, no. 51 (1995): 3278–84.

25. N. S. Jodha, 'Common property resources and rural poor in dry regions of India', *Economic and Political Weekly* 21 (1986): 169–81.

26. Satya Laxman, *Ecology, Colonialism and Cattle.*

27. Rahmani reports how blackbucks frequently and regularly graze on crops, resulting in crop damage in Rahmani, 'Conservation outside protected areas'.

28. Foundation for Ecological Security, *A Commons Story: In the rain shadow of green revolution* (New Delhi: Foundation for Ecological Security, 2011).

29. Anthra, 'Annual Report 2008–2009' (Pune and Hyderabad: Anthra, 2009).

30. In his studies on pastoral livelihoods in Rajasthan, Kavoori notes a change in composition in the flocks. In our studies with shepherds we observe a pressure on shepherds to sell lambs at a young age, responding possibly to policy change in India to encourage meat exports, and thus the need to shift to breeds that grow faster and reach a particular weight at a younger age. See Kavoori, *Pastoralism in Expansion.*

31. V. Switha and D. Srinivasarao, *Decanni Wool in Andhra Pradesh: A study* (Hyderabad: Anthra Publications, 2007), p. 13.

32. R. Aebi, *Sheep Husbandry on the Deccan Plateau in India: Recent developments and new challenges from keeping the native Deccani breed and the introduced Nellore breed* (Bern: Swiss College of Agriculture, 2009).

33. Foundation for Ecological Security, *A Commons Story.*

34. Foundation for Ecological Security, *A Commons Story.*

35. Directorate of Economics and Statistics, *Compendium of Area and Land Use Statistics of Andhra Pradesh 1955–56 to 2004–05* (Hyderabad: Directorate of Economics and Statistics, Government of Andhra Pradesh, 2007–08).

36. Foundation for Ecological Security, *A Commons Story.*

37. Rahmani, 'Conservation outside protected areas'.

38. M. D. Madhusudan and C. Mishra, 'Why big, fierce animals are threatened: conserving large mammals in densely populated landscapes' in Saberwal and Rangarajan (eds), *Battles Over Nature*, pp. 31–56.

39. Foundation for Ecological Security, *A Commons Story.*

40. Government of Andhra Pradesh, *Facts and Figures of Andhra Pradesh* (Hyderabad: Government of Andhra Pradesh, 2010).

41. Foundation for Ecological Security, *A Commons Story.*

42. A. Baviskar, 'States, communities and conservation' in Saberwal and Rangarajan (eds) *Battles Over Nature*, pp. 267–99.

43. Madhusudan and Mishra, 'Why big, fierce animals are threatened'.

44. M. Rangarajan, 'The politics of ecology: The debate on wildlife and people in India, 1970–1990' *Economic and Political Weekly*, 31 (1996): 2391–409.

45. Jhala, 'Status, ecology and conservation'.

46. Y. V. Jhala, 'Human-wolf conflict in India' presented at the Beyond 2000 Symposium, February 2000. Available at http://www.wolf.org/wolves/learn/intermed/inter_human/india_abstract_003.asp (accessed 20 July 2010).

47. Madhusudan and Mishra, 'Why big, fierce animals are threatened'.

48. S. Kumar and A. R. Rahmani, 'Predation by wolves (*Canis lupus pallipes*) on blackbuck (*Antilope cervicapra*) in the Great Indian Bustard Sanctuary, Nannaj, Maharashtra, India', *International Journal of Ecology and Environmental Sciences* 34 (2008): 99–112.

49. Kumar and Rahmani, 'Predation by Wolves'.

50. L.D. Mech and L. Boitani (eds), *Wolves: Behavior, ecology, and conservation.* (Chicago: University of Chicago Press, 2003).

51. R. Borges, 'The anatomy of ignorance or ecology in a Fragmented landscape: Do we know what really counts?' in Saberwal and Rangarajan (eds), *Battles Over Nature*, pp. 56–85.

52. J. Rong, *Wolf Totem* (London: Penguin, 2008).

53. Wolfsong, 'Wolves in Japan', 2010. Available at http://www.wolfsongalaska.org/Wolves_in_Japan (accessed 13 May 2014).

54. Rangarajan, *India's Wildlife History*.

55. M. Rangarajan, 'The raj and the natural world: "The war against dangerous beasts", in Colonial India' *Studies in History* 14 (1998): 265–99.

56. Jhala, 'Status, ecology and conservation'.

57. Anthra, 'Mid-Term Report, Pastoral Livelihoods' (Hyderabad: Anthra, 2008).

58. S. Ramesh, 'Control and prevention of epidemics and exotic diseases' in *Proceedings of the National Seminar on Sustainable Use and Conservation of the Deccani Sheep* (Hyderabad: Anthra Publications, 2007).

59. R. Krithivasan, V. Athreya and M. Odden, 'Human-wolf conflict in human dominated landscapes of Ahmednagar district, Maharashtra, India and possible mitigation measures', submitted to the Rufford Small Grants Foundation, 2009.

60. R. Guha, 'The authoritarian biologist and the arrogance of anti-humanism: Wildlife conservation in the third world' in Saberwal and Rangarajan (eds), *Battles Over Nature*, pp. 139–57.

61. K. Sivaramakrishnan, 'Conservation crossroads: Indian wildlife at the intersection of global imperatives, nationalist anxieties and local assertions' in Saberwal and Rangarajan (eds), *Battles Over Nature*, pp. 397–99.

62. M. Agarwala, S. Kumar, A. Treves and L. Naughton-Treves, 'Paying for wolves in Solapur, India and Wisconsin, USA: Comparing compensation rules and practice to understand the goals and politics of wolf conservation' *Biological Conservation* 143 (2010): 2945–55.

63. The Snow Leopard Trust, 'Livestock Insurance Programme Review', 2010. Availableathttp://www.snowleopard.org/programs/communitybasedconservation/livestockinsurance (accessed 28 July 2010).

64. Nature Conservation Foundation, 'People, livestock and snow leopards. Protecting livestock and snow leopards: Participatory conservation in the Trans Himalaya', 2010. Available at http://www.ncfindia org/projectoverview (accessed 31 July 2010).

65. Jhala, 'Status, ecology and conservation'.

66. S. Tug, *Conflicts between Humans and Wolf: A study in Bozdag, Konya Province, Turkey* (Ankara: University of Ankara, 2005).

67. Agarwala, et al., 'Paying for wolves'.

68. The Scheduled Tribes and Other Traditional Forest Dwellers (Recognition of Forest Rights) Act, 2006. Government of India.

69. Kavoori, 'Pastoralism in expansion'; Bhukya, *Subjugated Nomads*.

70. Foundation for Ecological Security, *A Commons Story*; S. R. Ramdas, 'Whose access and whose benefit: Securing customary rights in India' in *Biodiversity and Culture: exploring community protocols, PLA Notes 65* (London: Institute of Environment and Development): 55–64.

71. *Jagpal Singh and Others vs State of Punjab and Others*.

72. D. B. Botkin, *Discordant Harmonies: A new ecology for the twenty-first century* (New York: Oxford University Press, 1992), p. 256.

Seven

CONSERVATION WITHOUT FENCES

Project Snow Leopard

Yash Veer Bhatnagar and Charudutt Mishra

'We have abundant ibex and snow leopards near the Siachen glacier,' remarked a young Army captain who had just returned after serving his tenure in the world's highest battlefield. Numerous tourists traveling from Leh to Kargil notice herds of animals grazing near the road. They then move on, not realising that these are specimens of the endangered Ladakh urial, barely 3,000 of which survive in the entire world. In Sikkim, anyone travelling to the famous Gurudongmar Lake can easily see large herds of blue sheep or bharal, the most important wild prey of the snow leopard. The lucky ones also see the rare Tibetan argali and the Tibetan gazelle. And the most fortunate few are blessed with a fleeting glimpse of the globally endangered snow leopard.

As remarkable as these wild treasures are, the fact is that *none* of these places lie within the confines of any wildlife Protected Area. Such oases for wildlife dot the entire higher Himalayan landscape, from Arunachal Pradesh in the east to Jammu and Kashmir in the west, irrespective of their administrative status.

A study by the Wildlife Institute of India in Ladakh found that more than three-fourths of the landscape could be prioritised for wildlife, either due to the presence of a very rare species or a high diversity of large mammals.[1] A similar ongoing study by Nature Conservation Foundation (NCF) in Spiti has found numerous areas outside with superior wildlife values compared with the two existing PAs there. If we were to go by the existing conservation model, almost the whole of eastern Ladakh (>22,000 square km) and Spiti (c. 7,000 square km) would need to be designated as Protected Areas. Does it then make sense to follow the conventional Protected Areas approach to conserve the magnificent wildlife of the higher Himalaya?

It was in recognition of these incongruities that innovative conservation initiatives are now taking shape in Indian Himalaya and the Transhimalaya. In January 2009, Ministry of Environment and Forests launched an ambitious conservation programme for Indian high altitude areas called Project Snow Leopard.[2] This unique endeavour was catalysed by the Wildlife Institute of India, Nature Conservation Foundation and the Snow Leopard Trust, all voluntary organisations, with active participation of the five Himalayan state governments, the union Ministry of Environment and Forests and a select group of organisations and individuals, in a consultative process that lasted close to four years.[3] With a sizeable coverage of wildlife Protected Areas in the Indian high altitudes—that is just over nine per cent for the Transhimalayan zone—the question is why such a scheme was required; what were the attributes of the region that necessitated an alternative outlook? This leads us into the salient features of the snow leopard initiative and the challenges ahead.

Project Snow Leopard is not a species-centric programme but one that uses snow leopards as a 'flagship species' to draw conservation attention to the entire region that it represents—namely, the non-forested areas above the tree line in the Himalaya and the Transhimalaya. It was also observed that in the entire (rather vibrant) conservation discourse in India, often obsessed with the tiger and its fate, these areas and its issues were either absent or were only given passing reference.[4]

The Indian High Altitudes

The Indian Himalaya extends in a huge arc from the Nanga Parbat in the west to the Namche Barwa in the east, covering over 2,500 km and passing through five Indian states—Jammu and Kashmir, Himachal Pradesh and Uttarakhand in the west, and Sikkim and

Arunachal Pradesh in the east. The Himalaya and Transhimalaya cover over twelve per cent of India's geographical area, which is more land than the entire area of the Gangetic valley. This comes to a total area of 4,00,000 square km, part of a contiguous landscape that borders and includes other countries such as Pakistan, Nepal, Bhutan and China. The high altitudes are quite heterogeneous in topography, climate, flora and fauna from east to west and from south to north. In general, the climate and habitat become drier from east to west and from south to north. Dense forests are replaced by open scrub and meadows or steppes along both these gradients.

Inhabiting this diversity of habitats is a fascinating variety of fauna, including several globally endangered species.[5] The Himalaya is home to a unique and large assemblage of hoofed mammals (ungulates), with forest dwelling goat-antelopes such as goral, serow and takin occupying lower and middle zones, and wild goats and sheep such as ibex, markhor, blue sheep, Ladakh urial and Tibetan argali occurring in the open steppes of the Greater Himalayan and Transhimalayan zones. The Tibetan gazelle, Tibetan wild ass (or kiang), wild yak (or dong) and the Tibetan antelope (or chiru) also occur in parts of the Transhimalaya, though larger numbers are in Tibet. The Indian high altitudes have over ten species of wild ungulates, making them among the richest areas for mountain ungulates in the world.[6] Being from the same taxonomic groups as the primary livestock (wild sheep, goats, cattle and equids), wild ungulates form an important, but often neglected genetic resource. All species mostly occur at low densities due to the limited plant productivity, with plant growth confined to three to four months of summer.

Preying upon these wild herbivores is the snow leopard, the apex predator in these mountains. This elusive predator is known to occur in an area of over two million square km, spanning twelve countries of Central and South Asia; yet the global population estimate remains below 8,000 animals. By way of contrast, the more well known tiger, of which close to 4,000 survive in thirteen Asian countries spread over approximately 9,14,000 square km commands far more attention.[7] To place this in perspective, the global range of the snow leopard spreads over an area equivalent to two-thirds that of India: the tiger's lands now cover an expanse only one-third of India's size.

The snow leopard is a medium sized cat that is characterised by its thick fur, stocky limbs and long tail. It shares its habitat with other predators such as the Tibetan wolf, brown and black bears, the lynx and wild dogs. Individual snow leopards have relatively large home ranges over which they utilise the sparse prey. Recent home range estimates from Mongolia, for example, average 365 square km, varying from a 140 square km expanse to an expanse of over 900 square km.[8] Our camera trapping studies in Spiti too suggest that although there is considerable overlap among individual cat home ranges, they range across large areas. A study by the Snow Leopard Trust in Pakistan showed that a female snow leopard used an area of over 1,500 square km and travelled all the way to northern Afghanistan, spending considerable time in unprotected areas. She crossed borders and boundaries of provinces and nation states for her home range spanned these human drawn frontiers.[9] Snow leopards are thus species that have home range sizes exceeding that of most other large cats such as the tiger and leopard. Snow leopards are more peripatetic than many other large carnivores. They represent areas with complex ecologies with a spectrum of diversity even in terms of large fauna, a fact that needs wider appreciation. In this respect the Transhimalaya and Himalaya may have much in common with semi-arid regions like the Deccan plateau where the wolf ranges over large areas spanning field, forest and pasture.[10]

Project Snow Leopard encompasses the non-forested zone above the tree line (that occurs roughly around 3,200 metres in the western Himalaya and around 4,200 metres in the eastern Himalaya), going over the Greater Himalayan crest into the Transhimalayan region.[11] This region, which constitutes the headwaters of all North Indian rivers, has certain distinctive features that set it apart from other areas in the country. One crucial feature is that the population connectivity of wildlife populations is primarily broken only by natural features such as permafrost areas, glaciers or large rocky areas. This effectively translates to approximately 2,00,000 square km of almost continuous wildlife habitat. This is unlike the lowland forested and grassland areas where human-dominated landscapes fragment wilderness areas into ecological 'islands'. For instance, all the Elephant reserves in India total 1,10,000 square km, are distributed over some connected habitats but there are many unconnected and hold isolated wild elephant populations.[12] Similar is the case with many of the tiger reserves.[13] This is not to say there is no connectivity but to emphasise that movement and dispersal may entail greater hazard for the species in question. Thus, a tiger stepping out of a tiger reserve is very likely to face large expanses of cultivation or human habitation, while a snow leopard stepping out of a National Park may encounter large expanses of conducive habitat; very likely it will actually step into even better habitat!

The human density in the snow leopard's terrain is less than one person per square km in most areas, in sharp contrast to over 350 per square km in India as a whole. A similar contrast obtains in other Asian range states such as China. Many people inhabiting this landscape may be of different cultures and faiths (such as Tibetan Buddhist tribes, Kashmiris, pahadis), but essentially are agro-pastoralists dependent integrally on the meagre resources of the region. Various migrant herders such as Gujjars and Bakkarwals also depend on these tracts for their summer grazing. It can be safely said that in this region, people as well as wildlife use almost any usable piece of land.[14] This inescapable reality needs to be central to any effective action for conservation.

The Beginnings: Piecing Together the Ideas

The genesis of Project Snow Leopard goes much further back in time than the four years it took us with the government and other partners to have it launched. We started working in India's high altitude landscape in the 1990s, particularly in the Spiti Valley, a 7,000 square km landscape in northern Himachal Pradesh, and the adjoining region of Ladakh. We investigated the ecology of mountain ungulates,[15] tried to understand human ecology,[16] human-snow leopard conflicts,[17] and human impacts on wildlife and natural resources.[18] The close interaction of people with wildlife and natural resources makes it almost impossible for an ecologist to focus exclusively on wild species and natural processes. The widespread prevalence of Buddhism, which teaches compassion towards all forms of life, adds another interesting cultural dimension to issues of conservation and human-wildlife conflict in this region. There are also considerable possibilities in such contexts for adherents of different faiths and cultures to build on affinities with nature. Indeed, we have since spent a considerable amount of time and effort trying to understand human ecology, conflicts and societal transitions, as they have such a close bearing on wildlife conservation and ecology.[19]

Our research in Spiti established that a majority of the rangelands were overstocked with livestock, i.e., grazed at stocking densities so high that livestock production itself was getting compromised.[20] We found that this excessive livestock grazing was outcompeting and depleting the populations of Spiti's mountain ungulates, the bharal and the ibex,[21] and there were indications that several species such as Tibetan argali, wild yak and kiang, may also have gone extinct historically.[22] A further finding: some exceptions where the presence of livestock didn't appear a threat to wildlife, as in the case of the Pin Valley National Park where close to 400 local livestock did not seem to negatively impact ibex, but the large herds of migratory livestock did. There were thus different kinds of domestic stock with varying kinds of impacts on wild flora and fauna.[23] High density of livestock and impoverishment of wild prey populations turned out to be the most important cause of the high levels of livestock depredation by snow leopards and wolves, leading to an acute human-wildlife conflict in parts of the landscape.[24] Examining resource use and livestock grazing patterns also implicated poor anti-predatory herding practices as the other cause of livestock depredation.[25] Snow leopards and wolves were killed occasionally in retaliation to livestock depredation by local herders, and officials and defence personnel also engaged in some hunting of ungulates. While much of our research extended over most of Spiti's landscape, a substantial part of our work was also conducted within the confines of the Kibber Wildlife Sanctuary and the Pin Valley National Park. However, the Protected Areas then did not seem to make a difference, either in terms of the status of wildlife, or in terms of the presence and resource use by people, which was prevalent over the entire landscape. Both the problem (livestock versus wild ungulates and livestock depredation by wild carnivores), and the intervention (reducing livestock population and diffusing conflicts) thus had to address the issues beyond the confines of parks and sanctuaries. While livestock continued grazing in the pastures in areas designated protected, the wild animals ranged over areas not under any kind of governmental protection.

Our experience also showed that managing even Protected Areas in the high altitudes using the conventional exclusionary strategy had had limited success, since it has not been possible to exclude human use in any of the high altitude parks, which now cover as much as nine per cent of the Transhimalaya. Every area designated protected in the Transhimalaya and most of the Himalaya has a continuing year round or seasonal presence of humans. There has been some success in the Great Himalayan and Nanda Devi National Parks, but this may have more to do with the fact that both include lower forested tracts within their boundaries. The lower areas in general offer more livelihood alternatives thus enabling villagers to move out. In the high altitudes, as mentioned above, each patch of land is already under some community-based ownership or use, and large scale relocations are difficult and often not needed.[26] Even the existing Protected Areas remain heavily understaffed, often averaging up to 1000 square km to be managed by a single forest frontline staff. In addition, the staff continuously needs to deal with human-wildlife conflicts and enforcement cases from outside the Protected Areas. The usually poor equipment, capacity and motivational levels to work in the difficult mountainous area further compound the problem of efficient wildlife management. The fact that some sanctuaries like Changthang and the Karakorum have unclear boundary demarcation makes any settlement and management planning work even more difficult.

The situation for conservation appeared grim, but there was also hope. The Buddhist beliefs in the area were strong, and there was a certain sense of compassion towards wildlife in the community. The local people's traditional resource use practices reflected some conservation objectives, indicating that sustainable use, even if not achieved adequately, was a community-level desire. Perhaps most importantly, we found that the traditional village administration bodies, which functioned relatively democratically and were mostly not divided on party political lines, were still quite strong and wielded considerable influence on collective resource management decisions.[27] The vibrancy of such institutions enabled us to intervene by working with them. The body of research over the years helped us understand the important threats to wildlife conservation in this landscape, suggested the possible ways forward and identified the stakeholder bodies one would need to work with to effect conservation. Indeed, our subsequent research in other parts of the high altitudes such as Pangi, Ladakh, Sikkim and Arunachal Pradesh, similarly helped identify threats to conservation, means to address human as well as wildlife issues and possible ways forward.[28]

Our research results showed that decreasing the extent of forage competition between wild ungulates and livestock was an important conservation imperative, which could also help in addressing deeper causes of human-carnivore conflicts. Paucity of wild prey is often a factor that exacerbates tensions. The ground reality was that decreasing the livestock population was not feasible as an immediate solution, as at the level of individual families the livestock holdings were not very large, even though at the rangeland level the region was overstocked. Instead, following the traditional practice of leasing out part of the grazing land to nomadic herders, we began to work with the Village Council of Kibber (Spiti) and established a 'village reserve', which would not be grazed by livestock.[29] Initially confined to an area of about 500 ha when it was set up in 2001, the Kibber reserve has since tripled in size. Protecting a part of the village land from livestock grazing and other forms of resource use has, within a few years, contributed to a fourfold increase in the population of bharal and a twofold increase in the small population of ibex nearby.[30] This small but significant step shows how highly focused efforts on ground can enable nature's recovery. This was not a painless transition and there was a concerted effort to address loss of amenity to livestock owners. The closure of livestock grazing was compensated initially for Rs 50,000 a year as a contribution to the community fund that was used for various village developmental and cultural purposes. Our team is further working on linking establishment of reserves to other community based incentive programmes. These will not be limited to just direct cash payments.

While the village reserve protection was on, we also worked with the people of Kibber and a few other villages to establish a community-managed livestock insurance programme, which came to the assistance of families whose livestock was killed by wild carnivores. The reserve complemented this scheme, as with an increase in wild prey damage to domestic stock is likely to decline though not disappear. Further, the insurance programme addressed the issue of conflicts by direct compensation of the losses, but in a manner that was mostly self-managed.[31] Over time, a comprehensive and sustained education and awareness programme was also started. This helped people (as well as our team members) to engage with the genesis of the conflicts better while helping to improve their larger understanding of nature. This is not a scheme or a short term programme but a long term continuous effort based on cooperation to address and reduce human-animal conflict in a shared landscape.

Positive outcomes of efforts like these spurred us on and gave us the confidence that strong community involvement is the only reasonable way to effectively protect our high altitude wildlife. Owing to the increase in wild ungulate population and better herd protection, the level of livestock predation by wild carnivores annually came down from an estimated twelve per cent of the livestock holding in the early 2000s to less than four per cent by 2011. The insurance programme and conservation education initiatives have helped contribute to a greater tolerance and engendered more positive attitudes towards conservation and towards carnivores.[32] Today, five different villages in Spiti and Ladakh have established village reserves of this kind, helping in recovery of species such as the bharal, ibex, argali and Tibetan gazelle, and creating pockets of high prey density for snow leopards and wolves. At the time of writing, the first village reserve of Kibber has been extant for eleven years. The insurance programme has been expanded to ten villages of Spiti and Ladakh, and has now also been piloted in Mongolia by the Snow Leopard Trust. Our conservation education programme has reached out to over thirty schools, 100 teachers, and over 2000 children and youth in fifty villages in Spiti and Ladakh. In Spiti the efforts have covered over sixty per cent of all children since 2007, thus ensuring a substantial and sustained impact in the area. In Mongolia, the Snow Leopard Trust and other partners have been engaged with conservation in the South Gobi region through research, conservation and awareness programmes. It is now evident that conservation beyond parks can also work. Such tracts show not only species recovery, with more prey species and snow leopards, but also the spreading of a more positive attitude among herders towards conservation compared to a strictly Protected Area where their issues are rarely addressed.[33]

Scientific research gave us insights into the kind of interventions that were needed and our relationships with local communities, often based on personal bonds, provided us with the opportunity to experiment with community based conservation. The outcomes of these initiatives in multiple sites gave us the confidence and showed us the need for catalysing a national policy that enabled such science based, landscape level and inclusive conservation efforts. The open and broad view of key decision makers in the union government and equally so at the state government levels was instrumental in taking this initiative forward at a macro scale. From the earliest, officials as well as elected representatives in Arunachal Pradesh, Himachal Pradesh, Jammu and Kashmir, Sikkim and Uttarakhand (and we list them in alphabetical order here) saw this as a positive effort. Given the immense pressures for economic growth and limited financial resources of these hill states, their attempts to adapt, innovate and incorporate new ideas into conservation is commendable. The union government provided a platform and the finances, both vital to begin work.

Emergent Threats from Infrastructure Development

While competition from livestock and human-wildlife conflicts are matters of concern in the region,[34] the emergent threats from developmental projects, defence establishments and changing lifestyles are becoming far more serious. Socioeconomic and developmental pressures contribute to this.

These underdeveloped areas of the Himalaya and Transhimalaya have recently seen a spurt of developmental efforts from both government and the voluntary sectors. The much needed improvements in infrastructure invariably cause disturbances to habitats and bring in poor migratory labourers from outside.[35] Further, poaching for wild meat remains an issue in areas such as Lahaul and Kinnaur in Himachal, Doda, Kargil and the Kashmir Valley in Jammu and Kashmir, upper Uttarakhand and most of Arunachal Pradesh. There have been recent confiscations of illegal wildlife products from the region that include shahtoosh, tiger parts, red sanders and other products, thus increasing the importance of law enforcement in the region.

Because the resident people enjoy a high degree of economic mobility, they often employ migrant labourers for domestic help, cultivation and herding. Our recent surveys from 2012 in Kinnaur have shown that most resident people have not taken livestock herds grazing for over a decade. Virtually all livestock are taken care of by herders hired from lower Himachal Pradesh and Nepal. Many of them are also accomplished hunters. Spiti, with a population of merely about 10,000 people has close to 1,000 labourers from outside, often working on contracts in remote parts of the region.

Some policy changes may have unintended negative impacts on the landscape, wildlife and ecological integrity and legislation like the Border Infrastructure Bill, can also have serious implications for conservation in the region as it would dilute the environmental clearance requirements. Often, some realignments may be enough to safeguard conservation concerns without compromising defence needs. While defence needs are critical, ecological issues do need to be kept in mind to achieve a balance.

The Himalayan river systems are expected to provide over seventy-five per cent of India's hydropower requirements as per the National Electricity Policy of 2005[36], to meet the goal of 1,000 units of per capita power by 2012. The policy sees this as a tool for the development of poor sections of the society in the Himalayan states, particularly in Sikkim and Arunachal Pradesh, which are proposed to contribute over forty per cent of this need. The recent clearance of the Chamoli-GMR hydel project despite opposition by wildlife scientists and a statutory committee, the Forest Advisory Committee, in November 2011 is a case in point.[37] Initially turned down by the same committee after an in-depth study by the Wildlife Institute of India, it was cleared after reconsideration. The project will adversely affect parts of the Nanda Devi Biosphere Reserve. Many of the high altitude areas of the northeastern Himalayan states of Sikkim and Arunachal Pradesh that may have high biodiversity and many surprises in terms of occurrence of species, remain largely unexplored. The situation may be more critical in these ranges from where even preliminary aspects such as previously unknown occurrence of wildlife are just coming to light, and serious threats from both traditional and developmental causes seem to be severe.[38]

While the large people-wildlife interface is expected to generate some conflict, the tolerance level of people for wildlife-caused losses is in a disturbing decline. Given a thriving meat market and the increased value of animals such as pashmina goats and horses, any loss today has an understandably greater impact on a household compared with, say, twenty years ago. With increased job opportunities and increased proportion of nuclear families, there is a dearth of labour to herd livestock effectively, thereby adding to instances of conflict. In areas like Spiti and lower Ladakh, damage to high value cash crops such as green peas and apricots by wildlife causes significant resentment.

The spread of security establishments and tourism facilities in the region not only causes localised damage to wildlife habitats, but may also lead to other significant problems. One such issue is the drastic increase in feral dog population that thrives on garbage and regularly preys upon livestock. Free-ranging dogs are increasingly reported to prey on wild ungulates and compete with or directly attack wild predators including snow leopards.[39] Further, there is a constant influx of dogs that accompany the migratory herders from foothills and possibly bring new diseases that can affect wild carnivores.

The Way Ahead: Going Beyond Borders

Similar to our conservation efforts in Spiti and Ladakh, efforts by the Snow Leopard Conservancy in the Hemis National Park, in Ladakh have resulted in freeing up over 1,000 ha of open rolling steppe habitat, which a population of the Tibetan argali had colonised in the mid-1970s, and the small but stable population is already showing signs of increase in less than three years of management. Recent reports suggest that the population may have doubled after remaining close to just twenty-two for almost thirty years! The argali is one of the rarest animals in South Asia and this commendable effort requires closer study and replication. Owing to these efforts, and those by the Jammu and Kashmir Department of Wildlife Protection, these areas are also seeing an increased presence of predators. Already the communities are able to take advantage of improved wildlife sightings and a hitherto nonexistent wildlife tourism sector is emerging, thus augmenting the income of the local people.

These organisations have also demonstrated suitable conflict mitigation mechanisms. Even though the government has a mechanism of compensation, it is usually difficult to implement, in part because of the widespread and large number of cases of wildlife-caused damage. In any case, the amount of compensation sanctioned by the government authorities is usually much lower than the market price of the livestock lost. These projects by the Snow Leopard Trust and the Snow Leopard Conservancy both demonstrate how better corrals can reduce livestock losses significantly,[40] while community-managed insurance programmes catalysed by the NCF-SLT have helped in efficiently compensating the losses in a decentralised manner. Similar efforts in Pakistan[41] and Nepal[42] have also been successful in reducing monetary losses of herders and have also helped in improving their attitudes.

Though these experiments are all localised in scope, they do hold great promise at a much wider level. Community support combined with a sound understanding of local issues can enable success in high altitude conservation. It is obvious where the path takes us from here—mutually beneficial agreements coupled with comprehensive awareness programmes, which ultimately increase wildlife populations and helps local people with material gains and improved tolerance towards wildlife.

When wildlife is considered an important or at least a significant subject in the larger landscape, other government departments and agencies too need to be consulted and their participation sought in implementing conservation programmes. Often, these agencies may already have environmental concerns in their mandate or carry out activities that are environment friendly.[43] On the flip side, they may also be carrying out activities that may cause damage to the environment or harm wildlife. A recent assessment in Spiti for preparing a management plan for the Upper Spiti Landscape by the NCF and the Himachal Pradesh forest department[44] showed that departments such as horticulture, agriculture and rural development already acknowledge environmental concerns, for instance, through promotion of activities like organic agriculture, fodder supplementation and water conservation. The *Sarva Shiksha Abhiyan* (Universal Literacy Campaign) of the education department wishes to promote environment education as well as hold nature camps for children, while the Himurja (the government department responsible for alternative energy) is covering huge areas under its programmes for alternate sources of energy that include harnessing solar power and micro-hydroelectric projects. The idea of convergence or 'mainstreaming' biodiversity concerns in development is not a new idea, but under the project there are explicit bodies and mechanisms suggested that can help in coordination of efforts. While these structures are important, it is also recognised that core agencies such as the forest departments and other partner voluntary organisations will need to play a key role in persisting with the coordination efforts.

A more detailed analysis shows many other areas of convergences as well as some divergence. Once these are acknowledged and a mechanism of cooperation is put in place, conservation efforts can be made more effective and result in saving precious conservation resources for activities that other agencies are not doing. Rough calculations suggest that over fifty per cent of the normal annual plan of operations of the forest department for conservation work in Spiti consist of activities that can be funded through such departmental cooperation. If this is channelled, conservation funds can be more efficiently used for core activities such as capacity enhancement, managing conflicts, protection and staff motivation. While convergences are desirable and possible, the assessment in Spiti has highlighted the divergences too. These include large scale construction plans, in or near sensitive habitats such as moist meadows, roads through sensitive wildlife areas or into pristine areas that can open up valleys for exploitation and, as said earlier, the influx of outside labour.

Project Snow Leopard has been developed by experts and decision-makers from range states and the Centre, and it hopes to streamline conservation in the larger landscape, including the Protected Areas, in a manner that is landscape-based and participatory. It emphasises the identification of suitable landscapes and provides guidelines for the preparation of scientific management plans for them. The project also sets up a four-tier structure, from the village level up to the national steering committee, through a landscape level committee and a state level society, that will help in planning and implementation of all activities. The structure at all levels aims to be sensitive to all partners, with local village communities playing a key role in conservation efforts. Improved capacity among staff and local volunteers for participatory planning, action and monitoring wildlife form an important part of the scheme.

In a large landscape where wildlife occurs in a continuum, it would thus be ideal to visualise a system like this.

A functional scientific management plan is prepared with due participation by all concerned agencies and community members. A mosaic of well-researched small and large 'cores'—inviolate areas that have higher wildlife values compared to the adjacent valleys—are in place. These are 'socially fenced' and managed with the support of local communities with the objective that the wildlife population remains stable or increases. The 'spillover' of any increasing wildlife population that does take place finds the larger landscape fit to inhabit (as it is already suitable habitat, but may have some disturbances). In these areas, community based conflict mitigation systems that include protection of property, compensation and awareness are already in place. Suitable wildlife and nature based tourism programmes are put in place to augment incomes wherever possible.

Awareness programmes for school children, local youth, officials and others are in place that fosters a better appreciation of the wildlife and better understanding of human-wildlife conflicts. The other government agencies and civil society organisations understand where they are helping with environment and conservation work and this is acknowledged by the conservation agencies too. For any environment unfriendly activities, the participatory structures are used to discuss and find alternatives. The management plans also identify threats posed by local people and find ways of reducing dependence on natural resources and provision of alternative livelihoods. The entire programme is supported by constant knowledge and monitoring-based decisions as a result of research programmes that are encouraged by the establishment. The state level 'society' not only helps in planning and advice, but also helps in channelising resources from the central government and other national and international sources in a timely manner. All facilitators from the nongovernmental organisations, village committees and forest departments have improved capacity for working together on innovative participatory planning and action for the common goal of conservation.

This is how Project Snow Leopard conceives of wildlife conservation. But it faces some challenges. For one, it is a new and untested programme. Given the uncertain nature of official tenure within the government, there is a risk of losing the fundamental philosophy with time. There is a danger that the innovative programme may get trapped in the usual rigid official funding cycles. This may dilute its salient features. In the larger landscape, while the forest department needs to take the lead, and hopefully will have the capacity to lead, eliciting other agencies' cooperation can remain a challenge. However, these issues can all be sorted out, though it will require good cooperation between the government, conservationists and scientists. Indeed, the NCF and the Wildlife Institute of India have recently been appointed as technical organisations to advise the Government of India and the states in all matters related to snow leopard conservation, and in assisting Project Snow Leopard to move forward. The human and institutional challenges are real, but so is the promise and the potential.

With Project Snow Leopard, the primary agencies responsible for conservation in the states and the country now have an alternative model for landscape level, participatory, knowledge based conservation of the great heights of the Himalaya that go far beyond the Protected Area borders. Conservation beyond borders is not wishful thinking in this landscape, but probably the only way forward. Given time, effort and application, there is every reason to believe that it will work.

Notes

1. R. S. Chundawat and Q. Qureshi, *Planning Wildlife Conservation in Leh and Kargil Districts of Ladakh, Jammu and Kashmir* (Dehradun: Wildlife Institute of India, 1999).

2. Ministry of Environment and Forests, *The Project Snow Leopard* (New Delhi: Ministry of Environment and Forests, Government of India, 2008).

3. Project Snow Leopard, *Towards Project Snow Leopard: Report of the national workshop on Project Snow Leopard 10th–11th July, 2006, Leh, Ladakh* (Ministry of Environment and Forests, Government of India, Department of Wildlife Protection, Jammu and Kashmir and Nature Conservation Foundation, International Snow Leopard Trust, Mysore, India, 2006)

4. For example, see V. Thapar, *Land of the Tiger: A natural history of the Indian subcontinent* (Berkeley and Los Angeles: University of California Press, 1998); Saberwal and Rangarajan (eds), *Battles Over Nature*; Shahabuddin and Rangarajan, *Making Conservation Work*; A. Kothari, *Understanding Biodiversity: Life, sustainability, and equity* (New Delhi: Orient Longman, 1997); B. Seshadhri, *The Twilight of India's Wildlife* (London: John Baker, 1969); E. P. Gee, *The Wildlife of India* (London: Fontana, 1964), p. 224.

5. Ministry of Environment and Forests, *The Project Snow Leopard*.

6. G. B. Schaller, *Mountain Monarchs: Wild sheep and goats of the Himalaya* (Chicago: University of Chicago Press, 1977).

7. Global Tiger Initiative Secretariat, *Global Tiger Recovery Program, 2010–2022* (Washington DC: World Bank, 2011) ; E. Sanderson, J. Forrest, C. Loucks, J. Ginsberg, E. Dinerstein, J. Seidensticker, J, Forrest, G. Bryja, A. Heydlauff, S. Klenzendorf, P. Leimgruber, J. Mills, T. G. O'Brien, M. Shrestha, R. Simons and M. Songer, *Setting Priorities for the Conservation and Recovery of Wild Tigers: 2005–2015* (New York and Washington DC: Wildlife Conservation Society, World Wide

Fund For Nature, Smithsonian, NFWF-STF, 2006); R. S. Chundawat, B. Habib, U. Karanth, K. Kawanishi, J. Ahmad Khan, T. Lynam, D. Miquelle, P. Nyhus, S. Sunarto, R. Tilson and S. Wang, '*Panthera tigris*' in: IUCN, *IUCN Red List of Threatened Species, version 2013.2.* Available at www.iucnredlist.org (accessed 7 May 2014).

8. T. McCarthy, K. Murray, K. Sharma and O. Johansson, 'Preliminary results of a long-term study of snow leopards in South Gobi, Mongolia', *Cat News* 53 (2010): 15–19.

9. T. McCarthy, J. Khan, J. Ud-Din and K. McCarthy, 'First study of snow leopards using GPS-satellite collars underway in Pakistan', *Cat News* 46 (2007): 22–23.

10. Ghotge and Ramdas, this volume.

11. Ministry of Environment and Forests, *The Project Snow Leopard.*

12. M. Rangarajan, A. Desai, D. S. Vincent, et al., *Gajah*; R. Sukumar, *The Asian Elephant: Ecology and management* (Cambridge: Cambridge University Press, 1993).

13. K. U. Karanth, *The Way of the Tiger: Natural history and conservation of the endangered big cat* (Stillwater, USA: Voyageur Press, 2001); Y. V. Jhala, Q. Qureshi and P. R. Sinha, *Status of Tigers, Co-predators and Prey in India* (New Delhi and Dehradun: National Tiger Conservation Authority, Government of India, and the Wildlife Institute of India, 2011); J. S. C. Seidensticker, S. Christie and P. Jackson, 'Preface' in J. Seidensticker, S. Christie and P. Jackson (eds), *Riding the Tiger: Tiger conservation in human-dominated landscapes* (Cambridge, UK: Cambridge University Press, 1999).

14. Chundawat and Qureshi, *Planning wildlife conservation in Leh and Kargil*; Y. V. Bhatnagar and R. Wangchuk, 'Status survey of large mammals in eastern Ladakh and Nubra. Conservation biodiversity in the Trans-Himalaya: New initiatives for field conservation in Ladakh (Dehradun: Wildlife Institute of India, 2001); Y. V. Bhatnagar, V. B. Mathur and T. McCarthy, 'A regional perspective for snow leopard conservation in the Indian Trans-Himalaya' in Y. V. Bhatnagar, and S. E. Sathyakumar (eds), *WII ENVIS Bulletin* (Dehradun: Wildlife Institute of India, 2003); C. Mishra, P. Allen, T. McCarthy, M. D. Madhusudan, A. Bayarjargal and H. H. T. Prins, 'The role of incentive programs in conserving the snow leopard', *Conservation Biology* 17 (2003): 1512–20.

15. Y. V. Bhatnagar, 'Ranging and Habitat Use by Himalayan Ibex (*Capra ibex sibirica*) in Pin Valley National Park' (PhD thesis, Saurashtra University, Rajkot, India, 1997).

16. C. Mishra, H. H. T. Prins and S. E. Van Wieren, 'Diversity, risk mediation, and change in a Trans-Himalayan agropastoral system', *Human Ecology* 31 (2003): 595–609.

17. C. Mishra, 'Livestock depredation by large carnivores in the Indian Trans-Himalaya: Conflict perceptions and conservation prospects', *Environmental Conservation* 24 (1997): 338–43; Y. V. Bhatnagar, R. Wangchuk and R. Jackson, *A Survey of Depredation and Related Human-Wildlife Conflicts in Hemis National Park, Ladakh, Jammu and Kashmir* (Seattle, WA, USA.: International Snow Leopard

Trust, 1999); S. Bagchi and C. Mishra, 'Living with large carnivores: Predation on livestock by the snow leopard (*Uncia uncia*)', *Journal of Zoology* 268 (2006): 217–24.

18. Y. V. Bhatnagar, G. S. Rawat, A. J. T. Johnsingh and M. Stuwe, 'Ecological separation between ibex and resident livestock in a Trans-Himalayan Protected Area', *Grassland Ecology and Management in Protected Areas of Nepal* 3 (2000): 70–84; C. Mishra, 'High altitude survival: Conflicts between pastoralism and wildlife in the Trans-Himalaya' (PhD thesis, Wageningen University, Wageningen, Netherlands, 2001); C. Mishra, H. Prins and S. E. Van Wieren, 'Overstocking in the Trans-Himalayan rangelands of India', *Environmental Conservation* 28 (2001): 279–83.

19. Mishra, et al., 'Diversity, risk mediation'; C. Mishra, 'Socioeconomic transition and wildlife conservation in the Indian Trans-Himalaya', *Journal of the Bombay Natural History Society* 97 (2000): 25–32; T. Namgail, Y. V. Bhatnagar, C. Mishra and S. Bagchi, 'Pastoral nomads of the Indian Changthang: Production system, landuse and socio-economic changes', *Human Ecology* 35 (2007): 497–504; Y. V. Bhatnagar and N. J. Singh, 'Nomadism in the Indian Changthang: Changes and implications on society and biodiversity' in K. G. Saxana, L. Liang and X. Xue (eds), *Global Change, Biodiversity and Livelihoods in Cold Desert Regions of Asia*, (Dehradun: Bishen Singh Mahendra Pal Singh, 2011), pp. 135–46.

20. Mishra, et al., 'Overstocking'.

21. S. Bagchi, C. Mishra and Y. V. Bhatnagar, 'Conflicts between traditional pastoralism and conservation of Himalayan ibex (*Capra sibirica*) in the Trans-Himalayan mountains, *Animal Conservation* 7 (2004): 121–28; C. Mishra, S. E. Van Wieren, P. Ketner, I. Heitkönig and H. H. T. Prins, 'Competition between domestic livestock and wild bharal *Pseudois nayaur* in the Indian Trans-Himalaya', *Journal of Applied Ecology* 41 (2004): 344–54.

22. C. Mishra, S. E. Wieren, I. Heitkönig and H. H. T. Prins, 'A theoretical analysis of competitive exclusion in a Trans-Himalayan large-herbivore assemblage', *Animal Conservation* 5 (2002): 251–58.

23. Bhatnagar, *Ranging and Habitat* Use; Bagchi, et al., 'Conflicts between traditional pastoralism'; Y. V. Bhatnagar, G. S. Rawat, A. J. T. Johnsingh and S. Michael, 'Ecological separation between ibex and resident livestock in a Trans-Himalayan Protected Area' in C. Richard, K. Basent, J. P. Sah and Y. Raut (eds), *Grassland Ecology and Management in Protected Areas of Nepal. Volume 2. Technical and status papers on grasslands of mountain Protected Areas. Royal Bardia National Park, Thakurwara, Bardia, Nepal* (Kathmandu: ICIMOD, 2000), pp. 71–84.

24. Mishra, 'Livestock depradation'; Bagchi and Mishra, 'Living with large carnivores'.

25. Mishra, et al., 'The role of incentive programs'.

26. Y.V. Bhatnagar, 'Relocation from wildlife reserves in the Greater and Trans-Himalayas: Is it necessary?' *Conservation and Society* 6 (2008): 263.

27. Mishra, 'Livestock depredation'.

28. For examples, see Y. V. Bhatnagar, R. Wangchuk and C. Mishra, 'Decline of the Tibetan gazelle *Procapra picticaudata* in Ladakh, India', *Oryx* 40 (2006): 229–32;

C. Mishra, M. D. Madhusudan and A. Datta, 'Mammals of the high altitudes of western Arunachal Pradesh, eastern Himalaya: An assessment of threats and conservation needs', *Oryx* 40 (2006): 29–35; T. Namgail, S. Bagchi, C. Mishra and Y.V. Bhatnagar, 'Distributional correlates of the Tibetan gazelle *Procapra picticaudata* in Ladakh, northern India: Towards a recovery programme', *Oryx* 42 (2008): 107–12; TMI-NCF, 'Non-invasive monitoring to support local stewardship of snow leopards and their prey', submitted to Critical Ecosystem Partnership Fund (CEPF) and Ashoka Trust for Research in ecology and the Environment (ATREE), (2010).

29. Mishra, et al., 'Diversity, risk mediation'.

30. C. Mishra, S. Bagchi, T. Namgail and Y. V. Bhatnagar, 'Multiple use of Trans-Himalayan rangelands: Reconciling human livelihoods with wildlife conservation' in J. T. Du Toit, R. Kock and J. Deutsch (eds), *Wild Rangelands: Conserving wildlife while maintaining livestock in semi-arid ecosystems* (London: Wiley-Blackwell, 2010), pp. 291–311.

31. P. Trivedi, 'Heights of success: Conservation success at the high altitudes', *Hornbill* (2006): 36–40.

32. Bagchi and Mishra, 'Living with large carnivores'.

33. L. Purevjav, 'Snow leopard site occupancy survey in South Gobi, Mongolia' (PhD thesis, University of Minnesota, USA, 2011); B. Mijiddorj, *Pastoral Practice and Herders' Attitude Towards Wildlife in South Gobi, Mongolia* (Rajkot: Saurashtra University, 2011).

34. Mishra, et al., 'The role of incentive programs'; Mishra, 'Livestock depredation'; M. K. Oli, I. R. Taylor and M. E. Rogers, 'Snow leopard (*Panthera uncia*) predation of livestock: An assessment of local perceptions in the Annapurna Conservation Area, Nepal', *Biological Conservation* 68 (1994): 63–68; R. M. Jackson and R. Wangchuk, 'A community-based approach to mitigating livestock depredation by snow leopards', *Human Dimensions of Wildlife* 9 (2004): 1–16; T. Namgail, Y. V. Bhatnagar and J. L. Fox, 'Carnivore-caused livestock mortality in Trans-Himalaya', *Environmental Management* 39 (2007): 490–96; S. Hussain, 'The status of the snow leopard in Pakistan and its conflict with local farmers', *Oryx* 37 (2003): 26–33; N. Ikeda, 'Economic impacts of livestock depredation by snow leopard *Uncia uncia* in the Kanchenjunga Conservation Area, Nepal Himalaya', *Environmental Conservation* 31 (2004): 322–30; C. Mishra and A. Fitzherbert, 'War and wildlife: A post-conflict assessment of Afghanistan's Wakhan Corridor', *Oryx* 38 (2004).

35. Y.V. Bhatnagar, 'Relocation from wildlife reserves'.

36. Available at http://www.cea.nic.in/reports/national_elec_policy.pdf (accessed 7 May 2014)

37. Available at http://www.hindustantimes.com/India-news/NewDelhi/Rejected-by-panel-hydro-project-gets-ministry-nod/Article1-777909.aspx (accessed 7 May 2014).

38. Mishra, Madhusudan and Datta, 'Mammals of the high altitudes'; TMI-NCF, 'Non-invasive monitoring'; S. Sathyakumar, T. Bashir, T. Bhattacharya and K. Poudyal, 'Assessing mammal distribution and abundance in intricate eastern

Himalayan habitats of Khangchendzonga, Sikkim, India', *Mammalia* 75 (2011): 257–68.

39. A. Ghoshal, 'Wild blames wild', *Care4nature* (2011): 26–28.

40. Jackson and Wangchuk, 'A community-based approach'; R. Jackson and R. Wangchuk, 'Linking snow leopard conservation and people-wildlife conflict resolution: Grassroots measures to protect the endangered snow leopard from herder retribution', *Endangered Species Update* 18 (2001): 138–41.

41. Hussain, 'The status of the snow leopard'; S. Hussain, 'Protecting the snow leopard and enhancing farmers' livelihoods: A pilot insurance scheme in Baltistan', *Mountain Research and Development* 20 (2000): 226–31.

42. Ikeda, 'Economic impacts'; G. S. Gurung, K. Thapa, K. Kunkel, G. J. Thapa, M. Kollmair and U. M. Boeker, 'Enhancing herders' livelihood and conserving the snow leopard in Nepal', *Cat News* 55 (2011): 17–21.

43. Ministry of Environment and Forests, 'The Project Snow Leopard'.

44. Anonymous, *Management Plan for the Upper Spiti Landscape Including the Kibber Wildlife Sanctuary* (Mysore: Wildlife Wing, Himachal Pradesh Forest Department & Nature Conservation Foundation, 2011).

Eight
RESTORING NATURE
Wildlife Conservation in Landscapes Fragmented by Plantation Crops in India

Divya Mudappa, M. Ananda Kumar and T. R. Shankar Raman

Introduction: Conservation and the Countryside

Agricultural expansion has historically been a major global cause for the loss and fragmentation of natural ecosystems, and remains one of the largest threats to the world's remaining tropical forests today.[1] In tropical regions, conservation concerns have arisen over the implications of the anticipated increase in the area under agriculture by as much as twenty-five per cent.[2] Concomitant with biodiversity loss due to extinctions,[3] the loss of tropical forests may lead to decrease in ecosystem services of great value to humanity such as carbon storage in biomass and soils, watershed regulation and rainfall, modulation of climate and river flows, and amelioration of infectious disease and human-wildlife conflicts.[4] The primary conservation response to such trends has been the creation of Protected Areas such as National Parks, sanctuaries and nature reserves with restrictions on resource use to protect threatened species and ecosystems. Over 1,00,000 Protected Areas covering roughly 18.8 million square km (or twelve per cent of the earth's terrestrial surface area) have been set aside worldwide to preserve natural areas under various management regimes.[5]

Still, most Protected Areas are relatively small (over fifty-eight per cent are less than 10 square km), continue to face internal and external threats and remain susceptible to influences from surrounding landscapes.[6] These include habitat loss, conversion to other land uses, fragmentation and degradation, spread of invasive species, hunting, timber logging, disruption of animal corridors, unregulated harvest of forest products, fires, tourism and various developmental activities. Even when deforestation within Protected Areas is curtailed, surrounding areas continue to face forest loss and conversion, further isolating these parks and highlighting the need for a broader conservation approach that considers surrounding landscapes, poverty and livelihoods, and unsustainable land-uses.[7] There is now global interest in these surrounding landscapes, including those with resident or itinerant people and agriculture. They have the potential to complement wildlife conservation in Protected Areas by preserving the habitats adjoining them, increasing landscape level connectivity of patches and restoring degraded areas.[8]

Considerable biological diversity also exists outside the boundaries of designated conservation areas in human-modified habitats and secondary forests. The assessment of conservation values and forms or practices of land use that sustain higher levels of native biodiversity in the landscape of productive agriculture and protected or restored natural areas has been termed 'countryside biogeography' and has stimulated much recent research.[9] In tropical forest regions, numerous studies have focused on tropical agroforestry crops and commodity plantations such as coffee, cocoa, tea, rubber, oil palm, cardamom and vanilla, which occupy large areas in regions of high conservation significance. Frequently, plantations adjoin protected conservation reserves or contain embedded remnants of forests or other natural ecosystems known to be significant for conservation of biological diversity.[10] These studies seek to understand the conservation values of various plantations relative to unaltered forests in Protected Areas, identify better production or cultivation practices, potential costs and conflicts, as well as economic and ecosystem service benefits accruing to plantations from conservation. In this essay, we examine the context of conservation in landscapes with plantations and Protected Areas, taking the specific case of a region of great global and regional conservation significance: the Western Ghats range of mountains in India, a global biodiversity hotspot[11] and World Heritage Site, containing some of the world's most irreplaceable Protected Areas for species at risk of extinction.[12] We highlight research findings and ongoing interventions relevant to extending conservation beyond borders into plantation landscapes.

Plantations and Conservation in the Tropics

In the context of forests and conservation, the word 'plantation' often appears in the term 'plantation forests' established for timber and fuel wood, and 'plantation crops' such as tea, coffee, cocoa, rubber and oil palm. Plantation forests established through various forestry practices, often as monocultures of a small number of alien and native species, occupy some 140 million ha (c. 3.5 per cent of the world forest area) and are increasing annually by about 2–3 million ha (two per cent), even as world forest cover is in decline.[13] Keeping plantation forests outside the scope of this essay, we examine here some tropical commodity crops in terms of their conservation values relative to unaltered forests in Protected Areas, potential benefits and conflicts of such cultivation, and better production or cultivation practices.

Tropical plantation crops are globally significant for conservation because of the area they occupy, location in significant biodiversity hotspots, and land-use practices. For instance, globally, around 11 million ha is under coffee cultivation, almost entirely in tropical forest regions.[14] With an annual value of over $100 billion, coffee is the second highest traded commodity in international trade after oil, making assessment of its impacts on biodiversity imperative.[15] Traditional coffee growing areas also coincide closely with many of the global biodiversity hotspots.[16] Tea cultivation spans 2.3 million ha around the world, and conservation concerns include conventional cultivation as intensive monocultures, soil erosion and agrochemical inputs.[17] Similarly, cocoa is grown in over 7.5 million ha worldwide (principally in Africa and Brazil and

Mesoamerica), while cardamom is primarily cultivated in tropical forest areas, with the leading producing countries being Guatemala and India. A major conservation concern in recent years is the expansion and impact of oil palm (*Elaeis guineensis* and *E. oleifera*) in tropical forests, especially in South East Asia, with concomitant deforestation, loss of biodiversity, climate change impacts, and other social and environmental concerns.[18] Palm oil is a key commodity in intra-Asian trade and India is a major consumer of South East Asian edible oils.

Scenario in the Western Ghats

Around fifteen per cent of the land area of the Western Ghats currently receives some protection within sixty-eight wildlife sanctuaries and twenty national parks.[19] This region, occupying some 1,80,000 square km, holds about thirty per cent of India's plant and vertebrate species diversity in less than six per cent of its area.[20]

The Western Ghats faces continued forest loss, degradation and fragmentation, and only around a third of the area contains some form of natural vegetation. Menon and Bawa estimated that between 1920 and 1990, forest cover in the Western Ghats declined by forty per cent due to agriculture, plantations, hydroelectric projects and other activities, resulting in a fourfold increase in the number of fragments and an eighty-three per cent reduction in size of forest patches.[21] Similarly, Jha, Dutt and Bawa estimated that in a 40,000 square km area of the southern Western Ghats, 25.6 per cent of the forest cover was lost between 1973 and 1995, giving an annual deforestation rate of 1.16 per cent.[22] Large scale conversion to tea, coffee and other plantations had already occurred in many areas prior to 1920.[23] The substantial (and increasing) area under commercial plantations, adjoining key tropical forest conservation areas in the Western Ghats, is a matter of conservation concern (see Appendix).

Over the last two decades, much research has revealed the impact of plantations on biodiversity, and conversely, the conservation value of such plantations in the Western Ghats.[24] Some of the key findings are summarised below, with an emphasis on research on bird communities. The insights from these scholars make us critically re-examine a common view that plantations are ecological deserts or dead zones. Their distinct human-crafted ecosystems deserve a closer look as do cultivated spaces or pastures.[25]

The most striking effect of plantations is to cause habitat fragmentation, thereby leading to isolated populations and some local extinctions of species, especially if the remnants are not large enough to sustain individuals or groups of species such as primates.[26] Habitat degradation to more open, deciduous or secondary vegetation occurs due to human extraction of firewood and other forest products or the gradual replacement of mature forest species by pioneer, widespread and common species,[27] or spread of invasive alien species.[28] At the community level, even if the number of species (species richness) or overall abundance of taxa such as birds does not vary much between forests and plantations, there is invariably substantial alteration of species composition (identity of species that occur and their abundance) in these modified habitats. For instance, Bhagwat, et al. report that while plantations may hold between sixty-four per cent and 139 per cent of the number of species seen in forest reference sites, the compositional similarity with forest was lower at between twenty-five to sixty per cent.[29] As in other tropical regions,[30] when mature tropical rainforest is converted into plantations such as tea and coffee, species that are more common or widespread across a larger region gain ground, while range restricted or endemic species decline or disappear as they are less tolerant to alteration of the dense, closed canopy environment.[31] The extent of alteration in animal community composition is in turn related to the magnitude of change in the natural vegetation (e.g., forest) when plantations are established, as intensification of land use is accompanied by structural simplification of habitat.[32] In the Anamalai hills, Western Ghats, the proportion of rainforest bird species in the community increased from less than forty-three per cent in the open monoculture tea plantations[33] to fifty-nine per cent in shade coffee plantations with moderate tree cover to ninety per cent in rustic cardamom planted under denser shade of native rainforest trees.[34] In the Western Ghats of Karnataka, ninety per cent of bird species associated with regional forests also occurred in areca nut plantations.[35] Cardamom, coffee and areca nut plantations thus seem to hold more species, partly due to the extensive use of shade trees including native tree species, than is the case in more severely modified land use of tea plantations. However, such comparisons based on species presence still need to be complemented by analysing differences in abundance and breeding.[36] There has been little study of the effects of plantations such as rubber and oil palm on biological diversity in the Western Ghats, although a study from Thailand showed that rubber and oil palm plantations can have significant detrimental effects on biological diversity, especially species restricted to mature lowland forests.[37] Oil palm, because of the serious deforestation related concerns over this crop in South East Asia, has been the focus of many studies that have established its serious impacts on biological diversity, climate and implications for social justice.[38]

Plantations, usually under private ownership or lease, in the Western Ghats contain a large number of natural habitat remnants including rainforest fragments, shola grasslands and streams, which have considerable conservation value as refuges of biodiversity, including many charismatic and globally endangered and endemic species.[39] The fragments are important also as corridors for wide ranging species that move between surrounding wildlife sanctuaries across the fragmented landscape.[40] The more plantations are structurally and floristically similar to forests, the more similar they are in their animal community composition with forest.[41] Several studies have shown that plantations such as coffee and cardamom, which use native shade tree species, help support many forest species and act as a buffer habitat in the wider landscape context of cultivated areas, habitat remnants and Protected Areas.[42]

Besides differences in habitat structure or floristics, landscape context also matters: forest patches and plantations influence each other. For instance, while bird species richness and abundance in coffee plantations in Karnataka increases with increase in basal area of native tree species, it declines with increasing distance of the plantation from contiguous forest.[43] Plantations such as coffee that adjoin or are closer to forest patches may have enhanced conservation value for taxa such as birds,[44] even as the buffering role of shade coffee plantations around fragments may enable enhanced persistence of forest bird populations.[45] Still, many species are restricted to forests and will survive only if existing remnant forests such as Reserved Forests, Protected Areas, rainforest fragments and sacred groves are also protected in the landscape.[46] Thus, besides native shade trees, food resources, habitat and canopy connectivity in plantations, retention of forests in the wider landscape is essential to support large populations of sensitive species and increase the conservation potential of remnant habitats at the landscape level.[47] Presence of natural habitat fragments within plantations, control of wildlife poaching, maintenance of native shade tree cover, ability of species to use the plantation matrix itself as habitat or for movement—all of this contributes to the conservation values of plantation landscapes and persistence of many wildlife species in plantations.

Plantations and Human-Wildlife Conflict

Plantation landscapes in the Western Ghats often adjoin or occur as enclaves within wildlife Protected Areas. This interface brings wide ranging animals such as Asian elephants (*Elephas maximus*) and leopards (*Panthera pardus*) into greater contact with people and production landscapes. The presence of such species is pervasive, often with little or no conflict. Conflicts occur when there is damage or threat to the economy, livelihood and safety of people, or incidents leading to injury or death of wildlife. Understanding the nature of conflict and the species involved is necessary to identify preventive and mitigating actions and promote coexistence of people and wildlife.

In tea and coffee plantation landscapes, conflicts between people and elephants occur in the form of crop and property damage, injury and loss of lives.[48] However, there remains scope for coexistence between elephants and production as shown by studies of elephant movement, habitat use and conflict with people in these landscapes. In the Anamalai hills, Kumar, et al. tracked movements of elephant herds through a landscape dominated by tea plantations, with coffee, eucalyptus and interspersed natural vegetation in the form of rainforest fragments and riparian vegetation.[49] Although these natural vegetation remnants occupied a small fraction (less than five per cent) of the 220 square km landscape, elephants strongly preferred riparian vegetation and rainforest fragments (thirty-three per cent of observed elephant locations). Elephants avoided (in relation to area available) large tea monocultures and human settlements, particularly during the day, and used tea plantations more by night to move between natural refuges of riparian and remnant forests. Elephants use plantations as habitat not due to preference or attraction, but because plantations provide some resources.

In the coffee dominated landscape of Kodagu, Karnataka, area under coffee cultivation doubled over thirty years.[50] Elephants may enter coffee estates due to presence of palatable food such as rice paddies and fruit trees, and perennial water sources including artificial water bodies.[51] Bal, et al. argue that conflict mitigation must be based on stakeholders' awareness of the true nature of the problem and a combination of adaptive management strategies.[52] In addition, they call for better transparency in decision-making and solutions that increase public tolerance of elephants, possibly through provision of direct benefits, in such plantations. Still, smallholders in this landscape, who face higher costs and disincentives from conflict, hold positive attitudes towards conservation and express willingness to engage with participatory efforts and more decentralised government institutions.[53]

For leopards, different approaches may be required. The leopard is a wide ranging solitary and territorial carnivore, highly adaptable to changes in habitat and is known to live in close vicinity of human habitations, which sometimes leads to conflicts.[54] Leopards may also be attracted to human use areas, because of stray dogs, goats and cattle, and improper waste disposal, leading to incidence of injuries or fatal attacks on humans as well. Capture and translocation of so called 'problem leopards' is used as a management tool, often due to public pressure and media attention following leopard attacks on people. Recent research suggests however that such capture and translocation may actually increase conflicts at release sites (shifting conflict with the individual) or intervening areas (due to strong homing instinct of carnivores), and possibly increase density of leopards at the capture site due to vacant territories being filled by new individuals.[55] Leopard populations can persist in agricultural landscapes with little or no conflict if such improper management measures are avoided. Instead, efforts to proactively prevent conflict are required, such as better livestock herding and corrals, and basic precautionary measures in areas where people and leopards share spaces.[56]

In the plantation dominated Valparai plateau landscape surrounded by Protected Areas, large carnivores (mainly leopards) predominantly preyed upon available wild prey.[57] Over a three year period (2008–2010), thirty-two head of livestock (of a population of around 2,000 cows, buffalos and goats) were reported by respondents as lost to carnivore depredation. Over the same period, there were eight attacks on people, resulting in three fatalities (all children). To those households that kept livestock (less than five per cent of total households), livestock depredation was perceived to cause an estimated loss of thirteen per cent of the annual household income. People's attitudes toward leopards were not affected by monetary losses; however, in colonies where people were injured or killed by leopards, people held a negative attitude towards the species.

Clearly, if conservation is to extend into plantation landscapes the issue of conflict incidence needs to be squarely addressed. Measures need to be implemented based on scientific understanding of the landscape and social context, the patterns and magnitude of conflict, and the ecological and behavioural traits of the species concerned. A number of initiatives are currently being implemented in plantation landscapes, which appear to hold potential to positively involve plantations, local communities and government departments in conservation.[58]

Involving Plantations in Conservation

In the absence of adequate recognition, protection or habitat restoration, areas of conservation value in and around plantations continue to face threats, degradation and several other problems common to fragmented tropical landscapes.[59] Despite their considerable extent (more than 10,000 square km), plantation landscapes in the Western Ghats have seldom been directly incorporated in conservation policy and management. In this section, we describe efforts to involve plantations in conservation through the following interventions in plantation lands: 1) habitat restoration and native shade tree use, 2) fostering sustainable land use practices linked to certification, and 3) proactively minimising conflicts.

As the retention of existing forest remnants within plantations and enhancing habitat quality through ecological restoration and native shade tree use can have positive effects on biodiversity, these are essential components of wildlife conservation in private lands. Such a programme to restore degraded rainforest fragments within private plantations has been underway in the Anamalai hills, Western Ghats, in partnership with tea and coffee companies since 2001.[60] Until 2012, this effort has focused on ten rainforest fragments (sized between one and 100 ha), three sites contiguous with the Anamalai Tiger Reserve and one perennial stream in tea plantation, all identified and protected with support of plantation companies (Parry Agro Industries Ltd, Tata Coffee Ltd, Tea Estates India Ltd) and the Tamil Nadu Forest Department. While the total area of the sites is around 300 ha, restoration plantings targeted forty-five plots (with a total area of 50 ha) in the most degraded portions, especially fragment edges. Around 26,500 saplings of over 160 native rainforest tree and some liana species have been planted in these sites. Early monitoring showed that at the end of a two year period, sapling survival averaged around sixty-one per cent across forty-four species studied.[61] In early sites, many saplings of some particularly fast growing species (such as *Vernonia arborea*, *Bischofia javanica*, *Elaeocarpus tuberculatus* and *E. munronii*) have already attained tree dimensions with girths of over 30 cm at breast height (1.3 m from ground) and heights of over 6–8 m. This work has clearly established the possibility, potential and protocols for ecological restoration of degraded rainforest across a range of degraded sites, ranging from open grassy meadows, sites under erstwhile plantations of eucalyptus, sites invaded by alien species such as *Lantana camara*, *Mikania micrantha* and *Chromolaena odorata*, and other degraded rainforests and streamsides. Using developed protocols, such restoration can be applied to different areas in similar landscapes, which is likely to help conserve wildlife and watersheds and minimise human-wildlife conflicts in the long run.[62]

Restoration of rainforest fragments should ideally be complemented by enhancing land use practices, particularly involving tree cover, within the surrounding matrix of plantations. In the Anamalai hills, our experience has demonstrated that a large number of native tree species hold potential for use as shade trees in plantations, but have been hitherto ignored or seldom formally tried out. Between 2004 and 2012, over 12,300 saplings of sixty native rainforest tree species were supplied to and planted in coffee, vanilla and tea plantations (only five species in the latter). Observations suggest that in vanilla and cardamom plantations, most of these species do well, grow reasonably fast and provide suitable shade, while in tea plantations, at least two native species (of the five) appear as well suited or preferable to the conventionally used alien silver oak (*Grevillea robusta*). Similarly, research has shown that some native tree species may be superior to silver oak as shade in coffee plantations in southern India.[63] It is also increasingly evident that in the Western Ghats, use of native shade trees and presence of forests in the landscape can have direct benefits to farmers through enhanced pollination, yield and pest control services, particularly in crops such as coffee.[64] More research and trials using native shade tree species are needed, which requires the involvement of plantation crop research institutes and institutions such as United Planters' Association of South India (UPASI) and coffee and tea boards that can transmit research findings to planters for wider adoption in field practices. There is also a need for state and central governments to foster the use of native species and modify permit systems to allow planters to lop trees and carry out crop shade regulation. Presently, one of the reasons that planters seldom plant or use native shade tree species is the fear that they will never be permitted by the forest department authorities to fell or lop branches of native species to regulate shade.

Does Certification Provide a Way Forward?

In tropical plantations, can businesses and small farmers become involved in conservation and sustainability, where sustainability represents a triple bottomline of social, environmental and economic concerns? In more catchy terms, can plantations meld people, planet and profit? One approach to this is through certification of plantation business and produce, linked to growing markets for ethically and sustainably produced commodities. Certification has been criticised for the standards it uses (or fails to use), the reliability of the independent third party audit systems, as a non-tariff trade barrier and as costly for producers, but nevertheless remains the most extensive extant incentive system for sustainability in the plantation sector.

A variety of certification schemes is available, each with its own focus and limitations. This includes organic certification (emphasis on avoidance of chemicals for health and environmental reasons), Fair Trade certification (emphasis on social issues, worker welfare and safety), Utz Capeh (social and environmental concerns, but lax in criteria) and others (such as Ethical Tea Partnership, Starbucks's Cafe Practices, 4C Code of Conduct and Nespresso AAA Sustainable Quality Program in Coffee) evaluated on farms through self-assessment questionnaires or possibly third party 'verification'. However, these schemes are generally weak on environment and wildlife criteria. The Smithsonian Bird-Friendly Coffee Certification is strong on stipulating organic agriculture and specific conditions related to shade tree cover but ignores other aspects of sustainability such as the hunting of wildlife and social welfare. Rainforest Alliance (RA) certification, perhaps the largest certification programme in tea and coffee plantations at present, includes social, environmental and economic criteria in a set of standards for individual farms or groups developed by a network on nonprofit organisations, called the Sustainable Agriculture Network (SAN).[65] Farms that meet required criteria, screened by third party auditors, can become Rainforest Alliance Certified™ and apply for use of the 'frog' seal on packets and bags to market their produce.

Since 2007, the authors engaged with RA (and NCF also became a member of SAN in 2009) to work to raise awareness on better social, environmental, and land use practices, especially those pertaining to ecosystems, wildlife, soil and water, based on adoption of the SAN Sustainable Agriculture Standard, linked to market benefits for producers from RA certification.[66] Social aspects, including workers rights, freedom, welfare, and living and working conditions, continue to remain vital concerns in India's plantations, requiring attention in sustainability efforts, but these are outside the scope of this essay.

Under the SAN Standard, in certified farms, critical criteria prohibit hunting of wildlife, destruction of high value ecosystems and pollution of water bodies. Other criteria require certified farms to retain all existing natural ecosystems, plant native shade trees (at least twelve species per hectare in coffee and agroforestry crops), and retain animal corridors and habitat connectivity through plantations. These measures are in consonance with research cited earlier on the values of plantations for conservation and vice versa. Additional criteria on human-wildlife coexistence are proposed for inclusion in the 2014 version of the SAN Standard. These require farms to be aware of potential conflict species and design and deploy proactive prevention and emergency response measures appropriate for those species. Instead of detrimental reactive responses such as blocking or deflecting movements of animals such as elephants, or capture, translocation and lynching of wildlife such as leopards, proactive measures need to prevent or minimise conflict incidence. These include improving livestock corrals, restricting the use of barriers and fences to sensitive property and housing areas, installing early-warning systems to detect wildlife entry before damage is caused, avoiding wildlife deaths due to farm infrastructure (deep drainage ditches, illegal electrified fences), and cooperating with state authorities in neighbouring Protected Areas in implementing wildlife management plans in the wider landscape.

Through stakeholder consultation and outreach, aspects related to conservation were also discussed and disseminated widely in the plantation sector in numerous training events, workshops, presentations, field audits, posters, detailed local interpretation guidelines document, and a comprehensive website and visual guide on sustainable agriculture in tea and coffee.[67] As a result, some plantations began reaching out to regional civil society organisations (e.g., Keystone Foundation in the Nilgiris, Ecosystems India in Assam) for issues such as wildlife inventory, ecosystems protection, sourcing native shade tree seedlings and waste management. Since 2008, several estates applied for certification, underwent certification or recertification audits and became Rainforest Alliance certified (e.g., Valparai Coffee of Tata Coffee Ltd, a large estate with seventeen rainforest fragments adjoining the Anamalai Tiger Reserve). Commitments from global buyers such as Unilever, Tetley and Kraft, spurred the growing market for certified tea and coffee. By December 2013, the certified operations had expanded to include twenty-two farms and thirty-one groups occupying 1,04,605 ha (c. 72,000 ha in actual production), primarily tea and coffee plantations and limited pepper and cardamom, in southern and eastern India. Although certified produce from these farms have started appearing in foreign markets, the effects of changes due to certification on conservation at the ground level remain to be seen. There have been no targeted studies so far exploring the economic or ecological benefits from certification in Indian farms and many problematic issues remain (see Appendix). Also, because a large volume of Indian tea and coffee is sold for domestic consumption, often in auctions, certification is of little interest to many companies particularly in southern India, due to lack of domestic awareness of the sustainability issues and low domestic demand for certified produce.

Living with Wildlife: From Conflict to Coexistence

Several science based conservation efforts appear to hold promise in reducing incidence of conflicts between people and wildlife in plantation landscapes. For instance, in the Valparai plateau in the Anamalai hills, conflicts between people and elephants are mainly in the form of property damage in food storage areas, with most incident locations centred in the middle of the plateau and some specific locations repeatedly damaged by elephants.[68] This suggested that targeted measures at food storage locations can help reduce conflicts. Several food storage sites were shifted, patterns of storage changed, and buildings insured by plantations and government authorities, leading to reduced costs and incidence of damage in subsequent years.

The major concern in human-elephant conflict in plantation areas is the loss of human life due to elephants. In the Valparai plantations between 1994 and 2012, a total of thirty-seven people lost their lives in unexpected encounters with elephants. A majority (sixty-five per cent) of the deaths occurred over a three month period between December and February and many (twenty-five per cent) occurred in a small area (Ryan division of TANTEA [Tamil Nadu Tea Plantation Corporation]). This suggested that providing early warning systems for local people of elephant movement can help reduce conflict incidents while allowing elephant movement through the larger landscape.[69] We therefore set up an 'information network' to communicate about elephant presence to people in order to avoid fatal encounters with elephants, coupled with 'in house' warning systems for people living along elephant movement routes. An experimental study revealed that communication about elephant presence and movements through plantations to people over local television media as a 'crawl' and through a daily bulk SMS service to individual people's mobile numbers were received positively by the community.[70] Mobile-operated red LED flashing lights were installed in strategic locations to indicate elephant presence in the vicinity at night as an in house early warning system that is now largely operated by local people themselves. These systems, which now benefit nearly 70,000 people living in habitations across the Valparai plantation landscape, appear to be cost effective and sustainable solutions for human-elephant coexistence.[71] In addition, the Tamil Nadu Forest Department (TNFD) set up a conflict response unit with forest watchers and vehicle support, to respond to calls for assistance from local people. For the conflict prone and remote areas of TANTEA, the TNFD ordered closure of around 128 ha of tea plantation in 2012 and handover of these and other unplanted areas within TANTEA to the Anamalai Tiger Reserve. People living in remote labour colonies may also be relocated to better housing in an adjoining division of TANTEA with better road access and amenities. Such measures are also likely to reduce conflicts in the long run.

Other landscape level issues do remain in addressing human-wildlife conflicts. For instance, in many plantation areas, there has also been a proliferation of the use of power fences around private estates, creating barriers to animal movement. Fences erected between Protected Areas and private plantations are also often poorly maintained or ineffective because of lack of community participation.[72] Fences may reduce conflict if implemented in a participatory manner around specific property or crop fields, but may be ineffective or exacerbate conflict if used to fence off large areas including remnant natural forests, swamps and water sources. Proper deployment of fences for protection, leaving spaces for movement and access to water bodies by wildlife, will help in reducing costs and inefficiency (associated with long fences), mitigating conflicts better and supporting the conservation of wide ranging large mammals.

For carnivores such as leopards, addressing conflict with people requires a shift away from reactive measures such as providing compensation or capture and translocation of leopards after incidents occur. Instead, reducing incidence of human-leopard conflict requires proactive and precautionary mitigation measures such as improved livestock corrals, managing waste disposal, basic safety precautions for people especially young children,[73] creating awareness among local people to promote social acceptance of leopards in human use areas, and strict prohibition on stealing or removal of leopard kills.[74] Studies in the plantation areas of the Anamalai hills have similarly proposed conflict management based on leopard biology through proactive measures mentioned above. Safer living conditions for both the wild animals and a secure life for human co-inhabitants, especially children, are both goals to be pursued concomitantly. In common with the Deccan[75] and the Himalaya and Transhimalaya,[76] there are large, critical areas of overlap of people with large vertebrates, and conflict reconciliation with respect to life is a continuing challenge.

Property damage and human deaths cause economic losses, pain and trauma among residents, and other opportunity costs, resulting in undesirable retaliatory measures against wildlife. The loss of human life is tragic and irreversible, and efforts to minimise and eliminate such losses are imperative. Preventing human fatalities through appropriate measures, in particular, can also help increase greater tolerance levels of people. Community involvement and awareness in dealing with human-wildlife conflict has been crucial in developing a positive attitude among local communities and human co-inhabitants of the plantations. Living and working as we do in such a landscape, we are deeply aware of and sensitive to safety concerns at a human level even as we hope to work out ways in which neither animals nor people put each other's lives at risk.

Concluding Comments

A wide variety of approaches is being evolved globally to address the challenges of extending conservation to non-traditional arenas and production landscapes. These include approaches such as conservation easements, direct payments or credits for biodiversity services, carbon sequestration and trading, purchase of lands, conservation certification of commodities and produce, mitigation banking or compensatory mitigation, corporate social responsibility initiatives, and voluntary efforts.[77] Such initiatives have scarcely been tried in tropical Asia, particularly in India, where the mainstream conservation movement is still overly focused on Protected Areas (wildlife sanctuaries, National Parks, tiger reserves) under a protectionist paradigm.[78] Globally, evidence on the economic value of biodiversity and forests to plantations mediated by ecosystem services such as pollination, carbon sequestration and watershed benefits, also suggests that such landscape scale conservation can bring direct benefits to production, businesses and local residents.[79]

Better land use and business practices addressing issues such as water and soil conservation, ecosystems and wildlife protection, agrochemical use and safety, and worker welfare and community relations are sorely needed for Indian commodity plantations such as tea and coffee. Yet, in regions of high conservation importance such as the Western Ghats or North East India, there has been little effort to minimise negative impacts and enhance beneficial aspects of plantations for conservation through appropriate landscape and farm level management and agricultural practices. Our experiences suggest that effective and lasting changes, if they are to come to Indian plantations, cannot come from just the companies or farmers alone, or by any single means such as certification taken in isolation. A farmer primarily concerned with profit or yield or a company mainly concerned about an annual financial bottom line often allots little time or resources to finding and applying the various changes in land use and business practices, consumer awareness and market linkages, required for conservation and sustainability concerns to become mainstream. A mix of approaches is the need of the hour, including legal requirements and sanctions, certification based incentives, continuous civil society engagement to evolve better land use practices and act as watchdogs, and increased research and development in sustainability by plantation industry associations, boards and research institutions (see review of major stakeholders and issues in a SLOT Table in the Appendix). In addition, we require mechanisms of adaptive management of the human-wildlife interface by stakeholders to promote successful and sustainable human-wildlife coexistence.[80] Such holistic and inclusive approaches are required if we are to conserve wildlife at the landscape level, minimise conflicts and costs associated with ecologically insensitive land use, and sustain businesses and livelihoods profitably in the long haul.

Finally, we also note that, although rarely discussed, there is a deeper, more substantive and desirable approach that can lead to better outcomes. This is when businesses or farmers adopt better land use practices based on their own growing awareness of the need for conservation and the benefits such as watershed protection, pollination and pest control that are provided by diverse natural ecosystems. Farmers can additionally harness their own skills to mitigate the impact of plantations on people and the environment without compromising long term productive capacity of land. As Aldo Leopold wrote in a prescient essay titled

'The Farmer as Conservationist', 'Subsidies and propaganda may evoke the farmer's acquiescence, but only enthusiasm and affection will evoke his skill. It takes something more than a little "bait" to succeed in conservation.'[81]

Acknowledgements

We thank the Critical Ecosystems Partnership Fund (CEPF), IUCN Netherlands Ecosystems Grant Programme and Ecosystem Alliance Programme (with BothEnds and Wetlands International), Mohamed bin Zayed Species Conservation Fund and Rufford Small Grants Foundation for financial support for our work. We are grateful to Elephant Family, UK, and Dan Bucknell for partnering and supporting our work on human-elephant coexistence. The elephant early warning SMS service is enabled due to the support of GupShup Enterprises and Bharat Sanchar Nigam Ltd. We greatly appreciate the support and involvement of the TNFD for providing research permits and field collaboration and support in implementing the human-wildlife coexistence measures. We are grateful to a number of plantation companies, farmers, managers (too numerous to mention here individually), and our partners in RA and the SAN for participation and collaboration in our work. Our project colleagues Joke Aerts, Ganesh Raghunathan, P. Jeganathan, Nisarg Prakash, Kalyan Varma, Pavithra Sankaran, Ranjini Murali and Mathew James, helped enormously at various stages and we could not have accomplished the work without them. Ghazala Shahabuddin, M. D. Madhusudan and Mahesh Rangarajan patiently reviewed and shepherded this manuscript through its revision and we are indebted to them for their inputs and interest.

Appendix

Plantations in Southern India: Area, Growth and Conservation Concerns

Tea plantations occupied a total area of over 1,19,740 ha in southern India in 2007, having increased in coverage by around 6,280 ha (5.5 per cent) in the period between 2000 and 2007, despite a downturn in the industry for much of that period.[82] This is a matter of high environmental concern as tea plantations are grown as intensive monocultures, with no native shade tree cover and only very sparse shade represented by planted and annually lopped Australian silver oak (*Grevillea robusta*) trees. Tea thus represents more extreme habitat modification from natural forests of the region than is the case for plantations that normally have higher shade tree cover, including native tree species such as coffee and cardamom.

Coffee plantations in India span at least 3,41,518 ha having increased from around 2,70,821 ha in 1990–91 to span over 4,00,000 ha in 2010–11, of which eighty-five per cent of the production area lies in and adjoins the Western Ghats of Karnataka, Kerala and Tamil Nadu.[83] While part of the increase in coffee production area is due to increase in coffee growing in non-traditional areas, such as Andhra Pradesh, Orissa and eastern India, even in traditional areas in southern India there has been increase in coffee, often accompanied by loss of forest cover and loss or gradual conversion of private forests or sacred groves. For instance, Kodagu in Karnataka, one of the major coffee growing districts in India, lost an estimated thirty per cent of its forest cover between 1977 and 1997, when the area under coffee almost doubled and coffee cultivation expanded into new areas and evergreen forests.[84] Coffee plantations now abut all Protected Areas in the district, but forest loss seems to have now stabilised due to forest laws and lack of land availability. Among coffee areas, over half is under Robusta coffee (*Coffea canephora*), a species grown under less shade, with lower biodiversity conservation value[85] and higher invasive potential[86] than shade-grown Arabica coffee (*Coffea arabica*).

Small cardamom (*Elettaria cardamomum*) is mainly grown in the three southern states of Tamil Nadu, Kerala and Karnataka, where it spans over 73,228 ha.[87] Small cardamom, a native plant of the Western Ghats, now cultivated as several varieties in the region, requires denser shade for cultivation and offers opportunity for mixed native tree species agroforestry in the region. On the other hand, conventional cultivation requires high inputs of toxic agrochemicals in cardamom, which is a serious concern.

While tea, coffee and cardamom plantations are the major plantations in the middle and higher elevations of the Western Ghats, considerable expanses of other plantations occur in the lower elevations, foothills and adjoining plains. Important among these are plantations of rubber (*Hevea brasiliensis*), arecanut (*Areca catechu*) and cocoa (*Theobroma cacao*).

Rubber plantations occupy over 6,15,000 ha in India, mainly in southern India (around three fourths of the area is in the state of Kerala alone). India is the world's leading producer of areca nut, cultivated over an area of 3,54,000 ha, mainly in the states of Karnataka (leading producer), Kerala, Assam, Tamil Nadu, Meghalaya and Maharashtra.

Cocoa plantations occupy over 32,000 ha (2007), primarily in the states of Kerala, Karnataka and Andhra Pradesh. These are sometimes grown with areca nut as a shade crop as well as in home gardens, especially in Kerala and Karnataka along the western aspect of the Western Ghats and Malabar Coast. Other cultivated plantation crops in the region include coconut (*Cocos nucifera*), vanilla (*Vanilla sp.*) and pepper (*Piper nigrum*), the latter usually intercropped in coffee, cardamom and other plantations and home gardens.

Oil palm cultivation in India spanned about 53,161 ha in 2004, of which oil fruits production area was about 40,650 ha.[88] It is cultivated mainly in the states of Andhra Pradesh, Karnataka, Tamil Nadu, Kerala and Maharashtra, with smaller areas in Orissa, Gujarat, Tripura, Mizoram and the Andaman and Nicobar Islands. While the crop failed to gain initial acceptance by farmers (with substantial areas under oil palm being uprooted by farmers between 2001 and 2003 due to poor prices and other factors), there is a push to increase the area under oil palm in India, partly to reduce the growing dependency on imports. The Government of India has however identified around 7,96,000 ha as suitable for oil palm. In the Western Ghats, some of this increase is likely to occupy locations within or adjoining tropical forest areas in Kerala, Karnataka and Tamil Nadu. Cultivation of oil palm is already seen in landscapes adjoining Protected Areas in many districts of southern Karnataka (e.g., Mysore: Bandipur TR, Kodagu: Nagarahole NP) and Kerala (e.g., Waynad: Wayanad WLS, Trichur: Parambikulam TR).

Rainforest Alliance Certification and Conservation in Indian Tea and Coffee Plantations

The global SAN Standards underlying RA certification developed mainly on the basis of experiences from the neotropics and has lacunae in local contexts in Asia and Africa. In the environmental context, for instance, are issues related to conservation of large wildlife species like elephants, human-wildlife conflicts and animal corridors. Many farms in Africa and Asia are also much older and therefore there is a need to integrate traditional practices (higher diversity of native shade trees in traditional coffee estates, sacred groves, home gardens) and knowledge of local communities.

Introducing and fostering adoption of sustainable agriculture practices among Indian tea and coffee plantations faces challenges on social, environmental and economic fronts. In India, social concerns are sought to be addressed by legislation, particularly the Plantation Labour Act, 1951 (amendments up to 2010), Minimum Wages Act, 1948, and Factories Act, 1948. Despite the legislations, a number of vital social concerns remain on payment of living wages, adequate housing and sanitation facilities for workers, situation of contract workers and good working conditions.

Concerns over environmental sustainability arise from many of the present production practices in plantations. Threats to biodiversity include hunting of wildlife and land clearing leading to habitat fragments such as forests, grasslands and wetlands in plantations being degraded or converted to land uses that canno[illegible] endemic species. Examples include clearing fores[illegible] growth to establish monocultures of tea, the [illegible] species such as eucalyptus in grasslands, swamps and along streams, and draining of swamps or overuse of water or pollution of wetlands. The spread of invasive alien species introduced in plantation areas (e.g., as crops or cover crops, or for biological control), or which have established following disturbances is another serious concern with spillover effects in surrounding landscapes. A key issue in agroforestry plantations such as coffee and cardamom, where shade trees are integrated in the production area, is the intensification of production accompanied by removal of shade trees or the gradual replacement of diverse native shade trees with fewer or single tree species, often alien or exotic species such as silver oak or eucalyptus or *Maesopsis eminii*. Water conservation and pollution is another key issue. Waste water runoff into fresh water sources from coffee wet pulping or from washing of tea factories, especially the former, can be a significant source of water pollution. Groundwater use and surface water diversion and overuse, for irrigation, sprinkling and washing are also concerns from environmental as well as social (community relations) perspectives. Opportunities for improving water use efficiency, reducing wastage, water reuse, rainwater harvesting and better treatment systems exist, but are yet to see widespread implementation.

Certified farms are not allowed to use any of the agrochemicals (insecticides, acaricides, fungicides, herbicides, plant growth promoters, manures and fertilisers) listed in the periodically updated SAN List of Prohibited Pesticides (November 2011, revision due 2014). Although the standards do not stipulate organic cultivation, the list of prohibited pesticides ensures that the worst agrochemicals, internationally screened and prohibited, are not used for cultivation and additionally that chemicals falling within the highest toxicity classes are gradually reduced and replaced. In India, the (over)use or dependence on agrochemicals is also a major concern from environmental, economic and social (toxicity, health) perspectives. The use of pesticides is regulated by the Insecticide Act and Rules, but rather inadequately in comparison with international standards. For instance, paraquat (gramaxone), a herbicide on the dirty dozen [illegible] Pesticide Action Network,[89] is approved within India [illegible] in tea and coffee plantations. Chemicals such as endosulfan are also widely used in plantations, especially in rubber and cocoa, with the manufacture and use of this chemical prohibited by the Supreme Court only in 2011. Monocrotophos (toxic organophosphate) and carbofuran (furadan) are still recommended for use in cardamom plantations under conventional practices, to name just a few examples.

Further, certified farms are expected to maintain narrow strips of natural vegetation (buffer zones) to separate crop production areas from rivers, natural ecosystems, or intensive human use areas such as schools and public roads. This is to prevent exposure of people and ecosystems to harmful effects of agrochemical drift, besides helping maintain soil and water quality along streams and rivers, and provide spaces for wildlife movement. Tea and coffee estates in India are, however, notorious for planting the crop on every possible inch of land up to the edge of streams and even occasionally on land in the middle of rivers. Despite the fact that the required land area for buffer zones is usually a small fraction of the land area (less than two per cent including unplanted area), even large estates are loath to ensure such protection of people and ecosystems through buffer zones, due to various misgivings and the belief that the only way to run the business is to plant up all available area.

Economic concerns at the farm level, especially when viewed in terms of long term sustainability rather than exclusively on annual bottomlines, also predicate the need to adopt extensive ecological solutions to issues rather than intensive engineering solutions. The adoption of integrated farm management can increase the economic efficiency of many plantations, such as use of regular soil testing to determine exact fertiliser requirements, regulated and targeted spraying of pesticides on pest attack rather than preemptive spraying of entire fields, use of alternatives such as pheromone and sticky traps rather than expensive chemicals, proper assessment of social and environmental impact and suitability of new crops and new production areas before planting, and the use of appropriate soil cover, mulching and shading to address soil erosion, soil health and weed proliferation rather than using concrete revetments, artificial fertilisers and chemical herbicides.

SLOT Table of various stakeholders to achieve goals of conservation and sustainability in plantations in the region

Stakeholder	Strength	Limitations	Opportunities	Threats/Costs	Required Changes
Producers, farmers and workers' unions	Well organised sector with capacity to adopt and implement better practices if they desire. Supported by government, boards and agricultural research institutions. Close relationship with land.	History and colonial legacy of practices and inertia. Poor awareness of ecosystems and wildlife issues, animal corridors. Dominant/ unidimensional focus on intensification and yield per hectare. Dependence on agrochemicals.	Access to new and growing markets of informed consumers via certification. Improving worker welfare and safety. Ethical positioning and worker empowerment. More stable market linkages. Better relations with local community and workers.	Resistance to change, including organised change. Perverse subsidies to intensify improper land use. Conflicts with wildlife. Financial costs of compliance, audit and improvement.	Respecting habitat remnants as ecosystems. Being sensitive to animal corridors and movement through farms. Reducing toxic chemicals. Adopt integrated farm management. Collaborate with NGOs and civil society to remove weaknesses.

(Contd)

Table (Contd)

Stakeholder	Strength	Limitations	Opportunities	Threats/Costs	Required Changes
Producer associations and cooperatives	Well placed, strong voice and influence with government and planter communities.	Often biased towards larger estates and influential companies.	Bringing industry-wide changes in practices to leverage emerging market opportunities.	View of worker welfare costs primarily as a liability rather than as social capital.	Move members towards sustainability and show top management commitment.
	Represents huge worker population acting as social capital.	Representation of entrenched vested interests, especially over land and natural resources.	Sustainability and geographical branding and positioning.	Lobbying with government to increase subsidy and reduce interventions.	Lobby not only for subsidies or sharing of labour 'burdens' by state but for better research and development support related to sustainability.
	Negotiating powers with unions and state on wages.	Lobbying for subsidies, exemptions, often on basis of worker population.	Increased domestic markets for sustainable produce.	Negative attitude towards conservation due to inability to deal effectively with conflicts.	Take proactive stance towards enhancing worker welfare and dignity to counteract labour shortage.

(Contd)

Table (Contd)

Stakeholder	Strength	Limitations	Opportunities	Threats/Costs	Required Changes
Government boards and industry research institutions	Financially supported. Well equipped and staffed. Excellent access to wide variety of plantations and landscapes across India.	Very poor engagement on social sustainability issues, such as household energy needs, agrochemical impacts on worker health and soils. Almost lacking in wildlife research, and ecosystem services and impact studies. Limited engagement with organic and sustainable agriculture and overreliance on engineering techno-fixes and agrochemical solutions.	Exceptional native biological diversity may hold species of value for shade, pest management, cover crops and others. Boards under Ministry of Commerce can incentivise adoption of good land use (e.g., linking subsidy or tax/customs exemptions to adoption of sustainable practices). Foster domestic markets and labelling for sustainably produced commodities.	Industry membership based institutions have more unidimensional focus on yields and chemical inputs. Paradigmatic approach to mode of intensive industrial agriculture. Costs of broadening research capacity in the institutions to include social and environmental sciences.	Rethink and remove perverse subsidies that cause more land clearing, introduce inappropriate new crops or foster unsustainable land use intensification. Enhance research capacity and agenda to include environmental concerns (agrochemical impacts and alternatives, wildlife and ecosystems research). Develop effective solutions for worker health and safety (e.g., fuel efficient safer fuels/stoves, personal protective equipment).

(Contd)

Table (Contd)

Stakeholder	Strength	Limitations	Opportunities	Threats/Costs	Required Changes
NGOs, civil society and independent research institutions	Large number of independent and credible institutions in the region. Wide experience in issues such as wildlife and ecosystems, social and welfare, development alternative, waste management, native plant and animal species.	Constrained by funding. Poor leverage with industry bodies and boards. Lack of access to plantations to carry out enabling research, often due to mistrust by planters.	Contribute to conservation across a larger landscape. Research to foster native species use and minimise aliens and invasives. Enhance worker welfare and dignity, and reduce impacts on natural areas. Identify animal corridors and minimise conflicts.	Reluctance to engage with plantations, seen as a damaging sector. Maintaining independence and credibility in working with corporates and businesses.	Carry out ecosystems and wildlife studies, surveys and identification of suitable native plant species useful in farms. Form partnerships with planters for habitat restoration and mapping animal movement routes. Help develop locally appropriate guidelines and best practices. Play watchdog role on issues such as land clearing, encroachments. Create better awareness among producers, consumers and local communities.

(Contd)

Table (Contd)

Stakeholder	Strength	Limitations	Opportunities	Threats/Costs	Required Changes
Forest and environment departments	Strong supporting legislation on forest and wildlife conservation. Widespread presence in plantation landscapes that are also biodiversity rich.	Failure to integrate larger landscapes outside protected areas in conservation. Widespread perception of corruption. Legislation inhibits private efforts at conservation (e.g., growing and managing native shade trees).	As forests are a state subject, site-specific solutions may be evolved. Expertise can be shared and local partnerships created to engage with plantations. Can assist in mitigating wildlife-human conflict in private lands.	Tendency to see private owners as adversaries and to be suspicious of private initiatives. Inability to understand and foster better land use practices. Delays in wildlife compensation payments.	Taking a larger landscape view, including collaboration with local stakeholders. Training officers and field staff to better deal with production sector, conflict management. Change from a focus on booking offences to also supporting positive changes.

(Contd)

Table (Contd)

Stakeholder	Strength	Limitations	Opportunities	Threats/Costs	Required Changes
Workers and local people	Large number of people, resident in the region, often for generations. Being a vulnerable segment as changes in land use practices and working conditions affect them directly, they are sensitive to these changes and more open to adoption of sustainable practices. Often intrinsically tolerant of wildlife and nature conservation.	Usually lack decision-making powers. Significant migrant and temporary worker population, often with limited capacity, vulnerable to exploitation. Lack of training or capacity-building opportunities to deal with skilled tasks or adopt newer sustainable practices.	Potential for empowerment through education, health, and community efforts and civil society involvement. Greater awareness of rights coupled with continued high dependence of plantations on labour in leveraging improvements in housing and working conditions (can benefit from certification). Rights for collective bargaining agreements and labour unions.	Limited understanding of wildlife and conservation issues, and optimal approach to conflict avoidance. Improvements in housing, sanitation (such as toilets), and safety necessitates significant financial cost (investment).	Closer involvement in decisions related to working and living conditions and wages. Constant and continuous training, using appropriate language and material, in sustainable practices and wildlife conservation. Proactive measures for better safety and emergency response procedures in areas with large wildlife species.

Notes

1. F. Achard, H. D. Eva, H. J. Stibig, P. Mayaux, J. Gallego, T. Richards, and J. P. Malingreau, 'Determination of deforestation rates of the world's humid tropical forests', *Science* 297 (2002): 999–1002; K. Norris, 'Agriculture and biodiversity conservation: Opportunity knocks', *Conservation Letters* 1 (2008): 2–11.

2. D. Tilman, K. G. Cassman, P. A. Matson, R. Naylor and S. Polasky, 'Agricultural sustainability and intensive production practices', *Nature* 418 (2002): 671–77; A. Balmford, R. Green and J. P. W. Scharlemann, 'Sparing land for nature: Exploring the potential impact of changes in agricultural yield on the area needed for crop production', *Global Change Biology* 11 (2005): 1594–605; Green, et al., 'Farming and the fate of wild nature'.

3. C. J. A. Bradshaw, N. S. Sodhi and B. W. Brook, 'Tropical turmoil: A biodiversity tragedy in progress', *Frontiers in Ecology and the Environment* 7 (2009): 79–87.

4. J. A. Foley, R. DeFries, G. P. Asner, C. Barford, G. Bonan, S. R. Carpenter, F. S. Chapin, M. T. Coe, G. C. Daily, H. K. Gibbs, J. H. Helkowski, T. Holloway, E. A. Howard, C. J. Kucharik, C. Monfreda, J. A. Patz and I. C. Prentice, 'Global consequences of land use', *Science* 309 (2005): 570–74; J. A. Foley, G. P. Asner, M. H. Costa, M. T. Coe, R. DeFries, H. K. Gibbs, E. A. Howard, S. Olson, J. Patz, N. Ramankutty and P. Snyder, 'Amazonia revealed: Forest degradation and loss of ecosystem goods and services in the Amazon Basin', *Frontiers in Ecology and the Environment* 5 (2007): 25–32.

5. S. Chape, S. Blyth, L. Fish, P. Fox and M. Spalding, *United Nations List of Protected Areas* (Gland, Switzerland and Cambridge, UK: IUCN, UNEP-WCMC, 2003); Chape, et al., 'Measuring the extent and effectiveness of protected areas'.

6. J. Terborgh, C. van Schaik, L. Davenport and M. Rao (eds), *Making Parks Work: Strategies for preserving tropical nature* (Washington DC: Island Press, 2002).

7. Naughton-Treves, Holland and Brandon, 'The role of protected areas in conserving biodiversity and sustaining local livelihoods'; Laurance, et al., 'Averting biodiversity collapse in tropical forest protected areas'.

8. W. F. Laurance and R. Bierregaard, *Tropical Forest Remnants: Ecology, management, and conservation of fragmented communities* (Chicago: University of Chicago Press 1997); L. P. Koh and T. A. Gardner, 'Conservation in human-modified landscapes', *Conservation Biology for All* (2010): 236–61.

9. For example, see G. C. Daily, G. Ceballos, J. Pacheco, G. Suzán and A. Sanchez-Azofeifa, 'Countryside biogeography of neotropical mammals: Conservation opportunities in agricultural landscapes of Costa Rica', *Conservation Biology* 17 (2003): 1814–26; W. J. Sutherland, 'Restoring a sustainable countryside', *Trends in Ecology and Evolution* 17 (2002): 148–50; S. A. Bhagwat, K. J. Willis, H. J. B. Birks and R. J. Whittaker, 'Agroforestry: A refuge for tropical biodiversity?', *Trends in Ecology & Evolution* 23 (2008): 261–67.

10. G. Schroth, G. A. B. da Fonseca, C. A. Harvey, C. Gascon, H. L. Vasconcelos and A. M. N. Izac (eds), *Agroforestry and Biodiversity Conservation in Tropical*

Landscapes (Washington DC: Island Press, 2004); A. Das, J. Krishnaswamy, K. S. Bawa, M. C. Kiran, V. Srinivas, N. S. Kumar and K. U Karanth, 'Prioritisation of conservation areas in the Western Ghats, India', *Biological Conservation* 133 (2006): 16–31.

11. A. Kumar, R. Pethiyagoda and D. Mudappa, 'Western Ghats and Sri Lanka' in R. Mittermeier, P. Gil, M. Hoffmann, J. Pilgrim, T. Brooks, C. Goettsch Mittermeier, J. Lamoreux, G. A. B. Da Fonseca and P. A. Seligmann (eds), *Hotspots Revisited: Earth's biologically richest and most endangered ecoregions* (Mexico: CEMEX, 2004), pp. 152–57.

12. S. Le Saout, M. Hoffmann, Y. Shi, A. Hughes, C. Bernard, T. M. Brooks, B. Bertzky, S. H. M. Butchart, S. N. Stuart, T. Badman, A. S. L. Rodrigues, 'Conservation. Protected areas and effective biodiversity conservation', *Science* 342 (2013): 803–05.

13. E. G. Brockerhoff, H. Jactel, J. A. Parrotta, C. P. Quine and J. Sayer, 'Plantation forests and biodiversity: Oxymoron or opportunity?', *Biodiversity and Conservation* 17 (2008): 925–51.

14. J. W. Clay, *World Agriculture and the Environment: A commodity-by-commodity guide to impacts and practices* (Washington DC: Island Press, 2004).

15. P. F. Donald, 'Biodiversity impacts of some agricultural commodity production systems', *Conservation Biology* 18 (2004): 17–38.

16. J. H. Rappole, D. I. King and J. H. Rivera, 'Coffee and conservation III: Reply to Philpott and Dietsch', *Conservation Biology* 17 (2003): 1847–49; R. A. Mittermeier, P. R. Gil, M. Hoffmann, J. Pilgrim, T. Brooks, et al., *Hotspots Revisited: Earth's biologically richest and most endangered ecoregions* (Mexico: CEMEX, 2004).

17. Clay, *World agriculture.*

18. D. S. Wilcove and L. P. Koh, 'Addressing the threats to biodiversity from oil-palm agriculture', *Biodiversity and Conservation* 19 (2010): 999–1007; L. P. Koh, J. Miettinen, S. C. Liew and J. Ghazoul, 'Remotely sensed evidence of tropical peatland conversion to oil palm', *Proceedings of the National Academy of Sciences* 108 (2011): 5127–32.

19. Kumar, et al., 'Western Ghats'; W. A. Rodgers, H. S. Panwar and V. B. Mathur, *Wildlife Protected Area Network in India: A review* (Dehradun: Wildlife Institute of India, 2000).

20. Critical Ecosystems Partnerships Fund, *Ecosystem Profile Western Ghats & Sri Lanka Biodiversity Hotspot: Western Ghats region* (Arlington, USA: CEPF, 2007).

21. S. Menon and K. S. Bawa, 'Applications of geographic information systems, remote-sensing, and a landscape ecology approach to biodiversity conservation in the Western Ghats', *Current Science* 73 (1997): 134–45.

22. C. S. Jha, C. B. S. Dutt and K. S. Bawa, 'Deforestation and land use changes in Western Ghats, India', *Current Science* 79 (2000): 231–37.

23. C. R. T. Congreve, *The Anamalais* (Madras: Associated Printers, 1942); R. Prabhakar and M. Gadgil, 'Maps as markers of ecological change: A case study of the Nilgiri hills of Southern India' in D. Arnold and R. Guha (eds), *Nature,*

Culture, Imperialism: Essays on the environmental history of South Asia (Delhi: Oxford University Press, 1995), pp. 152–84.

24. T. R. S. Raman, 'Effects of habitat structure and adjacent habitats on birds in tropical rainforest fragments and shaded plantations in the Western Ghats, India', *Biodiversity and Conservation* 15 (2006): 1577–607; D. Mudappa and T. R. S. Raman, 'Rainforest restoration and wildlife conservation on private lands in the Valparai plateau, Western Ghats, India' in Shahabuddin and Rangarajan, *Making conservation work*, pp. 210–40; M. O. Anand, J. Krishnaswamy and A. Das, 'Proximity to forests drives bird conservation value of coffee plantations: Implications for certification', *Ecological Applications* 18 (2008): 1754–63; J. Dolia, M. S. Devy, N. A. Aravind and A. Kumar, 'Adult butterfly communities in coffee plantations around a protected area in the Western Ghats, India', *Animal Conservation* 11 (2008): 26–34.

25. Sundar, this volume; Ghotge and Ramdas, this volume.

26. G. Umapathy and A. Kumar, 'The occurrence of arboreal mammals in the rain forest fragments in the Anamalai Hills, South India', *Biological Conservation* 92 (2000): 311–19.

27. R. J. R. Daniels, M. Gadgil and N. V. Joshi, 'Impact of human extraction on tropical humid forests in the Western Ghats Uttara Kannada, South India', *Journal of Applied Ecology* 32 (1995): 866–74; S. Muthuramkumar, N. Ayyappan, N. Parthasarathy, D. Mudappa, T. R. S. Raman, M. A. Selwyn and L. A. Pragasan, 'Plant community structure in tropical rain forest fragments of the Western Ghats, India', *Biotropica* 38 (2006): 143–60.

28. A. J. Hiremath and B. Sundaram, 'The fire-lantana cycle hypothesis in Indian forests', *Conservation and Society* 3 (2005): 26–42; A. A. Joshi, D. Mudappa and T. R. S. Raman, 'Brewing trouble: Coffee invasion in relation to edges and forest structure in tropical rainforest fragments of the Western Ghats, India', *Biological Invasions* 11 (2009): 2387–400.

29. Bhagwat et al., 'Agroforestry'.

30. J. H. Lawton, D. E. Bignell, B. Bolton, G. F. Bloemers, P. Eggleton, P. M. Hammond, M. Hodda, R. D. Holt, T. B. Larsen, N. A. Mawdsley, N. E. Stork, D. S. Srivastava and A. D. Watt, 'Biodiversity inventories, indicator taxa and effects of habitat modification in tropical forest', *Nature* 391 (1998): 72–76; C. A. Lindell, W. H. Chomentowski and J. R. Zook, 'Characteristics of bird species using forest and agricultural land covers in southern Costa Rica', *Biodiversity and Conservation* 13 (2004): 2419–41; C. A. Harvey and J. A. G. Villalobos, 'Agroforestry systems conserve species-rich but modified assemblages of tropical birds and bats', *Biodiversity and Conservation* 16 (2007): 2257–92; M. Waltert, K. S. Bobo, S. Kaupa, M. L. Montoya, M. S. Nsanyi and H. Fermon, 'Assessing conservation values: Biodiversity and endemicity in tropical land use systems', *PLoS One* 6 (2011): e16238.

31. Raman, 'Effects of habitat structure'; R. J. R. Daniels, M. Hegde and M. Gadgil, 'Birds of the man-made ecosystems: The plantations', *Proceedings of the Indian Academy of Sciences-Animal Sciences, 1990* 99 (1990): 79–89.

32. R. Greenberg, I. Perfecto and S. M. Philpott, 'Agroforests as model systems for tropical ecology', *Ecology* 89 (2008): 913–14.

33. S. Sidhu, T. R. S. Raman and E. Goodale, 'Effects of plantations and home-gardens on tropical forest bird communities and mixed-species bird flocks in the southern Western Ghats', *Journal of the Bombay Natural History Society* 107 (2010): 91.

34. Raman, 'Effects of habitat structure'.

35. J. Ranganathan, R. J. R. Daniels, M. D. S. Chandran, P. R. Ehrlich and G. C. Daily, 'Sustaining biodiversity in ancient tropical countryside', *Proceedings of the National Academy of Sciences (USA), 2008* 105 (2008): 17852–54.

36. H. Sridhar, 'Are arecanut plantations really suitable for biodiversity conservation?' *Proceedings of the National Academy of Sciences (USA), 2009* 106 (2009): E34.

37. S. Aratrakorn, S. Thunhikorn and P. F. Donald, 'Changes in bird communities following conversion of lowland forest to oil palm and rubber plantations in southern Thailand', *Bird Conservation International* 16 (2006): 71–82.

38. Wilcove and Koh, 'Addressing the threats'; Koh, et al., 'Remotely sensed evidence'; E. B. Fitzherbert, M. J. Struebig, A. Morel, F. Danielsen, C. A. Brühl, P. F. Donald and B. Phalan, 'How will oil palm expansion affect biodiversity?' *Trends in Ecology and Evolution* 23 (2008): 538–45.

39. Mudappa and Raman, 'Rainforest restoration'; M. N. Ishwar, R. Chellam, A. Kumar and B. R. Noon, 'The response of agamid lizards to rainforest fragmentation in the southern Western Ghats, India', *Conservation and Society* 1 (2003): 69–86; D. Mudappa, B. R. Noon, A. Kumar and R. Chellam, 'Responses of small carnivores to rainforest fragmentation in the southern Western Ghats, India', *Small Carnivore Conservation* 36 (2007): 18–26; H. Sridhar, T. R. S. Raman and D. Mudappa, 'Mammal persistence and abundance in tropical rainforest remnants in the southern Western Ghats, India', *Current Science* 94 (2008): 748–57; M.O. Anand, J. Krishnaswamy, A. Kumar and A. Bali, 'Sustaining biodiversity conservation in human-modified landscapes in the Western Ghats: Remnant forests matter', *Biological Conservation* 143 (2010): 2363–74.

40. T. R. S. Raman and D. Mudappa, 'Correlates of hornbill distribution and abundance in rainforest fragments in the southern Western Ghats, India', *Bird Conservation International* 13 (2003): 199–212; M. A. Kumar, D. Mudappa and T. R. S. Raman, 'Asian elephant *Elephas maximus* habitat use and ranging in fragmented rainforest and plantations in the Anamalai Hills, India', *Tropical Conservation Science* 3 (2010): 143–58.

41. Raman, 'Effects of habitat structure'; T. R. S. Raman and R. Sukumar, 'Responses of tropical rainforest birds to abandoned plantations, edges and logged forest in the Western Ghats, India', *Animal Conservation* 5 (2002): 201–16.

42. Mudappa and Raman, 'Rainforest restoration'; Mudappa, et al., 'Responses of small carnivores'; A. Bali, A. Kumar and J. Krishnaswamy, 'The mammalian communities in coffee plantations around a protected area in the Western Ghats, India'. *Biological Conservation* 139 (2007): 93–102; J. M. Thiollay, 'The role of traditional agroforests in the conservation of rain forest bird diversity in Sumatra',

Conservation Biology 9 (1995): 335–53; R. Greenberg, P. Bichier, A. C. Angon and R. Reitsma, 'Bird populations in shade and sun coffee plantations in central Guatemala', *Conservation Biology* 11 (1997): 448–59; N. S. Sodhi, M. C. Posa, T. Lee and I. G. Warkentin, 'Perspectives in ornithology: Effects of disturbance or loss of tropical rainforest on birds', *The Auk* 125 (2008): 511–19.

43. Anand, Krishnaswamy and Das, 'Proximity to forests'.

44. Raman, 'Effects of habitat structure'; B. M. Beehler, K. S. R. K. Raju and S. Ali, 'Avian use of man-disturbed forest habitats in the Eastern Ghats, India', *Ibis* 129 (1987): 197–211; J. Ranganathan, J. Krishnaswamy and M. O. Anand, 'Landscape-level effects on avifauna within tropical agriculture in the Western Ghats: Insights for management and conservation', *Biological Conservation* 143 (2010): 2909–17.

45. Raman, 'Effects of habitat structure'; G. Shahabuddin, 'Preliminary observations on the role of coffee plantations as avifaunal refuges in the Palani Hills of the Western Ghats', *Journal of the Bombay Natural History Society* 94 (1997): 10–21.

46. For examples, see Sridhar, Raman and Mudappa, 'Mammal persistence'; Anand, et al., 'Sustaining biodiversity'; S. Bhagwat, C. Kushalappa, P. Williams and N. Brown, 'The role of informal protected areas in maintaining biodiversity in the Western Ghats of India', *Ecology and Society* 1 (2005): 8.

47. Bhagwat, et al., 'Agroforestry'; R. DeFries, A. Hansen, A. C. Newton and M. C. Hansen, 'Increasing isolation of protected areas in tropical forests over the past twenty years', *Ecological Applications* 15 (2005): 19–26; C. H. Sekercioglu, S. R. Loarie, O. F. Brenes, P. R. Ehrlich and G. C. Daily, 'Persistence of forest birds in the Costa Rican agricultural countryside', *Conservation Biology* 21 (2007): 482–494.

48. D. Nath, R. Sukumar and D. L. Caudhurī, *Elephant-Human Conflict in Kodagu, Southern India: Distribution patterns, people's perceptions and mitigation methods* (Bangalore: Asian Elephant Conservation Centre, 1998); M. A. Kumar, D. Mudappa, T. R. S. Raman and M. D. Madhusudan, *The Elephant Hills: Conservation of wild Asian elephant in a landscape of fragmented rainforests and plantations in the Anamalais, India* (Nature Conservation Foundation, India, 2004); P. Bal, C. D. Nath, K. M. Nanaya, C. G. Kushalappa and C. Garcia, 'Elephants also like coffee: Trends and drivers of human–elephant conflicts in coffee agroforestry landscapes of Kodagu, Western Ghats, India', *Environmental Management* 47 (2011): 789–801.

49. Kumar, Mudappa and Raman, 'Asian elephant'.

50. C. Garcia, D. Marie-Vivien, C. G. Kushalappa, P. G. Chengappa and K. M. Nanaya, 'Geographical indications and biodiversity in the Western Ghats, India: Can labeling benefit producers and the environment in a mountain agroforestry landscape?', *Mountain Research and Development* 27 (2007): 206–10.

51. Nath, Sukumar and Caudhurī, *Elephant-Human Conflict*; Bal, et al., 'Elephants also like coffee'.

52. Bal, et al., 'Elephants also like coffee'.

53. K. N. Ninan and J. Sathyapalan, 'The economics of biodiversity conservation: A study of a coffee growing region in the Western Ghats of India', *Ecological Economics* 55 (2005): 61–72.

54. V. Athreya, S. S. Thakur, S. Chaudhuri and A. V. Belsare, 'A study of the man-leopard conflict in the Junnar Forest Division, Pune District, Maharashtra', submitted to the Office of the Chief Wildlife Warden, Nagpur, Maharashtra Forest Department, 2004.

55. J. D. C. Linnell, R. Aanes, J. E. Swenson, J. Odden and M. E. Smith, 'Translocation of carnivores as a method for managing problem animals: A review', *Biodiversity and Conservation* 6 (1997): 1245–57; Athreya, 'Is relocation a viable management option for unwanted animals?' V. Athreya and A. V. Belsare, *Human-Leopard Conflict Management Guidelines* (Pune: Kaati Trust, 2007).

56. V. Athreya, M. Odden, J. D. C. Linnell and K. U. Karanth, 'Translocation as a tool for mitigating conflict with leopards in human-dominated landscapes of India', *Conservation Biology* 25 (2011): 133–41.

57. S. Sidhu, D. Mudappa and T. R. S. Raman, 'People and predators: Leopard diet and interactions with people in a tea plantation dominated landscape in the Anamalai Hills, Western Ghats', technical report, Nature Conservation Foundation, Mysore, 2011.

58. See section titled 'Living with Wildlife: From Conflict to Coexistence', this volume, pp. 191–94.

59. Laurance and Bierregaard, *Tropical Forest Remnants*; Mudappa and Raman, 'Rainforest restoration'.

60. Described in Mudappa and Raman, 'Rainforest restoration'.

61. T. R. S. Raman, D. Mudappa and V. Kapoor, 'Restoring rainforest fragments: Survival of mixed native species seedlings under contrasting site conditions in the Western Ghats, India', *Restoration Ecology* 17 (2009): 137–47.

62. D. Lamb, P. D. Erskine and J. A. Parrotta, 'Restoration of degraded tropical forest landscapes', *Science* 310 (2005): 1628–32; D. Mudappa and T. R. S. Raman, *A Rainforest Restoration: A guide to principles and practice* (Mysore: Nature Conservation Foundation, 2010).

63. C. D. Nath, R. Pélissier, B. R. Ramesh and C. Garcia, 'Promoting native trees in shade coffee plantations of southern India: Comparison of growth rates with the exotic *Grevillea robusta*', *Agroforestry systems* 83 (2011): 107–19.

64. S. Krishnan and J. Ghazoul, 'Importance of bees, shade trees and forests in coffee production in Kodagu', *Indian Coffee* 76 (2012): 10–12; J. Aerts, D. Mudappa and T. Raman, 'Coffee, conservation, and Rainforest Alliance certification: Opportunities for Indian coffee', *Planters' Chronicle* 106 (2010): 15–26.

65. Available at http://www.sanstandards.org (accessed 6 May 2014).

66. Aerts, Mudappa and Raman, 'Coffee, conservation'.

67. See http://ecoagriculture.in (accessed 7 May 2014).

68. Wilcove and Koh, 'Addressing the threats'.

69. Kumar, Mudappa and Raman, 'Asian elephant'; M. A. Kumar and G. Raghunathan, *Human-Elephant Coexistence: Community involvement in conflict*

resolution in a land-use mosaic of the Anamalai Hills, Western Ghats, India (Mysore: Nature Conservation Foundation, 2012).

70. Kumar and Raghunathan, *Human-Elephant Coexistence.*

71. Kumar and Raghunathan, *Human-Elephant Coexistence.*

72. Rangarajan, Desai, Sukumar, Easa, Menon, et al., *Gajah.*

73. Sidhu, Mudappa and Raman, 'People and predators'.

74. Athreya, et al., 'Translocation as a tool'; Ministry of Environment and Forests, *Guidelines for Human-Leopard Conflict Management* (New Delhi: Ministry of Environment and Forests, Government of India, 2011).

75. Ghotge and Ramdas, this volume.

76. Bhatnagar and Mishra, this volume.

77. S. Pagiola, J. Bishop and N. Landell-Mills (eds), *Selling Forest Environmental Services: Market-based mechanisms for conservation and development* (London: Earthscan, 2004); W. Ginn, *Investing in Nature: Case studies of land conservation in collaboration with business* (Washington DC: Island Press, 2005).

78. M. D. Madhusudan and T. R. S. Raman, 'Conservation as if biological diversity matters: Preservation versus sustainable use in India', *Conservation and Society* 1 (2003): 49.

79. Millennium Ecosystem Assessment. 2005–6. Ecosystems and human well-being. Synthesis (Washington DC: Islamd Press, 2005).

80. Rangarajan, et al., *Gajah*; Ministry of Environment and Forests, *Guidelines for human-leopard conflict*; F. V. Osborn and G. E. Parker, 'Towards an integrated approach for reducing the conflict between elephants and people: A review of current research', Oryx 37 (2003): 80–84.

81. A. Leopold, 'The farmer as a conservationist', *American Forests* 45 (1939): 294–99.

82. Tea Board statistics. Available at http://teaboard.gov.in/pdf/stat/Growers%20&%20Area%20under%20Tea.pdf

83. Coffee Board database. Available at http://indiacoffee.org/userfiles/DATABASEJune11_I(1).pdf

84. C. A. Garcia, S. Bhagwat, J. Ghazoul, C. D. Nath, K. M. Nanaya, C. G. Kushalappa, Y. Raghuramulu, R. Naasi and P. Vast, 'Biodiversity conservation in agricultural landscapes: Challenges and opportunities of coffee agroforests in the Western Ghats, India', *Conservation Biology* 24 (2010): 479–88.

85. Joshi, Mudappa and Raman, 'Brewing trouble'.

86. Raman, 'Effects of habitat structure'.

87. 2011 Spices Board data. Available at http://www.indianspices.com/pdf/spice-state-arprd.xls.

88. T. R. Manoharan, 'Oil Palm Sector in India: The Scope of Influencing India's Ecological Footprint in South East Asia' (New Delhi: WWF-India, 2007).

89. For more information, see http://www.pesticideinfo.org (accessed 7 May 2014).

BIBLIOGRAPHY

Abraham T. J., S. K. Sil and P. Vineetha, 'A comparative study on the aquaculture practices adopted by fish farmers in Andhra Pradesh and West Bengal', *Indian Journal of Fisheries* 57 (2010), 41–48.

Achard, F., H. D. Eva, H. J. Stibig, P. Mayaux, J. Gallego, T. Richards and J. P. Malingreau, 'Determination of deforestation rates of the world's humid tropical forests', *Science* 297 (2002), 999–1002.

Aebi, R., *Sheep Husbandry on the Deccan Plateau in India: Recent developments and new challenges from keeping the native Deccani Breed and the introduced Nellore Breed*. Bern: Swiss College of Agriculture, 2009.

Aerts, J., D. Mudappa and T. Raman, 'Coffee, conservation, and Rainforest Alliance certification: Opportunities for Indian coffee', *Planters' Chronicle* 106 (2010), 15–26.

Agarwal, A., R. Chopra and K. Sharma, *The State of India's Environment: A citizens' report*. New Delhi: Centre for Science and Environment, 1982.

Agarwal, R., 'Fight for a Forest', *Seminar* 638, no. 613 (2010), 48–52.

Agarwala, M., S. Kumar, A. Treves and L. Naughton-Treves, 'Paying for wolves in Solapur, India and Wisconsin, USA: Comparing compensation rules and practice to understand the goals and politics of wolf conservation', *Biological Conservation* 143 (2010), 2945–55.

Agrawal, A. and E. Ostrom, 'Collective action, property rights, and decentralization in resource use in India and Nepal', *Politics and Society* 29 (2001), 485–514.

Agrawal, A., *Environmentality: Technologies of government and the making of subjects*. Durham: Duke University Press, 2005.

Allsen, T.T., *The Royal Hunt in Eurasian History*. Philadelphia: University of Pennsylvania Press, 2011.

Almitra Patel and another vs Union of India and Ors, IA by NGO Forum for the NCR (WPC 5236/2010), judgment of 26 May 2011. Available at http://toxicslink.org/delhiridge/wp-content/uploads/Landfill_Order_Dated_26.05.pdf (accessed 24 April 2014).

Anand, M. O., J. Krishnaswamy and A. Das, 'Proximity to forests drives bird conservation value of coffee plantations: Implications for certification', *Ecological Applications* 18 (2008), 1754–63.

Anand, M. O., J. Krishnaswamy, A. Kumar and A. Bali, 'Sustaining biodiversity conservation in human-modified landscapes in the Western Ghats: Remnant forests matter', *Biological Conservation* 143 (2010), 2363–74.

Annaswamy, T. V., *Bengaluru to Bangalore: Urban history of Bangalore from the pre-historic period to the end of the 18th century*. Bangalore: Vengadam Publications, 2003.

Anonymous, *A Gazetteer of Delhi District, 1883–84*. Originally published by the Punjab Government Reprint. Gurgaon, Haryana: Vintage Books, 1988.

Anonymous, *The Delhi Ridge Forest: Decline and Conservation*. New Delhi: Kalpavriksh, 1991.

Anonymous, 'Report on Constraint Area and M/s Unison Hotels Ltd, Vasant Kunj', Environment Pollution (Prevention and Control) Authority For the National Capital Region, New Delhi, 2000.

Anonymous, 'Environmental impact assessment study for proposed landfill facility at Bhatti Mines, Delhi'. Final report carried out for the Municipal Corporation of Delhi. New Delhi: Consulting Engineering Services (India) Pvt. Ltd, 2005.

Anonymous, *City Development Plan Delhi, for the Department of Urban Development*. New Delhi: Government of India, IL&FS Ecosmart Ltd, 2006.

Anonymous, 'Agricultural statistics at a glance 2010'. Available at http://eands.dacnet.nic.in/Advance_Estimate-2010.htm (accessed 22 April 2014)

Anonymous, *Management Plan for the Upper Spiti Landscape Including the Kibber Wildlife Sanctuary*. Himachal Pradesh and Mysore: Wildlife Wing, Himachal Pradesh Forest Department and Nature Conservation Foundation, 2011.

Anonymous, 'Court stops defense construction on Delhi ridge', *Indo Asian News Service*, 5 December 2011. Available at http://in.news.yahoo.com/court-stops-defence-construction-delhi-ridge-095855978.html (accessed 25 April 2014).

Anthra, 'Annual Report 2007–08', Pune and Hyderabad: Anthra, 2008.

Anthra, 'Mid-Term Report, Pastoral Livelihoods', Hyderabad: Anthra, 2008.

Anthra, 'Annual Report 2008–2009', Pune and Hyderabad: Anthra, 2009.

Aratrakorn, S., S. Thunhikorn and P. F. Donald, 'Changes in bird communities following conversion of lowland forest to oil palm and rubber plantations in southern Thailand', *Bird Conservation International* 16 (2006), 71–82.

Archibald, G. W., K. S. G. Sundar and J. Barzen, 'A review of the three subspecies of Sarus Cranes (*Grus antigone*)', *Journal of Ecological Society* 16 (2003), 5–15.

Arthington, A. H., S. E. Bunn, N. L. Poff and R. J. Naiman, 'The challenge of providing environmental flow rules to sustain river ecosystems', *Ecological Applications* 16 (2006), 1311–1318.

Arthur, R., 'Patterns and processes of reef recovery and human resource use in the Lakshadweep Islands, Indian Ocean'. PhD thesis, James Cook University, Australia, 2005.

Ashraf, J., *Studies in Historical Ecology of India*. New Delhi: Sunrise Publications, 2004.

Assam Tribune, 'Translocated rhinos rehab prog receives big boost', 8 July 2013.

Athreya, V., 'Is relocation a viable management option for unwanted animals?: The case of the leopard in India', *Conservation and Society* 4 (2006), 419–23.

Athreya, V., and A. V. Belsare, *Human-Leopard Conflict Management Guidelines*, Pune: Kaati Trust, 2007.

Athreya, V., M. Odden, J. D. C. Linnell and K. U. Karanth, 'Translocation as a tool for mitigating conflict with leopards in human-dominated landscapes of India', *Conservation Biology* 25 (2011), 133–41.

Athreya, V., M. Odden, J. D. C. Linnell, J. Krishnaswamy and U. Karanth, 'Big cats in our backyards: Persistence of large carnivores in a human dominated landscape in India', *PLoS ONE* 8 (2013), e57872.

Athreya, V., S. S. Thakur, S. Chaudhuri and A. V. Belsare, 'A study of the man-leopard conflict in the Junnar Forest Division, Pune District, Maharashtra', submitted to the Office of the Chief Wildlife Warden, Nagpur, Maharashtra Forest Department, 2004.

Athreya, V. R., S. S. Thakur, S. Chaudhuri and A. V. Belsare, 'Leopards in human-dominated areas: A spillover from sustained translocations into nearby forests?', *Journal of the Bombay Natural History Society* 104 (2007), 45–50.

Bagchi, S., C. Mishra and Y. V. Bhatnagar, 'Conflicts between traditional pastoralism and conservation of Himalayan ibex (*Capra sibirica*) in the Trans-Himalayan mountains', *Animal Conservation* 7 (2004), 121–28.

Bagchi, S. and C. Mishra, 'Living with large carnivores: Predation on livestock by the snow leopard (*Uncia uncia*)', *Journal of Zoology* 268 (2006), 217–24.

Bal, P., C. D. Nath, K. M. Nanaya, C. G. Kushalappa and C. Garcia, 'Elephants also like coffee: Trends and drivers of human-elephant conflicts in coffee agroforestry landscapes of Kodagu, Western Ghats, India', *Environmental Management* 47 (2011), 789–801.

Bali, A., A. Kumar and J. Krishnaswamy, 'The mammalian communities in coffee plantations around a protected area in the Western Ghats, India', *Biological Conservation* 139 (2007), 93–102.

Balmford, A., R. Green and J. P. W. Scharlemann, ' Sparing land for nature: Exploring the potential impact of changes in agricultural yield on the area needed for crop production', *Global Change Biology* 11 (2005), 1594–605.

Bandyopadhyay, J., and S. Perveen, *The Interlinking of Indian Rivers: Some questions on the scientific, economic and environmental dimensions of the proposal.* London: SOAS Water Issues Study Group, School of Oriental and African Studies, King's College, 2004.

Banks, J. E., 'Divided culture: Integrating agriculture and conservation biology', *Frontiers in Ecology and the Environment* 2 (2004), 537–45.

Banerjee, M., 'A report on the impact of Farakka barrage on the human fabric'. New Delhi: South Asia Network on Dams, Rivers and People, 1999.

Bavinck, M., 'Changing balance of power at sea: Motorization of artisanal fishing craft', *Economic and Political Weekly* 32 (1997), 198–200.

Bavinck, M., *Marine Resource Management: Conflict and regulation in the fisheries of the Coromandel Coast.* New Delhi: Sage, 2001.

Bavinck, M., 'Understanding fisheries conflicts in the south: A legal pluralist perspective', *Society and Natural Resources* 18 (2005), 805–20.

Baviskar, A., 'The politics of the city', *Seminar* 516 (2002). Available at http://india-seminar.com/2002/516/516%20amita%20baviskar.htm (accessed 10 February 2012).

Baviskar, A., 'States, communities and conservation, the practice of ecodevelopment in the Great Himalayan National Park' in V. Saberwal and M. Rangarajan (eds), *Battles Over Nature: Science and the politics of conservation.* Delhi: Permanent Black, 2003, pp. 267–99.

Baviskar, A., 'What the eye does not see: The Yamuna in the imagination of Delhi', *Economic and Political Weekly* 46 (2011): 45–53.

Beehler, B. M., K. S. R. K. Raju and S. Ali, 'Avian use of man-disturbed forest habitats in the Eastern Ghats, India', *Ibis* 129 (1987), 197–211.

Bengtsson, J., P. Angelstam, T. Elmqvist, U. Emanuelsson, C. Folke, M. Ihse, F. Moberg and M. Nyström, 'Reserves, resilience and dynamic landscapes', *AMBIO: A Journal of the Human Environment* 32 (2003), 389–96.

Berger, J., B. Buuveibataar and C. Mishra, 'Globalization of the cashmere market and the decline of large mammals in Central Asia', *Conservation Biology* 27 (2013), 679–89.

Bhaduri, A., *The Face You Were Afraid to See: Essays on the Indian economy*. New Delhi: Penguin Books India, 2009.

Bhagwat, S., C. Kushalappa, P. Williams and N. Brown, 'The role of informal protected areas in maintaining biodiversity in the Western Ghats of India', *Ecology and Society* 1 (2005), 8.

Bhagwat, S. A., K. J. Willis, H. J. B. Birks and R. J. Whittaker, 'Agroforestry: A refuge for tropical biodiversity?', *Trends in Ecology and Evolution* 23 (2008), 261–67.

Bhathal, B., and D. Pauly, 'Fishing down marine food webs and spatial expansion of coastal fisheries in India, 1950–2000', *Fisheries Research* 91 (2008), 26–34.

Bhatnagar, Y. V., 'Relocation from wildlife reserves in the Greater and Trans-Himalaya: Is it necessary?', *Conservation and Society* 6 (2008), 263–70.

Bhatnagar, Y. V., and N. J. Singh, 'Nomadism in the Indian Changthang: Changes and implications on society and biodiversity', in K. G. Saxana, L. Liang, and X. Xue (eds), *Global Change, Biodiversity and Livelihoods in Cold Desert Regions of Asia*. Dehradun: Bishen Singh Mahendra Pal Singh, 2011, pp. 135–46.

Bhatnagar, Y. V., and R. Wangchuk, 'Status survey of large mammals in eastern Ladakh and Nubra.Conservation biodiversity in the Trans-Himalaya: New initiatives for field conservation in Ladakh'. Dehradun: Wildlife Institute of India, 2001.

Bhatnagar, Y. V., V. B. Mathur, T. McCarthy, 'A regional perspective for snow leopard conservation in the Indian Trans-Himalaya', in Y. V. Bhatnagar and S. E. Sathyakumar (eds), *WII ENVIS Bulletin*. Dehradun: Wildlife Institute of India, 2003.

Bhatnagar, Y. V., G. S. Rawat, A. J. T. Johnsingh and S. Michael, 'Ecological separation between ibex and resident livestock in a Trans-Himalayan Protected Area' in C. Richard, K. Basent, J. P. Sah and Y. Raut (eds), *Grassland Ecology and Management in Protected Areas of Nepal. Volume 2. Technical and status papers on grasslands of mountain Protected Areas.*

Royal Bardia National Park, Thakurwara, Bardia, Nepal. Kathmandu: ICIMOD, 2000, pp. 71–84.

Bhatnagar, Y. V., G. S. Rawat, A. J. T. Johnsingh and M. Stüwe, 'Ecological separation between ibex and resident livestock in a Trans-Himalayan Protected Area', *Grassland Ecology and Management in Protected Areas of Nepal* 3 (2000), 70–84.

Bhatnagar, Y. V., R. Wangchuk and R. Jackson, *A Survey of Depredation and Related Human-Wildlife Conflicts in Hemis National Park, Ladakh, Jammu and Kashmir.* Seattle, WA, USA: International Snow Leopard Trust, 1999.

Bhatnagar, Y. V., R. Wangchuk and C. Mishra, 'Decline of the Tibetan gazelle *Procapra picticaudata* in Ladakh, India', *Oryx* 40 (2006), 229–32.

Bhatnagar, Y. V., 'Ranging and Habitat Use by Himalayan Ibex (*Capra ibex sibirica*) in Pin Valley National Park'. PhD Thesis, Saurashtra University, Rajkot, 1997.

Bhatnagar, Y. V., 'Relocation from wildlife reserves in the Greater and Trans-Himalayas: Is it necessary?', *Conservation and Society* 6 (2008), 263.

Bhukya, B., *Subjugated Nomads: The Lambadas under the rule of the Nizam.* Hyderabad: Orient Blackswan, 2010.

Biggs, D., *Quagmire: Nation-building and Nature in the Mekong Delta.* Seattle: University of Washington Press. 2012.

Bijoy, C. R., 'The great Indian tiger show', *Economic and Political Weekly* 46 (2011), 36–41.

BirdLife International, *State of the World's Birds 2004: Indicators for our changing world.* Cambridge: BirdLife International, 2004.

Bonhommeau, S., L. Dubroca, O. Le Pape, J. Barde, D. M. Kaplan, E. Chassot and A. E. Nieblas, 'Eating up the world's food web and the human trophic level', *Proceedings of the National Academy of Sciences* (USA) 110 (2013), 20617–20.

Borges, R., 'The anatomy of ignorance or ecology in a fragmented landscape: Do we know what really counts?', in V. Saberwal and M. Rangarajan (eds), *Battles Over Nature: Science and the politics of conservation.* Delhi: Permanent Black, 2003, pp. 56–85.

Botkin, D. B., *Discordant Harmonies: A new ecology for the twenty-first century.* New York: Oxford University Press, 1992.

Bradshaw, C. J. A, N. S. Sodhi and B. W. Brook, 'Tropical turmoil: A biodiversity tragedy in progress', *Frontiers in Ecology and the Environment* 7 (2009), 79–87.

Branch, T. A., O. P. Jensen, D. Ricard, Y. Ye and R. Hilborn, 'Contrasting global trends in marine fishery status obtained from catches and from stock assessments', *Conservation Biology* 25 (2011), 777–86.

Branch, T. A., A. S. Lobo and S. W. Purcell, 'Opportunistic exploitation: An overlooked pathway to extinction', *Trends in Ecology and Evolution* 28, no. 7 (2013), 409–13.

Branch, T. A., 'Not all fisheries will be collapsed in 2048', *Marine Policy* 32 (2008), 38–39.

Briggs, J., 'Marine extinctions and conservation', *Marine Biology* 158 (2011), 485–88.

Brockerhoff, E. G., H. Jactel, J. A. Parrotta, C. P. Quine and J. Sayer, 'Plantation forests and biodiversity: Oxymoron or opportunity?', *Biodiversity and Conservation* 17 (2008), 925–51.

Brockington, D., R. Duffy and J. Igoe, *Nature Unbound: Conservation, capitalism and the future of protected areas*. London: Earthscan, 2008.

Bruhat Bangalore Mahanagara Palike (BBMP), *Namma Bengaluru Nisarga: An action plan for development of Bangalore's lakes*. Bangalore: BBMP, 2010.

Buchanan, F., *A Journey from Madras through the Countries of Mysore, Canara, and Malabar*. New Delhi: Asian Educational Services, 1807.

Bunn, S. E., and A. H. Arthington, 'Basic principles and ecological consequences of altered flow regimes for aquatic biodiversity', *Environmental Management* 30 (2002), 492–507.

Carruthers, J., *The Kruger National Park: A social and political history*. Durban: University of Kwazulu-Natal Press, 1995.

Carson, R., *Silent Spring*. London: Hamish Hamilton, 1962.

Carter, N. H., B. K. Shrestha, J. B. Karki, N. M. B. Pradhan and J. Liu, 'Coexistence between wildlife and humans at fine spatial scales', *Proceedings of the National Academy of Sciences (USA)* 109 (2012), 15360–65.

Carter, N. H., B. K. Shrestha, J. B. Karki, N. M. B. Pradhan and J. Liu, 'Reply to Goswami et al., Harihar et al., and Karanth et al.: Fine-scale interactions between tigers and people', *Proceedings of the National Academy of Sciences (USA)* 110 (2013), E111–E112.

Castro, A. P., and E. Nielsen, 'Indigenous people and co-management: Implications for conflict management', *Environmental Science and Policy* 4 (2001), 229–39.

Catton, T., *Inhabited Wilderness: Indians, eskimos, and national parks in Alaska*. Albuquerque: University of New Mexico Press, 1997.

Cederlof, G., 'Fixed boundaries, fluid landscapes: British expansion into northern East Bengal in the 1820s', *Indian Economic and Social History Review* 4 (2009), 513–40.

Chang, T. T., 'The origin, evolution, cultivation, dissemination, and diversification of Asian and African rices', *Euphytica* 25 (1976), 425–41.

Chape, S., S. Blyth, L. Fish, P. Fox and M. Spalding, *United Nations List of Protected Areas*. Gland, Switzerland and Cambridge, UK: IUCN and UNEP-WCMC, 2003.

Chape, S., J. Harrison, M. Spalding and I. Lysenko, 'Measuring the extent and effectiveness of protected areas as an indicator for meeting global biodiversity targets', *Philosophical Transactions of the Royal Society Series B* 360 (2005), 443–55.

Chhatre, A., and V. K. Saberwal, *Democratizing Nature: Politics, conservation, and development in India*. New Delhi: Oxford University Press, 2006.

Chitampalli, M. B., *Nisargavachan* (Marathi). Nagpur: Sahitya Prasar Kendra, 2007.

Choudhary, S., S. Dey, S. Dey, V. Sagar, T. Nair and N. Kelkar, 'River dolphin distribution in regulated river systems: Implications for dry-season flow regimes in the Gangetic basin', *Aquatic Conservation: Marine and Freshwater Ecosystems* 22 (2012), 11–25.

Choudhary, S. K., B. D. Smith, S. Dey, S. Dey and S. Prakash, 'Conservation and biomonitoring in the Vikramshila Gangetic Dolphin Sanctuary, Bihar, India', *Oryx* 40 (2006), 189–97.

Chundawat, R. S., and Q. Qureshi, *Planning Wildlife Conservation in Leh and Kargil Districts of Ladakh, Jammu and Kashmir.* Dehradun: Wildlife Institute of India, 1999.

Chundawat, R. S., B. Habib, U. Karanth, K. Kawanishi, J. Ahmad Khan, T. Lynam, D. Miquelle, P. Nyhus, S. Sunarto, R. Tilson and S. Wang, 'Panthera tigris' in IUCN, *IUCN Red List of Threatened Species. Version 2013.2*, 2013. Available at www.iucnredlist.org (accessed 7 May 2014).

Cinner, J. E., T. R. McClanahan, M. A. MacNeil, N. A J. Graham, T. M. Daw, A. Mukminin, D. A. Feary, A. L. Rabearisoa, A. Wamukota, N. Jidawi, S. J. Campbell, A. H. Baird, F. A. Januchowski-Hartley, R. Lahari, T. Morove and J. Kuange, 'Comanagement of coral reef social-ecological systems', *Proceedings of National Academy of Sciences (USA)* 109 (2012), 5219–22:

Civil Society Magazine, 'Bhatti's odds in legal dilemma', August 2009. Available at http://www.civilsocietyonline.com/aug07/aug079.asp (accessed 21 March 2012)

Clay, J. W., *World Agriculture and the Environment: A commodity-by-commodity guide to impacts and practices.* Washington DC: Island Press, 2004.

Clover, C., *The End of the Line: How Overfishing is changing the world and what we eat*, London: Random House, 2004.

Central Marine Fisheries Research Institute (CMFRI), *Annual Report 2006–2007,* Cochin: CMFRI, Cochin, 2007.

Collen, B., L. McRae, G. Kothari, R. Mellor, O. Daniel, A. Greenwood, R. Amin, S. Holbrook and J. Baillie, *Living Planet Index 2010 and Beyond: Rising to the biodiversity challenge.* Gland, Switzerland: World Wildlife Fund, 2008.

Congreve, C. R. T., *The Anamalais.* Madras: Associated Printers, 1942.

Critical Ecosystems Partnerships Fund, *Ecosystem Profile Western Ghats & Sri Lanka Biodiversity Hotspot: Western Ghats region.* Arlington, USA: CEPF, 2007.

Cronon, W., 'The trouble with wilderness: Or, getting back to the wrong nature' in W. Cronon (ed.), *Uncommon Ground: Rethinking the human place in nature.* New York: W. W. Norton & Company, 1995, pp. 69–90.

D'Souza, R., and H. Nagendra, 'Changes in public commons as a consequence of urbanization', *Environmental Management* 47, no. 5 (2011), 840.

Daan, N., H. Gislason, J. G. Pope and J. C. Rice, 'Apocalypse in world fisheries?: The reports of their death are greatly exaggerated', *ICES Journal of Marine Science* 68 (2011), 1375–78.

Daily, G. C., G. Ceballos, J. Pacheco, G. Suzán and A. Sanchez-Azofeifa, 'Countryside biogeography of neotropical mammals: Conservation opportunities in agricultural landscapes of Costa Rica', *Conservation Biology* 17 (2003), 1814–26.

Dandekar, A., 'In the name of pastoralism: The early medieval Maharashtra', in S. Ratnagar and R. Heredia (eds), *Mobile and Marginalized Peoples: Perspectives from the past.* New Delhi: Manohar, 2003, pp. 65–88.

Daniels, R. J. R., M. Gadgil and N. V. Joshi, 'Impact of human extraction on tropical humid forests in the Western Ghats Uttara Kannada, South India', *Journal of Applied Ecology* 32 (1995), 866–74.

Daniels, R. J. R., M. Hegde and M. Gadgil, 'Birds of the man-made ecosystems: The plantations', *Proceedings of the Indian Academy of Sciences-Animal Sciences, 1990,* 99 (1990), 79–89.

Das, A., J. Krishnaswamy, K. S. Bawa, M. C. Kiran, V. Srinivas, N. S. Kumar and K. U. Karanth, 'Prioritisation of conservation areas in the Western Ghats, India', *Biological Conservation* 133 (2006), 16–31.

Das, S. K., 'Small-scale rural aquaculture in Assam, India: A case study', *NAGA: World Fish Center Quarterly* 29 (2006), 42–47.

Dasgupta, S., 'Accessing nature: Forest laws and their impact on an *Adivasi* economy in Central India', *Conservation and Society* 7 (2009), 227–38.

Datta, A., 'Science, policy, politics and human rights: Myriad dimensions of conservation in the real world', Public lecture at the Society for Conservation Biology (Asia) Meeting, Bangalore, 10 August 2012. Unpublished.

DeFries, R., A. Hansen, A. C. Newton and M. C. Hansen, 'Increasing isolation of protected areas in tropical forests over the past twenty years', *Ecological Applications* 15 (2005), 19–26.

Delgado, C. L., 'Rising consumption of meat and milk in developing countries has created a new food revolution', *The Journal of Nutrition* 133 (2003), 3907–10.

Development Department, 'Notification No F.10 (42)-I/PA/DCF/93/2012-17(1)', *Delhi Gazette*. New Delhi: Govt. of NCT of Delhi, 1994.

Directorate of Economics and Statistics, *Compendium of Area and Land Use Statistics of Andhra Pradesh 1955–56 to 2004–05*. Hyderabad: Directorate of Economics and Statistics, Government of Andhra Pradesh, 2007–08.

Dinerstein, E., C. Loucks, E. Wikramanayake, J. Ginsberg, E. Sanderson, J. Seidensticker, J. Forrest, G. Bryja, A. Heydlauft, S. Klenzendorf, P. leimgruber, J. Mills, T. G. O'Brien, M. Shreshtha, R. Simons and M. Songer, 'The fate of wild tigers', *BioScience* 57 (2007), 508–14.

Dinerstein, E., A. Rijal, M. Bookbinder, B. Kattel and A. Rajuria, 'Tigers as neighbours: Efforts to promote local guardianship of endangered species in lowland Nepal', in J. Seidensticker, S. Christie and P. Jackson (eds), *Riding the Tiger: Tiger conservation in human-dominated landscapes*. Cambridge: Cambridge University Press, 1999, pp. 316–33.

Dolia, J., M. S. Devy, N. A. Aravind and A. Kumar, 'Adult butterfly communities in coffee plantations around a protected area in the Western Ghats, India', *Animal Conservation* 11 (2008), 26–34.

Donald, P. F., 'Biodiversity impacts of some agricultural commodity production systems', *Conservation Biology* 18 (2004), 17–38.

Douglas, M. M., S. E. Bunn, R. J. W. Pidgeon, P. M. Davies, P. Barrow, R. O'Connor and M. Winning, 'Weed management and the biodiversity and ecological processes of tropical wetlands'. Draft final report, Australia: National Wetlands R&D Program, Environment Australia and Land and Water Australia, 2001.

Dreze, J., and A. Sen, *An Uncertain Glory: India and its contradictions*. New Delhi: Penguin India, 2013.

Dudgeon, D., 'Large-scale hydrological changes in tropical Asia: Prospects for riverine biodiversity', *BioScience* 50 (2000), 793–806.

Dudgeon, D., 'River rehabilitation for conservation of fish biodiversity in monsoonal Asia', *Ecology and Society* 10 (2005), 15.

Elphick, C. S., and L. W. Oring, 'Conservation implications of flooding rice fields on winter waterbird communities', *Agriculture, Ecosystems and Environment* 94 (2003), 17–29.

Feldhaus, A., A. Malik and B. Bruckner, 'Essays on Khandoba' in S. Gunther-Dietz (ed.), *King of Hunters, Warriors, and Shepherds.* New Delhi: Manohar, 1997, pp. 19–33.

Foundation for Ecological Security, *A Commons Story: In the rain shadow of green revolution*. New Delhi: Foundation for Ecological Security, 2011.

Fischer, J., B. Brosi, G. C. Daily, P. R. Ehrlich, R. Goldman, J. Goldstein, D. B. Lindenmayer, A. D. manning, H. A. mooney, L. Pejchar, J. Ranganthan and H. Tallis, 'Should agricultural policies encourage land sparing or wildlife-friendly farming?', *Frontiers in Ecology and the Environment* 6 (2008), 380–85.

Fitzherbert, E. B., M. J. Struebig, A. Morel, F. Danielsen, C. A. Brühl, P. F. Donald and B. Phalan, 'How will oil palm expansion affect biodiversity?', *Trends in Ecology and Evolution* 23 (2008), 538–45.

Foley, J. A., G. P. Asner, M. H. Costa, M. T. Coe, R. DeFries, H. K. Gibbs, E. A. Howard, S. Olson, J. Patz, N. Ramankutty and P. Snyder, 'Amazonia revealed: Forest degradation and loss of ecosystem goods and services in the Amazon Basin', *Frontiers in Ecology and the Environment* 5 (2007), 25–32.

Foley, J. A., R. DeFries, G. P. Asner, C. Barford, G. Bonan, S. R. Carpenter, F. S. Chapin, M. T. Coe, G. C. Daily, H. K. Gibbs, J. H. Helkowski, T. Holloway, E. A. Howard, C. J. Kucharik, C. Monfreda, J. A. Patz and I. C. Prentice, 'Global consequences of land use', *Science* 309 (2005), 570–74.

Freeman, R., 'Folk models of the forest environment' in M. Rangarajan and K. Sivaramakrishnan (eds), *India's Environmental History, Volume 2*. Ranikhet: Permanent Black, 2012, pp. 169–96.

Funge-Smith, S., E. Lindebo and D. Staples, *Asian Fisheries Today: The production and use of low value/trash fish from marine fisheries in the Asia-Pacific region*. Bangkok: Food and Agricultural Organization of the United Nations, 2005.

Gadgil, M., 'Ecology, science and democracy in India', 2013. Available at http://www.nehrumemorial.org/audio/(594)Lecture-by-Sh. Madhav-Gadgil-17-7-13.MP3 (accessed 5 February 2014).

Gadgil, M., *Ecological Journeys: The science and politics of conservation in India*. Ranikhet: Permanent Black, 2001.

Ganguli, U., *A Guide to the Birds of the Delhi Area*. New Delhi: Indian Council of Agricultural Research, 1975.

Garcia, C., D. Marie-Vivien, C. G. Kushalappa, P. G. Chengappa and K. M. Nanaya, 'Geographical indications and biodiversity in the Western Ghats, India: Can labeling benefit producers and the environment in a mountain agroforestry landscape?', *Mountain Research and Development* 27 (2007), 206–10.

Garcia, C. A., S. Bhagwat, J. Ghazoul, C. D. Nath, K. M. Nanaya, C. G. Kushalappa, Y. Raghuramulu, R. Naasi and P. Vast, 'Biodiversity conservation in agricultural landscapes: Challenges and opportunities of coffee agroforests in the Western Ghats, India', *Conservation Biology* 24 (2010), 479–88.

Gee, E. P., *The Wildlife of India*. London: Fontana, 1964.

Ghosh, A., *The Hungry Tide*. London: Harper Collins.

Ghoshal, A., 'Wild blames wild', *Care4nature* (2011), 26–28.

Gillet, P., *Small is Difficult: The pangs and success of small boat technology transfer in South India*, Rugby, UK: Intermediate Technology Development Group (ITDG), 1985.

Ginn, W., *Investing in Nature: Case studies of land conservation in collaboration with business*. Washington DC: Island Press, 2005.

Global Tiger Initiative Secretariat, *Global Tiger Recovery Program, 2010–2022*. Washington DC: World Bank, 2010.

Gold, A. G., and B. R. Gujjar, *In the Time of Trees and Sorrows: Nature, power, and memory in Rajasthan*. Durham: Duke University Press, 2002.

Gopal, B., 'Does inland aquatic biodiversity have a future in Asian developing countries?' *Hydrobiologia* 542 (2005), 69–75.

Gopalakrishnan, S., 'Conservation and democracy', *Seminar* 638 (2010), 66–71.

Goswami, V. R., D. Vasudev, D. Karnad, Y. C. Krishna, M. Krishnadas, M. Pariwakam, T. Nair, A. Andheria, S. Sridhara and I. Siddiqui, 'Conflict of human–wildlife coexistence', *Proceedings of the National Academy of Sciences (USA)* 110 (2013), E108–E110.

Government of Andhra Pradesh. *Facts and Figures of Andhra Pradesh*, Hyderabad, 2010.

Government of India. 'Indian Board for Wildlife (IBWL) Report of the Expert Committee'. New Delhi: Ministry of Agriculture, 1970.

Government of India. 'Joining the Dots: Report of the Tiger Task Force'. New Delhi: Ministry of Environment and Forests, 2005.

Government of India. 'Report of the High Level Working Group on the Western Ghats Ecology Expert Panel: Part 1 & 2'. New Delhi: Ministry of Environment and Forests, 2011.

Government of India. 'Report of the High Level Working Group on Western Ghats: Volumes I and II'. New Delhi: Ministry of Environment and Forests, 2013.

Government of National Capital Territory of Delhi (NCTD), 'Report of the committee to recommend the pattern of management of the Delhi Ridge', NCTD, New Delhi, 2004.

Government of NCT of Delhi, 'Recorded Forests'. Available at http://www.delhi.gov.in/wps/wcm/connect/doit_forest/Forest/Home/Forests+of+Delhi/Recorded+Forest (accessed 13 May 2014).

Gowda, K., and M. V. Sridhara, 'Conservation of tanks/lakes in the Bangalore metropolitan area', *Management of Environmental Quality* 18 (2007), 137–51.

Green, R. E., S. J. Cornell, J. P. W. Scharlemann and A. Balmford, 'Farming and the fate of wild nature', *Science* 307 (2005), 550–555.

Green, R. E., M. A. Taggart, D. Das, D. J. Pain, C. S. Kumar, A. A. Cunningham and R. Cuthbert, 'Collapse of Asian vulture populations: Risk of mortality from residues of the veterinary drug diclofenac in carcasses of treated cattle', *Journal of Applied Ecology* 43 (2006), 949–56.

Greenberg, R., P. Bichier, A. C. Angon and R. Reitsma, 'Bird populations in shade and sun coffee plantations in central Guatemala', *Conservation Biology* 11 (1997), 448–59.

Greenberg, R., I. Perfecto and S. M. Philpott, 'Agroforests as model systems for tropical ecology', *Ecology* 89 (2008), 913–14.

Grimm, N. B., S. H. Faeth, N. E. Golubiewski, C. L. Redman, J. Wu, X. Bai and J. M. Briggs, 'Global change and the ecology of cities', *Science* 319 (2008), 756–60.

Guha, R., 'The authoritarian biologist and the arrogance of anti-humanism: Wildlife conservation in the third world', in V. Saberwal, and M. Rangarajan (eds), *Battles Over Nature: Science and the politics of Conservation*. Delhi: Permanent Black, 2003, pp. 139–57.

Guha, S., *Health and Population in South Asia: From earliest times to the present*. New Delhi: Permanent Black, 2001.

Gupta, C., 'Unshackling the Ganga', *Down to Earth* 2 (1993), 22–24.

Gupta, N., 'Delhi's history as reflected in its toponymy', in Maya Dayal (ed.), *Celebrating Delhi*. New Delhi: Viking Books, 2010, pp. 96–97.

Gurung, G. S., K. Thapa, K. Kunkel, G. J. Thapa, M. Kollmair and U. M. Boeker, 'Enhancing herders' livelihood and conserving the snow leopard in Nepal', *Cat News* 55 (2011), 17–21.

Gutiérrez, N. L., R. Hilborn and O. Defeo, 'Leadership, social capital and incentives promote successful fisheries', *Nature* 470 (2011), 386–89.

Habib, I., and F. Habib, *The Atlas of Ancient India*. New Delhi: Oxford University Press, 2012.

Hall, M. A., D. L. Alverson and K. I. Metuzals, 'By-Catch: Problems and solutions', *Marine Pollution Bulletin* 41 (2000), 204–19.

Handschuh, M., V. Rours and H. Rainey, 'Clutch size of Sarus Crane *Grus antigone* in the Northern Plains of Cambodia and incidence of clutches with three eggs', *Cambodian Journal of Natural History* 103 (2010).

Harihar, A., P. Chanchani, R. K. Sharma, J. Vattakaven, S. Gubbi, B. Pandav and B. Noon, 'Conflating "co-occurrence" with "coexistence"', *Proceedings of the National Academy of Sciences (USA)* 110 (2013), E109.

Harvey, C. A., and J. A. G. Villalobos, 'Agroforestry systems conserve species-rich but modified assemblages of tropical birds and bats', *Biodiversity and Conservation* 16 (2007), 2257–92.

Hashmi, S., 'Death of a river', *Kafila*, February 2011. Available at http://kafila.org/2011/02/04/death-of-a-river-yamuna-jamuna-delhi/ (accessed 12 May 2014).

Hazzah, L., and S. Dolrenry, 'Coexisting with predators', *Seminar* 577 (2007), 21–27.

Hazzah, L., S. Dolrenry, D. Kaplan and L. Frank, 'The influence of park access during drought on attitudes toward wildlife and lion killing behaviour in Maasailand, Kenya', *Environmental Conservation* 40 (2013), 266–76.

Hecht, S. B. and A. Cockburn, *The Fate of the Forest: Developers, destroyers, and defenders of the Amazon*. Chicago: University of Chicago Press, 1990.

Herzon, I., and M. Mikk, 'Farmers' perceptions of biodiversity and their willingness to enhance it through agri-environment schemes: A comparative study from Estonia and Finland', *Journal for Nature Conservation* 15 (2007), 10–25.

Hetkert, J. R., 'Response of bird populations to farmland set-aside programs', *Conservation Biology* 23 (2009), 1036–40.

Hindu, 'Right to fly (advertisement by the Government of Rajasthan)', 5 June 2013.

Hiremath, A. J., and B. Sundaram, 'The fire-lantana cycle hypothesis in Indian forests', *Conservation and Society* 3 (2005), 26–42.

Hughes, J. E., *Animal Kingdoms: Hunting, the environment, and power in the Indian princely states*. Cambridge: Harvard University Press, 2013.

Hughes, L., *Moving the Maasai: A colonial misadventure*. Basingstoke: Palgrave Macmillan, 2006.

Hughes, L., 'Rough time in paradise: Claims, blames and memory making around some protected areas in Kenya', *Conservation and Society* 5 (2007), 307–30.

Hussain, S., 'Protecting the snow leopard and enhancing farmers' livelihoods: A pilot insurance scheme in Baltistan', *Mountain Research and Development* 20 (2000), 226–31.

Hussain, S., 'The status of the snow leopard in Pakistan and its conflict with local farmers', *Oryx* 37 (2003), 26–33.

Ikeda, N., 'Economic impacts of livestock depredation by snow leopard *Uncia uncia* in the Kanchenjunga Conservation Area, Nepal Himalaya', *Environmental Conservation* 31 (2004), 322–30.

Isenberg, A. C., *The Destruction of the Bison: An environmental history, 1750–1920*. Cambridge: Cambridge University Press, 2001.

Ishwar, N. M., R. Chellam, A. Kumar and B. R. Noon, 'The response of agamid lizards to rainforest fragmentation in the southern Western Ghats, India', *Conservation and Society* 1 (2003), 69–86.

Jackson, J. B. C., 'Ecological extinction and evolution in the brave new ocean', *Proceedings of the National Academy of Sciences (USA)* 105 (2008), 11458–65.

Jackson, R. and R. Wangchuk, 'Linking snow leopard conservation and people-wildlife conflict resolution: Grassroots measures to protect the endangered snow leopard from herder retribution', *Endangered Species Update* 18 (2001), 138–41.

Jackson, R. M., and R. Wangchuk, 'A community-based approach to mitigating livestock depredation by snow leopards', *Human Dimensions of Wildlife* 9 (2004), 1–16.

Jacoby, K., *Crimes Against Nature: Squatters, poachers, thieves, and the hidden history of American conservation*. Berkeley: University of California Press, 2003.

Jagpal Singh and Others vs State of Punjab and Others, Judgment for civil appeal no. 1132/2011 in SLP (C) no. 3109/2011. New Delhi: Supreme Court of India, 2011.

Jalais, A., 'Unmasking the cosmopolitan tiger', *Nature and Culture* 3 (2008), 25–40.

Jalais, A., *Forest of Tigers: People, politics and environment in the Sundarbans*. London: Routledge, 2011.

Janzen, D., 'The eternal external threat' in M. E. Soule (ed.), *Conservation Biology: The science of scarcity and diversity*. Sunderland: Sinauer Associates, 1986, pp. 286–303.

Jha, C. S., C. B. S. Dutt and K. S. Bawa, 'Deforestation and land use changes in Western Ghats, India', *Current Science* 79 (2000), 231–37.

Jhala, Y. V., 'Human-wolf conflict in India' presented at the Beyond 2000 Symposium, February 2000. Available at http://www.wolf.org/wolves/learn/intermed/inter_human/india_abstract_003.asp (accessed 20 July 2010).

Jhala, Y. V., 'Status, ecology and conservation of the Indian wolf *Canis lupus pallipes* (Sykes)', *Journal of the Bombay Natural History Society* 100 (2003), 293–307.

Jhala, Y. V., R. Chellam, B. Pathak, V. Meena and P. Basu, *Ecology of the lion in Greater Gir Landscape*. Dehradun: Wildlife Institute of India, 2011.

Jhala, Y. V., Q. Qureshi and P. R. Sinha, *Status of Tigers, Co-predators and Prey in India*. New Delhi and Dehradun: National Tiger Conservation Authority, Government of India, and the Wildlife Institute of India, 2011.

Jodha, N. S., 'Common property resources and rural poor in dry regions of India', *Economic and Political Weekly* 21 (1986), 169–81.

Jodha, N. S., 'Common property resources and the environmental context', *Economic and Political Weekly* 30 (1995), 278–84.

Johari, R., 'Paper tigers and invisible people: The cultural politics of nature' in G. Shahabuddin and M. Rangarajan (eds), *Making Conservation Work: Securing biodiversity in this new century*, pp. 48–80. New Delhi: Permanent Black, 2007.

Johnsingh, A. J. T., K. Ramesh, Q. Qureshi, A. David, S. P. Goyal, G. S. Rawat, K. Rajapandian and S. Prasad, *Conservation status of tiger and associated species in the Terai Arc Landscape, India, RR-04/001*, Wildlife Institute of India, Dehradun, 2004.

Joshi, A. A., D. Mudappa and T. R. S. Raman, 'Brewing trouble: Coffee invasion in relation to edges and forest structure in tropical rainforest fragments of the Western Ghats, India', *Biological Invasions* 11 (2009), 2387–400.

Kamath, S. U., *Karnataka State Gazetteer: Bangalore district*. Bangalore: Lotus Printers, 1990.

Kapoor, M., K. Kohli and M. Menon, *India's Notified Ecologically Sensitive Areas (ESAs)*. Pune: Kalpavriksh, 2009.

Karanth, K. K., and R. DeFries, 'Nature-based tourism in Indian protected areas: New challenges for park management', *Conservation Letters* 4 (2011), 137–49.

Karanth, K. U., and P. Bhargav, 'De-fragmenting nature', *Seminar* 552 (2005), 59–61.

Karanth, K. U., and K. K. Karanth, 'A tiger in the drawing room', *Economic and Political Weekly* 47 (2012), 38–43.

Karanth, K. U., A. M. Gopalaswamy, K. K. Karanth, J. Goodrich, J. Seidensticker and J. G. Robinson, 'Sinks as saviors: Why flawed inference cannot assist tiger recovery', *Proceedings of the National Academy of Sciences* 110 (2013), E110.

Karanth, K. U., *The Way of the Tiger: Natural history and conservation of the endangered big cat*. Stillwater, USA: Voyageur Press, 2001.

Karanth, K. U., *View from the machan: How science can save the fragile predator*. Ranikhet: Permanent Black, 2005.

Kavoori, P. S., *Pastoralism in Expansion: The transhuming herders of Western Rajasthan*. New Delhi: Oxford University Press, 1999.

Kelkar, N., J. Krishnaswamy, S. Choudhary and D. Sutaria, 'Coexistence of fisheries with river dolphin conservation', *Conservation Biology* 24 (2010), 1130–40.

Kelleher, K., 'Discards in the world's marine fisheries: An update' in Rep. 470. Rome: Food and Agriculture Organization of the United Nations, 2005.

Karnataka Elephant Task Force, *Report of the Karnataka Elephant Task Force appointed by the Karnataka High Court*. Bangalore: Government of Karnataka, 2012.

Kenneth Builders & Developers Ltd vs Union of India & Ors, WP(C) 10647/2009, judgment of 30 July 2010. Available at http://www.indiankanoon.org/doc/146778/ (accessed 24 April 2014).

Kleijn, D., M. Rundlöf, J. Scheper, H. G. Smith and T. Tscharntke, Does conservation on farmland contribute to halting the biodiversity decline?', *Trends in Ecology and Evolution* 26 (2011), 474–81.

Klein, C. J., A. Chan, L. Kircher, A. J. Cundiff, N. Gardner, Y. Hrovat, A. Scholz, B. E. Kendall and S. Airame, 'Striking a balance between biodiversity conservation and socioeconomic viability in the design of marine protected areas', *Conservation Biology* 22 (2008), 691–700.

Koh, L. P., and T. A. Gardner, 'Conservation in human-modified landscapes' in N. S. Sodhi and P. R. Ehrlich (eds), *Conservation Biology for All*. Oxford: Oxford University Press, 2010, pp. 236–61.

Koh, L. P., J. Miettinen, S. C. Liew and J. Ghazoul, 'Remotely sensed evidence of tropical peatland conversion to oil palm', *Proceedings of the National Academy of Sciences* 108 (2011), 5127–32.

Kohli, K., 'Landfill is minefield for MCD', *Civil Society Magazine* (2011), 31–35.

Kothari, A., N. Pathak, R. V. Anuradha and B. Taneja (eds), *Communities and Conservation: Natural resource management in South and Central Asia*. New Delhi: Sage, 1998.

Kothari, A., *Understanding Biodiversity: Life, sustainability, and equity*. New Delhi: Orient Longman, 1997.

Kothari, A., 'The many colours of environmentalism', *Economic and Political Weekly* 47 (2012).

Krishen, P., *Trees of Delhi: A Field Guide*. New Delhi: Penguin Books, 2006.

Krishen, P., 'Realising the ridge', *India Today, Delhi Special* (2012), 46–47.

Krishnan, M., *India's wildlife in 1959–70: An ecological survey of the larger mammals of Peninsular India*. Bombay: Bombay Natural History Society, 1975.

Krishnan, S., and J. Ghazoul, 'Importance of bees, shade trees and forests in coffee production in Kodagu', *Indian Coffee* 76 (2012), 10–12.

Krithivasan, R., V. Athreya and M. Odden, *Human-wolf conflict in human dominated landscapes of Ahmednagar District, Maharashtra, India and possible mitigation measures*, submitted to the Rufford Small Grants Foundation, 2009.

Kumar, A., R. Pethiyagoda and D. Mudappa, 'Western Ghats and Sri Lanka', in R. Mittermeier, P. Gil, M. Hoffmann, J. Pilgrim, T. Brooks, C. Goettsch Mittermeier, J. Lamoreux, G. A. B. Da Fonseca and

P. A. Seligmann (eds), *Hotspots Revisited: Earth's biologically richest and most endangered ecoregions*. Mexico: CEMEX, 2004, pp. 152–57.

Kumar, M. A., and G. Raghunathan, *Human-elephant coexistence: Community involvement in conflict resolution in a land-use mosaic of the Anamalai Hills, Western Ghats, India*. Mysore: Nature Conservation Foundation, 2012.

Kumar, M. A., D. Mudappa and T. R. S. Raman, 'Asian elephant *Elephas maximus* habitat use and ranging in fragmented rainforest and plantations in the Anamalai Hills, India', *Tropical Conservation Science* 3 (2010), 143–58.

Kumar, M. A., D. Mudappa, T. R. S. Raman and M. D. Madhusudan, *The Elephant Hills: Conservation of wild Asian elephant in a landscape of fragmented rainforests and plantations in the Anamalais, India*, Mysore: Nature Conservation Foundation, 2004.

Kumar, R., G. Shahabuddin and A. Kumar, 'How good are managed forests at conserving native woodpecker communities?: A study in sub-Himalayan dipterocarp forests of northwest India', *Biological Conservation* 144 (2011), 1876–84.

Kumar, S., and A. R. Rahmani, 'Predation by wolves (*Canis lupus pallipes*) on blackbuck (*Antilope cervicapra*) in the Great Indian Bustard Sanctuary, Nannaj, Maharashtra, India', *International Journal of Ecology and Environmental Sciences* 34 (2008), 99–112.

Kurien, J., 'Entry of big business into fishing: Its impact on fish economy', *Economic and Political Weekly* 13 (1978): 1557–65.

Kurien, J., 'Technical assistance projects and socioeconomic change: Norwegian intervention in Kerala's fisheries development', *Economic and Political Weekly* 20 (1985), A70–A88.

Lahiri-Dutt, K., and G. Samanta, *Dancing with the River: People and lives on the chars of South Asia*. Yale: Yale University Press, 2012.

Lal Mohan, R. S., and N. Kelkar, 'The Ganges River dolphin' in A. J. T. Johnsingh and M. Manjrekar (eds), *Mammals of South Asia*. Universities Press, 2014.

Lam, M. E., and D. Pauly, 'Who is right to fish?: Evolving a social contract for ethical fisheries', *Ecology and Society* 15 (2010), 16.

Lamb, D., P. D. Erskine and J. A. Parrotta, 'Restoration of degraded tropical forest landscapes', *Science* 310 (2005), 1628–32.

Laurance, W. F., and R. Bierregaard, *Tropical Forest Remnants: Ecology, management, and conservation of fragmented communities*. Chicago: University of Chicago Press, 1997.

Laurance, W. F., D. Carolina Useche, J. Rendeiro, M. Kalka, C. J. A. Bradshaw, et al., 'Averting biodiversity collapse in tropical forest protected areas', *Nature* 489 (2012), 290–94.

Lawton, J. H., D. E. Bignell, B. Bolton, G. F. Bloemers, P. Eggleton, P. M. Hammond, M. Hodda, R. D. Holt, T. B. Larsen, N. A. Mawdsley, N. E. Stork, D. S. Srivastava and A. D. Watt, 'Biodiversity inventories, indicator taxa and effects of habitat modification in tropical forest', *Nature* 391 (1998), 72–76.

Laxman, D. S., *Ecology, Colonialism and Cattle: Central India in the nineteenth century*. New Delhi: Oxford University Press, 2004.

Le Saout, S., M. Hoffmann, Y. Shi, A. Hughes, C. Bernard, T. M. Brooks, B. Bertzky, S. H. M. Butchart, S. N. Stuart, T. Badman and A. S. L. Rodrigues, 'Conservation. Protected areas and effective biodiversity conservation', *Science* 342 (2013), 803–05.

Leakey, R., 'Not-so-cold mountain', *Economist*, 18 November 2005. Available at http://www.economist.com/node/5134723 (accessed 8 April 2014).

Leakey, R. E., and R. Lewin, *The Sixth Extinction: Biodiversity and its survival*. New York: Anchor Books, 1996.

Leakey, R. E., and V. Morell, *Wildlife Wars: My battle to save Kenya's elephants*. London: Pan Macmillan, 2001.

Lear, L., *Rachel Carson: Witness for nature*. London: Macmillan, 1998.

Lees, A. C., and C. A. Peres, 'Habitat and life history determinants of antbird occurrence in variable-sized Amazonian forest fragments', *Biotropica* 42 (2010), 614–21.

Legg, S., *Spaces of Colonialism: Delhi's urban governmentalities*. London: Wiley-Blackwell, 2011.

Lenin, J., 'The song of the Ganges gharial: Reorienting conservation', *Seminar* 577 (2007), 34–38.

Leopold, A., 'The farmer as a conservationist', *American Forests* 45 (1939), 294–99.

Lewis, M., ' Cattle and conservation at Bharatpur: A case study in science and advocacy', *Conservation and Society* 1 (2003), 1–21.

Lindell, C. A., W. H. Chomentowski and J. R. Zook, 'Characteristics of bird species using forest and agricultural land covers in southern Costa Rica', *Biodiversity and Conservation* 13 (2004), 2419–41.

Linnell, J. D. C., R. Aanes, J. E. Swenson, J. Odden and M. E. Smith, 'Translocation of carnivores as a method for managing problem animals: A review', *Biodiversity and Conservation* 6 (1997), 1245–57.

Liu, J., M. Linderman, Z. Ouyang, L. An, J. Yang and H. Zhang, 'Ecological degradation in protected areas: The case of Wolong Nature Reserve for giant pandas', *Science* 292, no. 5514 (2001), 98–101.

Lobo, A. S., A. Balmford, R. Arthur and A. Manica, 'Commercializing bycatch can push a fishery beyond economic extinction', *Conservation Letters* 3 (2010), 277–85.

Madden, F., 'Creating coexistence between humans and wildlife: Global perspectives on local efforts to address human–wildlife conflict', *Human Dimensions of Wildlife* 9 (2004), 247–57.

Madhusudan, M. D., 'Recovery of wild large herbivores following livestock decline in a tropical Indian wildlife reserve', *Journal of Applied Ecology* 41 (2004), 858–69.

Madhusudan, M. D., 'The global village: Linkages between subsistence use and global markets in a forest-based rural economy in southern India', *Conservation Biology* 19 (2005), 411–20.

Madhusudan, M. D., and C. Mishra, 'Why big, fierce animals are threatened: Conserving large mammals in densely populated landscapes', in V. Saberwal and M. Rangarajan (eds), *Battles Over Nature: Science and the politics of conservation*. Delhi: Permanent Black, 2003, pp. 31–56.

Madhusudan, M. D., and T. R. S. Raman, 'Conservation as if biological diversity matters: Preservation versus sustainable use in India', *Conservation and Society* 1 (2003), 49–59.

Mahapatra, R., and K. S. Shrivastava, 'Bamboo rising'. *Down To Earth* (2013). Available at http://www.downtoearth.org.in/content/bamboo-rising (accessed 9 April 2014)

Mann, M., and S. Sehrawat, 'A city with a view: The afforestation of the Delhi Ridge, 1883–1913', *Modern Asian Studies* 43, no. 2 (2009), 543–70.

Manoharan, T. R., 'Oil Palm Sector in India: The Scope of Influencing Business and Industry to Reduce India's Ecological Footprint in South East Asia. New Delhi: WWF-India, 2007.

Masselos, J., and N. Gupta, *Beato's Delhi: 1857 and beyond*. New Delhi: Ravi Dayal and Penguin Viking, 2011.

M. C. Mehta vs Union of India, WP(C) 4677/1985, orders of 9 April 1996 and 9 May 1996. Delhi: Supreme Court of India, 1996.

M. C. Mehta vs Union of India, I.A. No. 1785/01, Judgement of 8 May 2009.

McCarthy, T., J. Khan, J. Ud-Din and K. McCarthy, 'First study of snow leopards using GPS-satellite collars underway in Pakistan', *Cat News* (2007), 22–23.

McCarthy, T., K. Murray, K. Sharma and O. Johansson, 'Preliminary results of a long-term study of snow leopards in South Gobi, Mongolia', *Cat News* 53 (2010), 15–19.

McClanahan, T. R., 'Effects of Fisheries Closures and Gear Restrictions on Fishing Income in a Kenyan Coral Reef', *Conservation Biology* 24, no. 6 (2010), 1519–28.

Mech, L. D., and L. Boitani (eds), *Wolves: Behavior, ecology, and conservation*. Chicago: University of Chicago Press, 2003.

Menon, S., and K. S. Bawa, 'Applications of geographic information systems, remote-sensing, and a landscape ecology approach to biodiversity conservation in the Western Ghats', *Current Science* 73 (1997), 134–45.

Mijiddorj, N., *Pastoral Practice and Herders' Attitude Towards Wildlife in South Gobi, Mongolia*. Rajkot: Saurashtra University, 2011.

Millennium Ecosystem Assessment, *Ecosystems and human well-being: Current States and Trends*, Volume 1, Island Press: Washington DC, 2005.

Ministry of Environment and Forests, Gazette Notification dated 7 May 1992.

Ministry of Environment and Forests, 'Joining the Dots: Report of the tiger task force'. Ministry of Environment and Forests, Government of India, New Delhi, 2005.

Ministry of Environment and Forests, *The Project Snow Leopard*. New Delhi: Ministry of Environment and Forests, Government of India, 2008.

Ministry of Environment and Forests, *Notification No. 521, 2009. Registered No. 33004/99*. New Delhi: Ministry of Environment and Forests, Government of India, 2009.

Ministry of Environment and Forests, *Guidelines for Human-leopard Conflict Management*. New Delhi: Ministry of Environment and Forests, Government of India, 2011.

Ministry of Rural Development. *Wastelands Atlas of India*. New Delhi: Ministry of Rural Development, Department of Land Resources, 2005.

Mishra, C, P. Allen, T. McCarthy, M. D. Madhusudan, A. Bayarjargal and H. H. T. Prins, 'The role of incentive programs in conserving the snow leopard', *Conservation Biology* 17 (2003), 1512–20.

Mishra, C., and A. Fitzherbert, 'War and wildlife: A post-conflict assessment of Afghanistan's Wakhan Corridor', *Oryx* 38 (2004).

Mishra, C, S. Bagchi, T. Namgail and Y. V. Bhatnagar, 'Multiple use of Trans-Himalayan rangelands: Reconciling human livelihoods with wildlife conservation' in J. T. Du Toit, R. Kock and J. Deutsch (eds), *Wild Rangelands: Conserving wildlife while maintaining livestock in semi-arid ecosystems*. London: Wiley-Blackwell, 2010, pp. 291–311.

Mishra, C., 'Livestock depredation by large carnivores in the Indian Trans-Himalaya: Conflict perceptions and conservation prospects', *Environmental Conservation* 24 (1997), 338–43.

Mishra, C., 'Socioeconomic transition and wildlife conservation in the Indian Trans-Himalaya', *Journal of the Bombay Natural History Society* 97 (2000), 25–32.

Mishra, C., 'High altitude survival: Conflicts between pastoralism and wildlife in the Trans-Himalaya'. PhD thesis, Waganingen, Netherlands: Wageningen University, 2001.

Mishra, C., M. D. Madhusudan and A. Datta, 'Mammals of the high altitudes of western Arunachal Pradesh, eastern Himalaya: An assessment of threats and conservation needs', *Oryx* 40 (2006), 29–35.

Mishra, C., H. Prins and S. E. Van Wieren, 'Overstocking in the Trans-Himalayan rangelands of India', *Environmental Conservation* 28 (2001), 279–83.

Mishra, C., H. H. T. Prins and S. E. Van Wieren, 'Diversity, risk mediation, and change in a Trans-Himalayan agropastoral system', *Human Ecology* 31 (2003), 595–609.

Mishra, C., S. E. Van Wieren, P. Ketner, I. Heitkönig and H. H. T. Prins, 'Competition between domestic livestock and wild bharal *Pseudois nayaur* in the Indian Trans-Himalaya', *Journal of Applied Ecology* 41 (2004), 344–54.

Mishra, C., S. E. Van Wieren, I. Heitkönig and H. H. T. Prins, 'A theoretical analysis of competitive exclusion in a Trans-Himalayan large herbivore assemblage', *Animal Conservation* 5 (2002), 251–58.

Mishra, M., 'Dreaming of a blue Yamuna', in Bharati Chaturvedi (ed.), *Finding Delhi: Loss and renewal in a megacity*. New Delhi: Viking Books, 2010, p. 74.

Misra, V. N., 'Prehistoric human colonization of India', *Journal of Biosciences* 26 (2001), 491–531.

Mitsch, W. J., and J. G. Gosselink, *Wetlands*. New Jersey: John Wiley and Sons, 2007.

Mittermeier, R. A., P. R. Gil, M. Hoffmann, J. Pilgrim, T. Brooks, C. Goettsch Mittermeier, J. Lamoreux, G. A. B. Da Fonseca and

P. A. Seligmann, *Hotspots Revisited: Earth's biologically richest and most endangered ecoregions*. Mexico: CEMEX, 2004.

Mondal, S. K., M. W. Bruford and U. Ramakrishnan, 'Demographic loss, genetic structure and the conservation implications for Indian tigers', *Proceedings of the Royal Society B* 280, no. 1762 (2013), 20130–96.

Morrison, K., 'Opening up the pre-colonial: Primeval forests, baseline thinking and other archives in environmental history' in M. Rangarajan and K. Sivaramakrishnan (eds), *Shifting Ground: People, mobility and animals in India's environmental pasts*. New Delhi: Oxford University Press, forthcoming.

Moulton, T. P., 'Defying water's end: Do we need different conservation strategies for aquatic systems compared with terrestrial?', *Aquatic Conservation: Marine and Freshwater Ecosystems* 19 (2009), 1–3.

Mudappa, D., B. R. Noon, A. Kumar and R. Chellam, 'Responses of small carnivores to rainforest fragmentation in the southern Western Ghats, India', *Small Carnivore Conservation* 36 (2007), 18–26.

Mudappa, D., and T. R. S. Raman, 'Rainforest restoration and wildlife conservation on private lands in the Valparai plateau, Western Ghats, India', in G. Shahabuddin and M. Rangarajan (eds), *Making Conservation Work*. Ranikhet, India: Permanent Black, 2007, pp. 210–40.

Mudappa, D., and T. R. S. Raman, *Rainforest Restoration: A guide to principles and practice*. Mysore: Nature Conservation Foundation, 2010.

Murali, A., 'Whose Trees?: Forest practices and local communities in Andhra, 1600–1922', in D. Arnold and R. Guha (eds), *Nature, Culture and Imperialism: Essays on the environmental history of South Asia*. New Delhi: Oxford University Press, 1995, pp. 46–122.

Muthuramkumar, S., N. Ayyappan, N. Parthasarathy, D. Mudappa, T. R. S. Raman, M. A. Selwyn and L. A. Pragasan, 'Plant community structure in tropical rain forest fragments of the Western Ghats, India', *Biotropica* 38 (2006), 143–60.

Myers, N., and J. Kent, 'New consumers: The influence of affluence on the environment', *Proceedings of the National Academy of Sciences (USA)* 100 (2003), 4963–68.

Nabhan, G. P., *Gathering the Desert*. Tucson: University of Arizona Press, 1987.

Nag S., *Pied pipers in North-East India: Bamboo-flower, rat-famine and the politics of philantrophy (1881–2007)*. New Delhi: Manohar Publishers, 2008.

Nagendra Harini, 'Maps, lakes and citizens', *Seminar* 613 (2010). Available at http://www.india-seminar.com/2010/613/613_harini_nagendra.htm (accessed 10 July 2012).

Nagendra, H., S. Paul, S. Pareeth and S. Dutt, 'Landscapes of protection: Forest change and fragmentation in northern West Bengal', *Environmental Management* 44 (2009), 853–64.

Nagendra, H., R. Sivaram and S. Subramanya, 'Lakes of Mahadevpura constituency, Bangalore: Current status, changes in distribution, and recommendations for restoration'. Bengaluru: BBMP, 2011.

Nagendra, H., and E. Ostrom, 'Applying the social-ecological systems framework to the diagnoses of urban commons', *Ecology and Society*, forthcoming.

Nair, J., *The Promise of the Metropolis: Bangalore's twentieth century*. New Delhi: Oxford University Press, 2005.

Nair, T., *Ecological and Anthropogenic Covariates Influencing Gharial* Gavialis gangeticus *Distribution and Habitat Use in Chambal River, India*. MSc Dissertation, Bengaluru: National Centre for Biological Sciences, 2010.

Namgail, T., S. Bagchi, C. Mishra and Y. V. Bhatnagar, 'Distributional correlates of the Tibetan gazelle *Procapra picticaudata* in Ladakh, northern India: Towards a recovery programme', *Oryx* 42 (2008), 107–12.

Namgail, T., Y. V. Bhatnagar and J. L. Fox, 'Carnivore-caused livestock mortality in Trans-Himalaya', *Environmental Management* 39 (2007), 490–96.

Namgail, T., Y. V. Bhatnagar, C. Mishra and S. Bagchi, 'Pastoral nomads of the Indian Changthang: Production system, landuse and socio-economic changes', *Human Ecology* 35 (2007), 497–504.

Nandeesha, M. C., 'Farmers as scientists: Andhra Pradesh fish farmers go into revolutionary carp research', *Aquaculture Asia* 6 (2001), 29–32.

Naoroji, R., 'Contamination in egg shells of Himayalayan grey headed eagle in the Corbett National Park, Uttar Pradesh', *Journal of the Bombay Natural History Society* 94 (1997), 398–400.

Naoroji, R., *Birds of prey of the Indian subcontinent*. New Delhi: Om Books International, 2007.

Nath, C. D., R. Pélissier, B. R. Ramesh and C. Garcia, 'Promoting native trees in shade coffee plantations of southern India: Comparison of growth rates with the exotic *Grevillea robusta*', *Agroforestry systems* 83 (2011), 107–19.

Nath, D., R. Sukumar and D. L. Caudhuri, *Elephant-Human Conflict in Kodagu, Southern India: Distribution patterns, people's perceptions and mitigation methods*. Bangalore: Asian Elephant Conservation Centre, 1998.

National Capital Region Planning Board, 'Functional plan for recharge of groundwater in NCR', 2010. Available at http://www.ncrpb.nic.in/Consolidate_pre_document.pdf (accessed 25 April 2014).

Nature Conservation Foundation, 'People, livestock and snow leopards. Protecting livestock and snow leopards: Participatory conservation in the Trans Himalaya', 2010. Available at http://www.ncfindia.org/projectoverview (accessed 31 July 2010).

Naughton-Treves, L., M. B. Holland and K. Brandon, 'The role of protected areas in conserving biodiversity and sustaining local livelihoods', *Annual Review Environment and Resources* 30 (2005), 219–52.

Ninan, K. N., and J. Sathyapalan, 'The economics of biodiversity conservation: A study of a coffee growing region in the Western Ghats of India', *Ecological Economics* 55 (2005), 61–72.

Norris, K., 'Agriculture and biodiversity conservation: Opportunity knocks', *Conservation Letters* 1 (2008), 2–11.

Novacek, M. J., and E. E. Cleland, 'The current biodiversity extinction event: Scenarios for mitigation and recovery', *Proceedings of the National Academy of Sciences (USA)* 98 (2001), 5466–70.

Office of the Development Commissioner, *Constitution of Ridge Management Board*. Delhi: Govt. of NCT of Delhi, No F.56 (225)/95/Dev./No/5596–5612.

Office of the Registrar General of India, 'Population of States/Union Territories by sex and percentage share of population in total population: 2011'. Available at http://www.censusindia.gov.in/2011-prov-results/DATA_FILES/Final PPT 2011_12.PDF

Oli, M. K., I. R. Taylor and M. E. Rogers, 'Snow leopard (*Panthera uncia*) predation of livestock: An assessment of local perceptions in the Annapurna Conservation Area, Nepal', *Biological Conservation* 68 (1994), 63–68.

Osborn, F. V., and G. E. Parker, 'Towards an integrated approach for reducing the conflict between elephants and people: A review of current research', *Oryx* 37 (2003), 80–84.

Ostrom, E., 'A general framework for analyzing sustainability of social-ecological systems', *Science* 325 (2009), 419–22.

Ostrom, E., and H. Nagendra, 'Insights on linking forests, trees, and people from the air, on the ground, and in the laboratory', *Proceedings of the National Academy of Sciences (USA)* 103 (2006), 19224–31.

Our Bureau, 'Javadekar clears Karwar Nath Naval Base Project', *Economic Times*, 10 June 2014.

Pagiola, S., J. Bishop and N. Landell-Mills (eds), *Selling Forest Environmental Services: Market-based mechanisms for conservation and development*. London: Earthscan, 2004.

Panigrahy, S., T. V. R. Murthy, J. G. Patel and T. S. Singh, 'Wetlands of India: Inventory and assessment at 1:50,000 scale using geospatial techniques', *Current Science* 102 (2012), 852–56.

Parthasarathy, D., 'Hunters, Gatherers and Foragers in a Metropolis: Commonising the Private and Public in Mumbai', *Economic and Political Weekly* 46 (2011), 54–63.

Patinkin, J., 'Tanzania's Maasai battle game hunters for grazing land', *BBC News*, 18 April 2013. Available at http://www.bbc.co.uk/news/world-africa-22155538 (accessed 13 May 2014).

Pauly, D., and J. Maclean, *In a Perfect Ocean: Fisheries and ecosystem in the North Atlantic*. Washington DC: Island Press, 2003.

Pauly, D., V. Christensen, J. Dalsgaard, R. Froese and F. Torres Jr., 'Fishing down marine food webs', *Science* 279 (1998), 860–63.

Pauly, D., V. Christensen, S. Guenette, T. J. Pitcher, U. Rashid Sumaila, C. J. Walters, R. Watson and D. Zeller, 'Towards sustainability in world fisheries', *Nature* 418 (2002), 689–95.

Payne, A. I., and S. A. Temple, *River and Floodplain Fisheries in the Ganges Basin*. London: Marine Resources Assessment Group Limited, Overseas Development Administration, 1996.

Perdue, P. C., *China Marches West: The Qing conquest of Central Eurasia*. Cambridge, MA: Harvard University Press, 2009.

Phalan, B., M. Onial, A. Balmford and R. E. Green, 'Reconciling food production and biodiversity conservation: Land sharing and land sparing compared', *Science* 333, no. 6047 (2011), 1289–91.

Pita, C., G. J. Pierce, I. Theodossiou and K. Macpherson, 'An overview of commercial fishers' attitudes towards marine protected areas', *Hydrobiologia* 670 (2011), 289–306.

Pomeroy, R. S., J. E. Parks and L. M. Watson, *How is your MPA doing?* Gland, Switzerland, and Cambridge, UK: International Union for Conservation of Nature (IUCN), 2007.

Pomeroy, R. S., B. D. Ratner, S. J. Hall, J. Pimoljinda and V. Vivekanandan, 'Coping with disaster: Rehabilitating coastal livelihoods and communities', *Marine Policy* 30 (2006), 786–93.

Prabhakar, R., and M. Gadgil, 'Maps as markers of ecological change: a case study of the Nilgiri hills of southern India' in D. Arnold and R. Guha (eds), *Nature, Culture, Imperialism: Essays on the environmental history of South Asia*. Delhi: Oxford University Press, 1995, pp. 152–84.

Prakash, V., 'Status of vultures in Keoladeo National Park, Bharatpur, Rajasthan, with special reference to population crash in *Gyps* species', *Journal of the Bombay Natural History Society* 96 (1999), 365–78.

Prasad, A., 'The political ecology of swidden cultivation: The survival strategies of the Baigas in the Central Provinces 1860–1960' in M. Rangarajan and K. Sivaramakrishnan (eds), *India's Environmental History, Volume 2*. Ranikhet: Permanent Black, 2012, pp. 246–80.

Pratap, A., *The Hoe and The Axe: An ethnohistory of shifting cultivation in Eastern India*. New Delhi: Oxford University Press, 1999.

Project Snow Leopard, *Towards Project Snow Leopard: Report of the national workshop on Project Snow Leopard 10th–11th July, 2006*, Leh, Ladakh: Ministry of Environment and Forests, Government of India, Department of Wildlife Protection, Jammu and Kashmir, Nature Conservation Foundation, International Snow Leopard Trust, Mysore, India, 2006.

Purevjav, L., 'Snow leopard site occupancy survey in South Gobi, Mongolia'. PhD thesis, University of Minnesota, Minneapolis, 2011.

Pyrovetsi, M., and G. Daoutopoulos, 'Contrasts in conservation attitudes and agricultural practices between farmers operating in wetlands and a plain in Macedonia, Greece', *Environmental Conservation* 24 (1997), 76–82.

Rahmani, A., 'Conservation outside protected areas: Case studies of Bustard Protection' in V. Saberwal and M. Rangarajan (eds), *Battles Over Nature: Science and the Politics of Conservation*. Delhi: Permanent Black, 2003, pp. 117–38.

Rajshekar, M., 'Posco's Orissa project: Many hurdles lie ahead despite environment ministry's approval', *Economic Times*, 8 May 2011.

Ramachandran, R., 'Ministry's "no" to neutrino observatory project in Nilgiris', *Hindu*, 21 November 2009.

Ramakrishna, R., 'Kolleru carp culture in India: An aquaplosion and an explosion', *Aquaculture Asia Magazine* 25 (2007), 12–18.

Raman, T. R. S., 'Effect of slash-and-burn shifting cultivation on rainforest birds in Mizoram, Northeast India', *Conservation Biology* 15 (2001), 685–98.

Raman, T. R. S., 'Effects of habitat structure and adjacent habitats on birds in tropical rainforest fragments and shaded plantations in the Western Ghats, India', *Biodiversity and Conservation* 15 (2006), 1577–607.

Raman, T. R. S., and D. Mudappa, 'Correlates of hornbill distribution and abundance in rainforest fragments in the southern Western Ghats, India', *Bird Conservation International* 13 (2003), 199–212.

Raman, T. R. S., and D. Mudappa, 'Island in peril: Conservation caveats', *Hindu*, 25 February 2012.

Raman, T. R. S., D. Mudappa and V. Kapoor, 'Restoring rainforest fragments: Survival of mixed native species seedlings under contrasting site conditions in the Western Ghats, India', *Restoration Ecology* 17 (2009), 137–47.

Raman, T. R. S., and R. Sukumar, 'Responses of tropical rainforest birds to abandoned plantations, edges and logged forest in the Western Ghats, India', *Animal Conservation* 5 (2002), 201–16.

Ramankutty, N., and J. A. Foley, 'Characterizing patterns of global land use: An analysis of global croplands data', *Global Biogeochemical Cycles* 12 (1998), 667–85.

Ramdas, S., 'Whose access and whose benefit: Securing customary rights in India', *Biodiversity and Culture: Exploring Community protocols, PLA Notes 65*. London: Institute of Environment and Development, 2012.

Ramesh Chopra and Ors vs Union of India and Ors, WP (civil) 11884–87/2006 in High Court of Delhi, Delhi.

Ramesh, S., 'Control and prevention of epidemics and exotic diseases', *Proceedings of the National Seminar on Sustainable Use and Conservation of the Deccani Sheep*. Hyderabad: Anthra Publications, 2007.

Ranganathan, J., R. J. R. Daniels, M. D. S. Chandran, P. R. Ehrlich and G. C. Daily, 'Sustaining biodiversity in ancient tropical countryside', *Proceedings of the National Academy of Sciences (USA)*, 105 (2008), 17852–4.

Ranganathan, J., J. Krishnaswamy and M. O. Anand, 'Landscape-level effects on avifauna within tropical agriculture in the Western Ghats: Insights for management and conservation', *Biological Conservation* 143 (2010), 2909–17.

Rangarajan, M., *Fencing the Forest: Conservation and ecological change in India's Central Provinces, 1860–1914*. New Delhi: Oxford University Press, 1996.

Rangarajan, M., 'The politics of ecology: The debate on wildlife and People in India, 1970–1995', *Economic and Political Weekly, Special Number* 31 (1996), 2391–409.

Rangarajan, M., 'The raj and the natural world: The war against "dangerous beasts" in Colonial India', *Studies in History* 14 (1998), 265–99.

Rangarajan, M., 'From princely symbol to conservation icon: The political history of the lion in India' in M. Hasan and N. Nazakato (eds), *Unfinished Agendas: Nationalism in South Asia*. New Delhi: Manohar Publishers, 2001, pp. 371–99.

Rangarajan, M., *India's Wildlife History: An introduction*. New Delhi: Permanent Black, 2001.

Rangarajan, M., 'Striving for a balance: Nature, power, science and India's Indira Gandhi, 1917–1984', *Conservation and Society* 7, no. 4 (2009).

Rangarajan, M., 'Contesting Conservation: Nature, politics and history in contemporary India' in T. S. Patel and T. Uys (eds), *Contemporary India and South Africa: Legacies, identities and dilemmas*. New Delhi: Routledge, 2012, pp. 241–58.

Rangarajan, M., 'Animals with rich histories: The case of the lions of Gir Forest, Gujarat, India', *History and Theory* 52 (2013), 109–27.

Rangarajan, M., 'Forest as Faunal Enclave' in S. B. Hecht, K. D. Morrison and C. Padoch (eds), The Social Life of Forests: The past, present and future of woodland resurgence (Chicago: University of Chicago Press, 2014), 190–98.

Rangarajan, M. and K. Sivaramakrishnan (eds), *India's Environmental History: From ancient times to the colonial period, Volume 1*. New Delhi: Permanent Black, 2012.

Rangarajan, M. and K. Sivaramakrishnan (eds), Shifting Ground: People, Mobility and Animals in India's Environmental Histories. New Delhi: Oxford University Press (forthcoming).

Rangarajan, M., A. Desai, R. Sukumar, P. S. Easa, V. Menon, D. S. Vincent, S. Ganguly, B. K. Talukdar, B. Singh, D. Mudappa, S. Chowdhary and A. N. Prasad, 'Gajah: securing the future for elephants in India'. New Delhi: Ministry of Environment and Forests, Government of India, 2010.

Ranjitsinh, M. K., *Beyond the Tiger: Portraits of Asian wildlife*. New Delhi: Brijbasi Publishers, 1995.

Ranjitsinh, M. K., and Y. V. Jhala, 'Assessing the potential for reintroducing the cheetah in India'. Noida and Dehradun: Wildlife Trust of India and Wildlife Institute of India, 2010.

Rao, G. S., 'Turtle Excluder Device (TED) in trawl nets: Applicability in Indian trawl fishery', *Indian Journal of Fisheries* 58 (2011), 115–24.

Rappole, J. H., D. I. King and J. H. Rivera, 'Coffee and conservation III: Reply to Philpott and Dietsch', *Conservation Biology* 17 (2003), 1847–49.

Reeves, P., 'Inland waters and freshwater fisheries: Issues of control, access and conservation in colonial India' in D. Arnold and R. Guha (eds), *Nature, Culture, Imperialism*. Oxford University Press, New Delhi, India, 1995, pp. 260–292.

Reeves, P. N., and P. D. Champion, 'Effects of livestock grazing on wetlands: Literature review' in *NIWA Client Report: HAM2004-059*. New Zealand: National Institute of Water and Atmospheric Research Limited, 2004.

Rice, B. L., *Mysore: A gazetteer compiled for government*, Westminister: Archibald Constable and Company, 1897.

Rice, B. L., *Epigraphica Carnatica Volume IX: Inscriptions in the Bangalore District*. Bangalore: Mysore Government Central Press, 1905.

Richter, B. D., and G. A. Thomas 'Restoring environmental flows by modifying dam operations', *Ecology and Society* 12 (2007), 12.

Richter, B. D., R. Mathews, D. L. Harrison and R. Wigington, 'Ecologically sustainable water management: Managing river flows for ecological integrity', *Ecological Applications* 13 (2003), 206–24.

Robb, P. G., 'Ancient rights and future comfort: Bihar, the Bengal Tenancy Act of 1885, and British rule in India', *London Studies on South Asia* 13 (1997).

Rodgers, W. A., D. Hartley and S. Bashir, 'Community approaches to conservation: Some comparisons between India and Africa' in V. Saberwal and M. Rangarajan (eds), *Battles Over Nature: Science and the politics of conservation*. Delhi: Permanent Black, 2003, pp. 324–82.

Rodgers, W. A., H. S. Panwar and V. B. Mathur, *Wildlife Protected Area Network in India: A review*. Dehradun, India: Wildlife Institute of India, 2000.

Roma, 'Forest justice movements', *Seminar* 638 (2010), 75–77.

Rong, J., *Wolf Totem*. London: Penguin, 2008.

Rosenzweig, M. L., *Win-Win Ecology: How the earth's species can survive in the midst of human enterprise*. New York: Oxford University Press, 2003.

Roy, A., *Listening to Grasshoppers: Field notes on democracy*. London: Penguin UK, 2009.

Runte, A., *National Parks: The American experience*. Boulder: Taylor Trade Publications, 2010.

Russ, G. R., and A. C. Alcala, 'Enhanced biodiversity beyond marine reserve boundaries: The cup spilleth over', *Ecological Applications* 21 (2011), 241–50.

Saberwal, V. K., *Pastoral Politics: Shepherds, bureaucrats and conservation in the Western Himalaya*. New Delhi: Oxford University Press, 1999.

Saberwal, V. K. and A. Chhatre, *Democratizing Nature*. New Delhi: Oxford University Press, 2006.

Saberwal, V., and M. Rangarajan (eds), *Battles Over Nature: Science and the politics of conservation*. Ranikhet: Permanent Black, 2003.

Saberwal, V. K., J. P. Gibbs, R. Chellam and A. J. T. Johnsingh, 'Lion-human conflict in the Gir forest, India'. *Conservation Biology* 8 (1994), 501–07.

Saberwal, V. K., M. Rangarajan and A. Kothari, *Towards Coexistence: People, parks and wildlife*. Hyderabad: Orient Longman, 2000.

Sahgal, B., *The Kaziranga Inheritance*. Mumbai: Sanctuary Books, 2005.

Saikia, A., 'Kaziranga National Park: Dynamics of social and political history', *Conservation and Society* 7 (2009), 113–29.

Saikia, A., 'Kaziranga National Park: History, landscape and conservation practices', *Economic and Political Weekly* 46 (2011), 12–13.

Sanderson, E., J. Forrest, C. Loucks, J. Ginsberg, E. Dinerstein, J. Seidensticker, J. Forrest, G. Bryja, A. Heydlauff, S. Klenzendorf, P. Leimgruber, J. Mills, T. G. O'Brien, M. Shrestha, R. Simons and M. Songer, *Setting Priorities for the Conservation and Recovery of Wild Tigers: 2005–2015*, New York and Washington DC: Wildlife Conservation Society, World Wide Fund For Nature, Smithsonian, NFWF-STF, 2006.

Sankaran, P., and M. D. Madhusudan, 'Desperate neighbours: Endangered wildlife and the rural poor', *The Hindu, Survey of the Environment 2010* (2010), 113–18.

Sathyakumar, S., T. Bashir, T. Bhattacharya and K. Poudyal, 'Assessing mammal distribution and abundance in intricate eastern Himalayan habitats of Khangchendzonga, Sikkim, India', *Mammalia* 75 (2011), 257–68.

Satya Laxman, D., *Colonialism and Cattle: Central India in the Nineteenth Century*. New Delhi: Oxford University Press, 2004.

Saunders, D. L., J. J. Meeuwig and A. C. J. Vincent, 'Freshwater Protected Areas: Strategies for conservation', *Conservation Biology* 16 (2002), 30–41.

Savyasaachi, 'The tiger and the honeybee', *Seminar* 423 (1995), 30–35.

Saxena, A., V. Prasad, I. B. Singh, M. S. Chauhan and R. Hasan, 'On the Holocene record of phytoliths of wild and cultivated rice from Ganga plain: Evidence for rice-based agriculture', *Current Science* 90 (2006), 1547–52.

Saxena, N. C., *Eucalytpus in India: The god that failed*. New Delhi: Sage, 1995.

Schaller, G. B., *Mountain Monarchs: Wild sheep and goats of the Himalaya*. Chicago: University of Chicago Press, 1977.

Scholtens, J., M. Bavinck and A. S. Soosai, 'Fishing in dire straits: Trans-boundary incursions in the Palk Bay', *Economic and Political Weekly* 47 (2012), 85–95.

Schroth, G., G. A. B. da Fonseca, C. A. Harvey, C. Gascon, H. L. Vasconcelos and A. M. N. Izac (eds), *Agroforestry and Biodiversity Conservation in Tropical Landscapes*. Washington DC: Island Press, 2004.

Secchi, S., and B. A. Babcock, *Impact of High Crop Prices on Environmental Quality: A case of Iowa and the Conservation Reserve Program*. Ames, Iowa: Center for Agricultural and Rural Development, Iowa State University, Ames, IA, 2007.

Seidensticker, J., S. Christie and P. Jackson, 'Preface' in J. Seidensticker, S. Christie, and P. Jackson (eds), *Riding the Tiger: Tiger conservation in human-dominated landscapes*. Cambridge, UK: Cambridge University Press, 1999.

Sekercioglu, C. H., S. R. Loarie, O. F. Brenes, P. R. Ehrlich and G. C. Daily, 'Persistence of forest birds in the Costa Rican agricultural countryside', *Conservation Biology* 21 (2007), 482–94.

Seshadhri, B., *The Twilight of India's Wildlife*. London: John Baker, 1969.

Shah, A., *In the Shadows of the State: Indigenous politics, environmentalism and insurgency in Jharkhand, India*. Durham: Duke University Press, 2010.

Shahabuddin, G., 'Preliminary observations on the role of coffee plantations as avifaunal refuges in the Palani Hills of the Western Ghats', *Journal of the Bombay Natural History Society* 94 (1997), 10–21.

Shahabuddin, G., *Conservation at the Crossroads: Science, society, and the future of India's wildlife*. New Delhi: Permanent Black, 2010.

Shahabuddin, G., and M. Rangarajan, *Making Conservation Work: Securing biodiversity in this new century*. New Delhi: Permanent Black, 2007.

Shahabuddin, G., and M. Rao, 'Do community-conserved areas effectively conserve biodiversity: Global insights and the Indian context', *Biological Conservation* 143 (2010), 2926–29.

Shahabuddin, G., and J. W. Terborgh, 'Frugivorous butterflies in Venezuelan forest fragments: Abundance, diversity and the effects of isolation', *Journal of Tropical Ecology* 15 (1999), 703–22.

Shanker, K., B. Pandav and B. C. Choudhury, 'An assessment of the olive ridley turtle (*Lepidochelys olivacea*) nesting population in Orissa, India', *Biological Conservation* 115 (2004), 149–60.

Sharma, A., 'Off to pastures new', *Hindu*, 9 June 2013.

Sharma, D. K., J. E. Maldonado, Y. V. Jhala and R. C. Fleischer, 'Ancient wolf lineages in India', *Proceedings of the Royal Society of London. Series B: Biological Sciences* 271 (2004), S1–S4.

Sharma, M., *Landscapes and Lives*. New Delhi: Oxford University Press, 2006.

Sharma, M., *Green and Saffron: Hindu nationalism and Indian environmental politics*. Ranikhet: Permanent Black, 2012.

Sharma, S., M. Joachimski, M. Sharma, H. J. Tobschall, I. B. Singh, C. Sharma, M. S. Chauhan and G. Morgenroth, 'Late glacial and Holocene environmental changes in Ganga plain, Northern India', *Quaternary Science Reviews* 23 (2004), 145–59.

Shrivastava, A., and A. Kothari, *Churning the Earth: The making of global India*. New Delhi: Penguin, 2012.

Sidhu, S., D. Mudappa and T. R. S. Raman, 'People and predators: Leopard diet and interactions with people in a tea plantation dominated landscape in the Anamalai Hills, Western Ghats'. Technical report, Nature Conservation Foundation, Mysore, 2011.

Sidhu, S., T. R. S. Raman and E. Goodale, 'Effects of plantations and home-gardens on tropical forest bird communities and mixed-species bird flocks in the southern Western Ghats', *Journal of the Bombay Natural History Society* 107 (2010), 91.

Sillero-Zubiri, C., M. Hoffmann and D. W. Macdonald (eds), *Canids: Foxes, Wolves, Jackals and Dogs. Status Survey and Conservation Action Plan*. Gland and Cambridge: IUCN/SSC Canid Specialist Group, 2004.

Singh, M., and H. N. Kumara, 'Distribution, status and conservation of Indian gray wolf (*Canis lupus pallipes*) in Karnataka, India', *Journal of Zoology* 270 (2006), 164–69.

Sinha, R., B. Smith, G. Sharma, G. Prasad, B. C. Choudhury, K. Sapkota, R. K. Sharma and S. K. Behera, 'Status and distribution of the Ganges susu (*Platanista gangetica*) in the Ganges River system of India and

Nepal', *Occasional Paper in IUCN Species Survival Communication* 23 (2000), 54–61.

Sivaramakrishnan, K., 'Conservation crossroads: Indian wildlife at the intersection of global imperatives, nationalist anxieties and local assertions', in V. Saberwal, and M. Rangarajan (eds), *Battles Over Nature: Science and the Politics of Conservation*. Delhi: Permanent Black, 2003, pp. 397–99.

Smith, A. M., and B. D. Smith, 'Review of status and threats to river cetaceans and recommendations for their conservation', *Environmental Reviews* 6 (1998), 189–206.

Smith, B. D., A. K. M. A. Haque, M. S. Hossain and A. Khan, 'River dolphins in Bangladesh: Conservation and the effects of water development', *Environmental Management* 22 (1998), 323–35.

Smith, B. D., and G. T. Braulik, '*Platanista gangetica*' in *IUCN Red List of Threatened Species*, version 2013.2. Available at www.iucnredlist.org (accessed 30 December 2013).

Snow Leopard Trust, The, 'Livestock Insurance Programme Review', 2010. Available at http://www.snowleopard.org/programs/community basedconservation/livestockinsurance (accessed 28 July 2010).

Sodhi, N. S., M. C. Posa, T. Lee and I. G. Warkentin, 'Perspectives in ornithology: Effects of disturbance or loss of tropical rainforest on birds', *The Auk* 125 (2008), 511–19.

Soni, V., 'Three waters: An evaluation of urban groundwater resource in Delhi', *Current Science* 93 (2007), 760–61.

Sontheimer, G. D., and M. L. K. Murty, 'Pre-historic background to pastoralism in the Southern Deccan in the light of oral traditions and cults of some pastoral communities' in H. Bruckner, A. Feldhaus and A. Malik (eds), *Essays on Religion, Literature and Law*, Delhi: Manohar, 2004, p. 161.

Soto, D., J. Aguilar-Manjarrez, J. Bermudez, C. Brugere, D. Angel, C. Bailey, K. Black, P. Edwards, B. Coste-Pierce, T. Chopin, S. Deudero, S. Freeman, J. Hambrey, N. Hishamunda, D. Knowler, W. Silvert, N. Marba, S. Mathe, R. Norambuena, F. Simard, P. Tett, M. Troell and A. Wainberg, 'Applying an ecosystem-based approach to aquaculture: principles, scales, and some management measures'. FAO/Universidat de les Illes Balears Expert Workshop Palma de Mallorca, Spain. In D. Soto, J. Aguilar-Manjarrez and N Hishamunda (eds), *Building an Ecosystem Approach to Aquaculture*. Rome: FAO Fisheries and Aquaculture Proceedings, UN, 2007, pp. 15–35.

Spence, M. D., *Dispossessing the Wilderness: Indian removal and the making of the national parks*. New York: Oxford University Press, 1999.

Sridhar, H., T. R. S. Raman and D. Mudappa, 'Mammal persistence and abundance in tropical rainforest remnants in the southern Western Ghats, India', *Current Science* 94 (2008), 748–57.

Sridhar, H., 'Are arecanut plantations really suitable for biodiversity conservation?', *Proceedings of the National Academy of Sciences (USA)* 106 (2009), E34.

Srinivas, S., *Landscapes of Urban Memory: The sacred and the civic in India's high-tech city*. Hyderabad: Orient Longman, 2004.

Srishti, 'The Delhi Ridge, Issues and Perspective—a paper'. New Delhi, Srishti, 1994.

Srishti, *Saving the Delhi Ridge, One Year of Conservation Action*. New Delhi: Srishti, 1994.

Srishti and Others v. Govt. of NCT of Delhi, chief of Army Staff and others, WP(C). Delhi: High Court of Delhi, 1996.

Srishti and Toxics Link, *Delhi Ridge Under Threat: Community conservation of Sanjay Van report*. New Delhi: Srishti and Toxics Link, 2011. Available at http://toxicslink.org/delhiridge/studies-and-reports/delhi-ridge-under-threat-community-conservation-of-sanjay-van-report/ (accessed 24 April 2014).

Stephen, J., A. Menon, J. Scholtens and M. Bavinck, 'Transboundary dialogues and the "politics of scale" in Palk Bay fisheries: Brothers at sea?', *South Asia Research*, 33, no. 2 (2013), 141–61.

Subramanian, A., 'Community, place and citizenship' in M. Rangarajan (ed.), *Environmental Issues in India: A Reader*. New Delhi: Dorling-Kindersey, 2007, pp. 444–53.

Subramanian, A., *Shore Lines, Space and rights in South India*. New Delhi: Yoda Press, 2013.

Sudhira, H. S., T.V. Ramachandra and B. H. S. Subrahmanya, 'City profile: Bangalore', *Cities* 24 (2007), 379–90.

Sukumar, R., *The Asian Elephant: Ecology and management*. Cambridge University Press, 1993.

Sundar, K. S. G., 'Effectiveness of road transects and wetland visits for surveying Black-necked Storks *Ephippiorhynchus asiaticus* and Sarus Cranes *Grus antigone* in India', *Forktail* 21 (2005), 27.

Sundar, K. S. G., 'Are rice paddies suboptimal breeding habitat for Sarus Cranes in Uttar Pradesh, India?', *The Condor* 111 (2009), 611–23.

Sundar, K. S. G., 'Cranes, cultivators and conservation', *Seminar* 638 (2010), 34–37.

Sundar, K. S. G., 'Agricultural intensification, rainfall patterns, and large waterbird breeding success in the extensively cultivated landscape of Uttar Pradesh, India', *Biological Conservation* 144 (2011), 3055–63.

Sundar, K. S. G., and B. C. Choudhury, 'Mortality of Sarus Cranes (*Grus antigone*) due to electricity wires in Uttar Pradesh, India', *Environmental Conservation* 32 (2005), 260–69.

Sundar, K. S. G., and B. C. Choudhury, 'Conservation of the Sarus Crane *Grus antigone* in Uttar Pradesh, India', *Journal of the Bombay Natural History Society* 103 (2006), 182–90.

Sundar, K. S. G., and S. Subramanya, 'Bird use of rice fields in the Indian subcontinent', *Waterbirds* 33 (2010), 44–70.

Sundara, R. B. N., *Bengalurina itihasa (A History of Bangalore)*. Bangalore: Vasanta Sahitya Granthamala, 1985.

Sundaram, B., and A. J. Hiremath, '*Lantana camara* invasion in a heterogeneous landscape: Patterns of spread and correlation with changes in native vegetation', *Biological Invasions* 14 (2012), 1127–41.

Sundaresan, J., 'Planning as commoning: Transformation of a Bangalore lake', *Economic and Political Weekly* 46 (2011), 71–79.

Sunquist, M. E., 'The social organization of tigers (*Panthera tigris*) in Royal Chitawan National Park, Nepal', *Smithsonian Contributions to Zoology* 98 (1981).

Sutherland, W. J., 'Restoring a sustainable countryside', *Trends in Ecology and Evolution* 17 (2002), 148–50.

Sutherland, W. J., 'A blueprint for the countryside', *Ibis* 146 (2004), 230–38.

Switha, V., and D. Srinivasarao, *Decanni Wool in Andhra Pradesh: A study*. Hyderabad: Anthra Publications, 2007.

Terborgh, J., C. van Schaik, L. Davenport and M. Rao (eds), *Making Parks Work: Strategies for preserving tropical nature*. Washington DC: Island Press, 2002.

Thapar, V., *Land of the Tiger: A natural history of the Indian subcontinent*. Berkeley and Los Angeles: University of California Press, 1998.

Thapar, V., *Battling for Survival: India's wilderness over two centuries*. New Delhi: Oxford University Press, 2003.

Thapar, V., *Ranthambhore: 10 days in the tiger fortress*. New Delhi: Oxford University Press, 2011.

Thapar, V., *The Last Tiger: Struggling for survival*. New Delhi: Oxford University Press, 2012.

Thenkabail, P. S., M. Schull and H. Turral, 'Ganges and Indus river basin land use/land cover (LULC) and irrigated area mapping using continuous streams of MODIS data', *Remote Sensing of Environment* 95 (2005), 317–41.

Thiollay, J. M., 'The role of traditional agroforests in the conservation of rain forest bird diversity in Sumatra', *Conservation Biology* 9 (1995), 335–53.

Tilman, D., K. G. Cassman, P. A. Matson, R. Naylor and S. Polasky, 'Agricultural sustainability and intensive production practices', *Nature* 418 (2002), 671–77.

Tilman, D., J. Fargione, B. Wolff, C. D'Antonio, A. Dobson, R. Howarth, D. Schindler, W. H. Schlesinger, D. Simberloff and D. Swackhamer, 'Forecasting agriculturally driven global environmental change', *Science* 292 (2001), 281–84.

Times of India, 'Tusker trail', 25 June 2013, Bengaluru edition.

TMI-NCF, 'Non-invasive monitoring to support local stewardship of snow leopards and their prey', submitted to Critical Ecosystem Partnership Fund (CEPF) and Ashoka Trust for Research in ecology and the Environment (ATREE), 2010.

T. N. Godavarman vs Union of India, Writ Petition (civil) 202 of 1995, judgments of 13 September 1996, 19 August 1997, 8 March 2004 and 17 January 2006, Delhi: Supreme Court of India.

Trivedi, P., 'Heights of success: conservation success at the high altitudes', *Hornbill* (2006), 36–40.

Tscharntke, T., Y. Clough, T. C. Wanger, L. Jackson, I. Motzke, I. Perfecto, J. Vandermeer and A. Whitbread, 'Global food security, biodiversity conservation and the future of agricultural intensification', *Biological Conservation* 151 (2012), 53–59.

Tug, S., *Conflicts between Humans and Wolf: A study In Bozdag, Konya Province, Turkey*. Ankara: University of Ankara, 2005.

Turvey S., *Witness to Extinction: How we failed to save the Yangtze River dolphin*. Oxford: Oxford University Press, 2008.

Turvey, S. T., R. L. Pitman, B. L. Taylor, J. Barlow, T. Akamatsu, L. A. Barrett, X. Zhao, R. R. Reeves, B. S. Stewart, K. Wang, Z. Wei, X. Zhang, L. T. Pusser, M. Richlen, J. R. Brandon and D. Wang, 'First human-caused extinction of a cetacean species?', *Biology Letters* 3 (2007), 537–540.

Umapathy, G., and A. Kumar, 'The occurrence of arboreal mammals in the rain forest fragments in the Anamalai Hills, South India. *Biological Conservation* 92 (2000), 311–19.

Unison Hotels Ltd. vs DDA and Ors, SLP (Civil) No 8960/97, Delhi: Supreme Court of India.

Vaillant, J. *The Tiger: A true story of vengeance and survival*. New York: Knopf, 2010.

van der Weijden, W., P. Terwan and A. Guldemond, *Farmland Birds Across the World*. Barcelona: Lynx Edicions, 2004.

Vass, K. K., S. K. Mondal, S. Samanta, V. R. Suresh and P. K. Katiha, 'The environment and fishery status of the River Ganges', *Aquatic Ecosystem Health and Management* 13 (2010), 385–94.

Vivekanandan, V., 'Trawl brawl', *Samudra report* 57 (2010), 24–27.

Waltert, M., K. S. Bobo, S. Kaupa, M. L. Montoya, M. S. Nsanyi and H. Fermon, 'Assessing conservation values: Biodiversity and endemicity in tropical land use systems', *PLoS One* 6 (2011), e16238.

Watling, L., and E. A. Norse, 'Disturbance of the seabed by mobile fishing gear: A comparison to forest clearcutting', *Conservation Biology* 12 (1998), 1180–97.

Watts J., *When a Billion Chinese Jump: Voices from the frontline of climate change*. New York: Scribner, 2010.

Weber, B., and A. Vedder, *In the Kingdom of Gorillas: The quest to save Rwanda's mountain gorillas*. New York: Simon and Schuster, 2012.

Western D., *In the Dust of Kilimanjaro*. Washington DC: Island Press, 2001.

Wilcove D. S., and L. P. Koh, 'Addressing the threats to biodiversity from oil-palm agriculture', *Biodiversity and Conservation* 19 (2010), 999–1007.

World Wildlife Fund and Mark McGinley, 'Deccan thorn scrub forests' in J. Cleveland Cutler (ed.), *Encyclopedia of Earth*. Washington, D.C.: Environmental Information Coalition, National Council for Science and the Environment. First published in *Encyclopedia of Earth*, 23 September 2008; last revised 21 January 2011; Available at http://www.eoearth.org/view/article/51cbed5f7896bb431f691d38/ (accessed 29 April 2014).

Worm, B., E. B. Barbier, N. Beaumont, J. E. Duffy, C. Folke, B. S. Halpern, J. B. C. Jackson, H. K. Lotze, F. Micheli, S. R. Palumbi, E. Sala, K. A. Selkoe, J. J. Stachowicz and R. Watson, 'Impacts of biodiversity loss on ocean ecosystem services', *Science* 314 (2006), 787–90.

Worm, B., R. Hilborn, J. K. Baum, T. A. Branch, J. S. Collie, C. Costello, M. J. Fogarty, E A. Fulton, J. A. Hutchings, S. Jennings, O. P. Jensen, H. K. Lotze, P. M. Mace, T. R. McClanahan, C. Minto, S. R. Palumbi, A. M. Parma, D. Richard, A. A. Rosenberg, R. Watson and D. Zeller, 'Rebuilding global fisheries', *Science* 325 (2009), 578–85.

Wolfsong, 'Wolves in Japan', 2010. Available at http://www.wolfsongalaska.org/Wolves_in_Japan (accessed 13 May 2014).

Xie S., Z. Li, J. Liu, S. Xie, H. Wang and B. R. Murphy, 'Fisheries of the Yangtze River show immediate impacts of the Three Gorges Dam', *Fisheries* 32 (2007), 343–44.

Zimmermann, F., *The Jungle and the Aroma of Meats: An ecological theme in Hindu medicine*. Berkeley: University of California Press, 1989.

NOTES ON THE CONTRIBUTORS

Aaron Savio Lobo is a marine conservation practitioner who works on issues of tropical coastal fisheries. He specialises in understanding the impacts of changing fisheries' practices on marine ecosystems and fishery dependent livelihoods.

M. Ananda Kumar is a scientist with the Nature Conservation Foundation, Mysore. He has been studying Asian elephants for the past ten years in the Anamalai hills, Western Ghats.

Charudutt Mishra works with Snow Leopard Trust, Seattle and Nature Conservation Foundation, Mysore. He studies carnivore ecology, large herbivore community ecology, rangeland and human ecology, and human-wildlife conflicts in snow leopard landscapes of the Himalaya and Central Asia.

Divya Mudappa is a scientist with the Nature Conservation Foundation, Mysore, based at the field research station, Valparai. She specialises in ecology, conservation, and restoration of tropical rainforest ecosystems.

Ghazala Shahabuddin is an independent researcher working on forest ornithology, urban biodiversity, sustainable forest use and conservation policy in India. She is affiliated with Centre for Ecology, Development and Research (CEDAR), Dehradun, Uttarakhand.

K. S. Gopi Sundar is the Director, Program SarusScape, International Crane Foundation and Scientist, Cranes and Wetlands Programme, Nature Conservation Foundation. His interests lie in the patterns determining water bird and wetland conservation in farmed landscapes.

Harini Nagendra is Professor of Sustainability Studies, Azim Premji University, Bengaluru. Her research examines trajectories of ecological sustainability in different parts of India and the conditions under which people can act as positive or negative agents of change.

Jagdish Krishnaswamy is Senior Fellow and Programme Leader, Ecosystem Services and Human Well-being, Ashoka Trust for Research in Ecology and Environment (ATREE), Bengaluru. His research interests are ecohydrology, landscape ecology, riverine biodiversity and applied Bayesian statistics.

M. D. Madhusudan is Senior Scientist, Nature Conservation Foundation, Mysore, and Adjunct Faculty, National Institute of Advanced Studies.

Mahesh Rangarajan is Professor of History and Environmental Studies at Ashoka University, Haryana, India. Educated at the universities of Delhi and Oxford, he has taught at Cornell, Jadavpur and Delhi universities. He has also been Director of the Nehru Memorial Museum and Library, New Delhi.

Nachiket Kelkar is a doctoral student with Ashoka Trust for Research in Ecology and Environment (ATREE), Bengaluru. His interests centre on socio-ecological research and conservation of freshwater and marine biodiversity.

Nitya Sambamurti Ghotge is founder director of Anthra, a voluntary organisation. She works on livestock development in the wider context of sustainable natural resource use.

Ramesh Sivaraman is a businessman, social worker and politician based in Bangalore.

Ravi Agarwal is an environmental activist and founder director of Toxics Link, an environmental nongovernmental organisation. He is deeply involved in the Ridge campaign.

Rohan Arthur heads the Oceans and Coasts Programme at Nature Conservation Foundation. His interests focus on the ecological and socioeconomic processes underlying large-scale changes in marine systems in the Lakshadweep, Andaman and Nicobar Islands, and other coastal systems in India.

Sagari R. Ramdas is a veterinary scientist and a member of the Food Sovereignty Alliance, India. She is former trustee and former director of Anthra.

T. R. Shankar Raman is a scientist with the Nature Conservation Foundation, Mysore, and based in the field research station in Valparai. He is interested in tropical forests, wildlife conservation, and human connections to nature.

S. Subramanya is an ornithologist based in Bangalore. His interests include wetlands and water birds with a focused interest on large colonial nesting water birds and threatened birds of India.

Yash Veer Bhatnagar works as the Management Planning Coordinator for the Global Snow Leopard Protection Programme and as Scientist at the Nature Conservation Foundation and Snow Leopard Trust. He is interested in snow leopard and mountain ungulate ecology, and effective conservation of high-altitude arid ecosystems using landscape-level participatory approaches.

INDEX